Marketing Concepts and Strategies in the next Decade

Marketing Concepts and Strategies in the next Decade

Edited by LESLIE W. RODGER

A HALSTED PRESS BOOK

74111

JOHN WILEY & SONS
New York

English language edition, except USA
Published by
Associated Business Programmes Ltd
17 Buckingham Gate, London SW1
Distributed by
Cassell and Co. Ltd.
35 Red Lion Square, London WC1R 4SJ

Published in the USA
by Halsted Press, a Division
of John Wiley & Sons, Inc.
New York

Library of Congress Number 73–1797

First published 1973

*This book has been set in Times New Roman type, printed in Great Britain
on antique wove paper by Anchor Press, and
bound by Wm. Brendon, both of Tiptree, Essex*

ISBN 0–470–72932–5

Contents

Introduction

It is commonplace to talk about the speed of change in our present-day industrial society and of the need of business to respond to its rapidly changing environment. Each decade of change has its doom-watchers with their dire warnings of social and economic disintegration; its optimists who see glorious vistas ahead and new opportunities for society to attain still higher planes of efficiency and achievement; the traditionalists and conservationists who think that all that makes life worth living, according to their own lights, is being eroded and who fear that society is prejudicing the future by its actions in the present; finally and perhaps the most numerous category of all, the confused and perplexed people caught up in a process which they can neither control nor influence, the massive fall-out victims of change. Every decade, according to one's point of view, probably appears either as the most doomladen, the most opportunistic, the most retrogressive and wasteful or the most perplexing of our lives.

Change is coming in on us so quickly from so many directions that it is now threatening to outstrip the rate at which our thinking and our actions can adapt to it. It is in the scale, direction and timing of the changes that we are seeing and are likely to see in the decade of the 70's and well into the 80's that this book has its origins. The economic and social life of Britain in the late 70's and 80's is likely to be so different in aggregate from what we have known in the past as to constitute a change of kind and not merely a change of degree. Among the major dimensions of this change are the following:

1. *The 'people' dimension*
   The younger people in particular have new outlooks, ideas, standards and aspirations and this has opened up the so-called generation gap with parents finding themselves on a different

wavelength to their children and unable to understand how their childrens' attitudes and beliefs have evolved from their own attitudes and beliefs.

These younger people are demanding something different from society, the Government and from their employers and showing increasing concern for the physical environment and their whole social and economic milieu.

At the other end of the age spectrum, people are living longer but we have not yet devised ways of keeping them from getting older and from becoming obsolete and redundant sooner. There are some disquietening structural changes at work in the economy affecting opportunities for employment and security of employment.

2. *The 'social' dimension*

Traditional modes and standards of behaviour by companies are being questioned at every turn – their behaviour towards employees, shareholders, the community and Government. New attitudes are being demanded from management towards the young, the old, the displaced and redundant employee.

The organisable power of the consumer is becoming an increasingly cogent fact in the business environment. A more broadly educated, better informed and more articulate consumer power due in large part to the development of communications media and technique, is making its presence felt in the boardrooms of more and more companies. In an economy dominated by advanced technology and big business wielding excessive market power, there is an undeniable need for a countervailing consumer power. This exists and is growing. It will not disappear simply by business men turning their backs on it.

A shift in the industrial power structure in favour of organised labour holds out the prospect of a protracted and arduous period in our industrial relations. Heavily capitalised industry which is necessary to achieve high and competitively efficient levels of output cannot for too long sustain the costs of interruptions to production flows. These high levels of output and the heavy costs involved require greatly increased marketing effort and expenditure to secure and retain markets in the face of vigorous international competition. Discontinuities in production flows and distribution channels (road, rail and sea) can be more expensive to the employer through loss of markets or market share, sometimes permanently, than the cost of a strike to the employees.

3. *The 'market' dimension*
   The Common Market which is in reality a most uncommon market in the sense that it represents the greatest market segmentation opportunity that has faced British industry this century, is by no means the only development requiring changes in Britain's traditional marketing methods. Markets are reflecting and being affected by the redisposition of the newer technologies around the world, e.g.: Japan and the Far East.

   The ability of the multi-national firm to transfer the latest in tools, managerial technique and technology around the world provides another dimension of global change to which our industry must find an effective response. The multi-national's ability to link low wage labour in the developing countries with sophisticated markets in the advanced countries – not to mention its ability to channel its profits into tax haven countries – opens up new threats and opportunities for all domestically based companies.

   Differences in culture, standards of behaviour and Government regulation between the low cost developing countries and the high cost advanced countries complicates marketing transactions and contractual relationships and adds an additional and high element of risk which the multi-national firm controlling both the manufacturing facility in the former and the marketing facility in the latter is better able to sustain than the domestic manufacturer or importer.

4. *The 'technological' dimension*
   Accelerated obsolescence which rapidly advancing technology brings in its train and changes in consumer tastes resulting from the more rapid dissemination of innovations make for greater uncertainty and risk in terms of the profitable life of present and future fixed investments, products, production processes and employee skills.

   Technology is increasingly an exportable item (as the multi-national company has already demonstrated) as well as being an eminently importable one (as the Japanese penetration of world markets with high-technology products based on 'bought-in' technology has demonstrated). Equally, technology alone is no longer a guarantee of commercial success for a company or a nation. Success is the result of the symbiosis of technology and marketing.

5. *The 'management' dimension*

   Clearly the management of business must itself change in response to changes in these other dimensions. Marketing, as an element of management, must also change both in concept and strategy.

   The time scale is vital. So far as the Common Market is concerned it is not just a question of biding our time to go after a share of European markets. The other members of the European community are out to get as big a share as possible of our market. The time scale is vital in getting managements to accept a greater share of responsibility for social welfare, and the protection of the environment as well as for safeguarding the interests of consumers. The time scale is vital in achieving a better symbiosis of technology and marketing than our competitors. Finally, the time scale is vital in working out a new pattern of industrial relations which best serves the interests of labour, business and the community at large.

The chapters cover both practical and philosophical aspects of marketing chosen not only for their relevance to some of the live issues and areas of immediate concern facing commercial, profit-motivated managements but also for their potential interest for top executives and administrators in Government, social and other organisations whose primary concerns and objectives may not be commercial at all.

The emphasis – marketing strategy for technology-based enterprises, planning diversification strategies, patterns and developments in multi-national enterprises, marketing non-differentiated industrial products, the contractual consequences of systems selling in purpose made capital goods marketing, developing effective pricing policies developments in physical distribution management – is primarily industrial. This reflects the fact that sales of industrial products – inter-industry, to public authorities and for purposes of fixed investment – contributes something of the order of 60 per cent, by value, of total UK output.

The two introductory chapters are philosophical in nature and look at how the marketing concept itself must change and become more sentient in relation to the new social imperatives – the responsibilities of business towards the community and the environment. The final chapter examines how the tools and techniques of commercial marketing can be adapted and used to promote social welfare and social programmes.

I have much reason to be grateful to my fellow authors and collaborators in giving of their valuable time, knowledge and expertise and for their patience in seeing this rather protracted project through. I hope that their reward will be a widespread readership of the book and of their individual contributions. I also hope they will agree that no attempt was made in the editing to alter in any material way the views which they wished to express, to dilute the strength of their declared convictions or to make their several contributions conform to an imposed pattern or editorial style.

I would also wish to thank Janet Judd for coping so efficiently with some of the more tedious administrative detail. And finally, but far from least, I wish to thank my wife for not protesting as much as she had cause to at my temporary but sometimes prolonged withdrawal from the family circle.

CHAPTER 1

The Coming Age of Marketing Maturity

By Leslie. W. Rodger

Marketing's Tarnished Image

Since the late 1960's the marketing concept has come under increasing questioning, criticism and outright attack from the public, organised consumer associations and groups as well as from business itself. In more recent times, which have been characterised by inflation without growth, marketing men have found themselves, along with their scientific, technical and engineering colleagues, unbelieving victims in the executive shake-out and have come to the shock realisation that no superior virtue or claim to indispensability attaches to their particular function and expertise within the business enterprise.

Marketing, as a separate discipline, appears to be moving out of fashion, if indeed, for the bulk of British companies it has ever been in fashion. But today even the hundred or so major companies that have really thought through the implications of a marketing approach to business are looking towards financial experts rather than marketing men to solve their problems.

Many companies pay lip service to the marketing concept – as though a new executive title or new department incorporating the word 'marketing' is all that is necessary – and then have the temerity to wonder why it does not appear to work for them. Their self-delusion has probably done more to damage their business than if they had gone on in their old production-orientated ways. Others have treated marketing as a sort of pep pill to reassure themselves that they are keeping up with modern techniques only to find that the supposed benefits have not been forthcoming. Disillusionment has followed swiftly without the reasons for the apparent failure having been analysed to see who or what was at fault.

The view that the marketing concept, as implemented at the operational level, has led unsuspecting companies up profitless alleys and organisational cul-de-sacs, is one that is increasingly being expressed by businessmen. James Gulliver, a former Director of Associated British Foods and Chairman of Fine Fare Limited, expressed the opinion that 'there is little evidence that strongly marketing-orientated companies have, in the absence of other efficiencies, produced good profits and, indeed, the experience of the food industry would suggest that the opposite is the case.'[1] He went on to say that the fashion of marketing orientation is passing quickly and all managers, including marketing men, will be measured on their total performance although, of course, this is not to say that marketing does not still have a major role to play.

Hugh Davidson[2] cited evidence to show that strongly marketing-orientated companies (chosen from the two hundred firms in the *Management Today* 1970 British Business Growth League over the period 1960 to 1969) failed to impress when judged by the ratio between increase in rpofits and increase in capital employed. He took the view that many companies take too narrow and specialist a view of marketing and fail to treat it as a total approach to the business.

Disenchantment with the marketing concept is not confined to practising businessmen and journalistic commentators on business and management affairs. One of America's foremost writers of marketing went on record as early as 1966, saying 'The marketing concept has led to organisational proposals, often followed by organisational changes, which have spawned much inter-departmental conflict and concern. The time is ripe to ask whether the company's interests are best advanced by requiring all departments to treat customers' intersts as paramount'.[3]

As a nation we do not appear to have reaped the benefits that might have been expected to follow the more widespread diffusion and adoption of the marketing concept. It has not elevated British

[1] *Management Myths.* An address given to The Marketing Society, 23rd February 1972.
[2] *Offensive Marketing: or how to make your competitors followers.* Cassell and Company Limited, London 1972.
[3] Philip Kotler – Diagnosing the Marketing Takeover, *Marketing*, August 1966.

industrial management to higher planes of performance or made it more able or better prepared. The UK's share of the world market in manufactured goods has declined from 18 per cent in 1959 to 10 per cent in 1971. Sales in the United Kingdom of foreign manufactured goods have been rising faster than sales of our own manufactured goods. The marketing approach has not improved our competitiveness in either our domestic market or in overseas markets it seems, although some might argue that the situation might have been a lot worse had we not taken even a few faltering steps in the direction of greater marketing orientation.

The particular views outlined above are symptomatic of a mounting tide of general criticism being levelled at marketing and marketing men. It finds expression in the following forms:

● That marketing, through its ill-used power and its misapplication of the tools of persuasion and manipulation such as advertising and all types of promotion, packaging and pricing, is guilty of deceiving the customer whose interests the marketing concept are purported to advance. Both in this country and more especially in the United States, leading companies are under strong attack for the use of misleading advertising in support of spurious product claims (e.g. slimming and nutritional products) for the use of harmful ingredients (e.g. certain drugs and food additives), the sale of unsafe products (e.g. vehicles, toys) and indestructible packaging, and for discharging harmful effluents and pollutants into our rivers, the air and the countryside. Some major companies are under attack from minority groups for making profits from ingenious lethal weapons (e.g. anti-personnel weapons) although ostensibly engaged in other main lines of business, for racial discrimination in employment, for investing in the 'wrong' country, (e.g. South Africa) or trading with the 'wrong' country (e.g. Rhodesia).

● That marketing places too much emphasis on material goals at the expense of more laudable non-material and social goals and that marketing is forcing the pace of technological change without regard to the consequences for the individual and for society. It is claimed that marketing is producing a society adapted to the demands of a technological imperative and that in the process the facts of marketing are making an ass of our 'whirling-dervish' technology – and a very expensive ass at that, as the Rolls-Royce and Concorde examples illustrate.

● That marketing has been insensitive and slow to respond to the public interest and the changing aspirations of society. The emergence of and the necessity for organised consumer power, so-called 'consumerism', is seen as an indictment of the marketing concept, as an indication of its own bankruptcy and inability to define for itself a socially responsible role. Customers are recognising and articulating their rights to demand better standards and not to be exploited or to be victims of social and environmental injury.[4]

● That even as a managerial concept marketing has failed to live up to its promises and that a number of organisational concepts introduced as part of a new 'marketing package' have simply not worked or have been found wanting. Such has been the case with the 'Brand Manager' concept.

Ten years ago, a 'Brand' or 'Product' managership was thought to constitute a passport to a successful marketing career. 'Managing Directors of brands' they were supposed to be, charged with the responsibility for making their particular brands or products profitable. Unfortunately, they were not given the wide-ranging powers that should go with such an exalted position. They did not command the production or financial resources of the business, nor in many cases, did they control the selling effort put behind their products – to name just three contributory factors to product profitability. A classic case of assigning responsibility without authority – bad practice and not even good theory. The brand or product manager concept frequently gave too much responsibility too early to relatively inexperienced, often immature and hence aggressive, young men straight from university. Educated as specialists, frequently in a non-commercial subject, they were expected to be instant generalists, able to co-ordinate and integrate diverse functions carried out by older, seasoned and, in many cases, fairly strong characters. Experts in their own product market they may have eventually become but as co-ordinators they proved, by and large, to be inadequate.

4 Ronald Hurst examines in the next chapter some of the main impacts on and implications for marketing of these social and environmental issues.

That they were placed in the position of having to coordinate at too low a level was reflected in the fact that it was considered necessary to impose higher level coordinating and supervisory marketing bodies over them, e.g. Group Brand Managers and marketing coordinating committees. Instead of becoming generals inside companies most of them turned out to be N.C.O.s.

In the early years of this decade, characterised by severe inflation and reduced profitability, companies have been occupied with revamping their marketing structures and in the process, the tried-and found-wanting product manager has been assigned to a different, more restricted role. Decisions taken by others at higher levels have superseded the product managers, product assistants, market planners or whatever one likes to call them, so that they are now brand or product progress monitors with much more closely defined responsibilities. Today's product manager is more of an information collator and analyst, studying form and documenting evidence for the policy-maker and decision-taker, liaising with the factory and development and applications laboratories and generating new product concepts. In this role and also as an ideas-man, he performs a vital function in backing up the selling organisation.

It is important in any sensible discussion of the foregoing criticisms of the marketing concept to reiterate that there are very few companies in Britain today, which can be said to be marketing orientated in any real sense. To take but another example, this time from the electronics industry, representative of advanced technology, the following editorial comment in a leading professional journal[5] is apposite. 'Taking this word (i.e. marketing) to include, in its broadest sense, all the factors which go to govern the outward appearance of a company, its products, the market area involved and so on, then there are still many in electronics who pay lip-service to the idea and still don't use it as the reliable management tool it is.'

Plenty of lip-service has been paid to the marketing concept. Executive titles have been changed on doors and business cards – for 'Sales Manager' or 'Product Manager' read 'Marketing Manager'. But the reality has too often been something quite different. Perhaps it is the difference between the idea and the reality which has created something of a credibility gap.

As anyone who has tried will confirm, implementing the marketing concept requires more than a change of title or the hiring of a few

[5] *Electronics Weekly*, 8th September 1971.

B

executives with the word 'marketing' somewhere in their titles. The existence of a so-called 'Marketing Director' or of a specialist marketing department is no guarantee that the marketing concept is really established and is influencing the management style of running the business. It doesn't even mean that the executive marketing function is being properly carried out. The chances are, that unless the basic concept is accepted and seen to be accepted by top management, then the executive marketing function is almost certainly bound to fail.

The panacea merchants of marketing have done great disservice by including practically every area of the business as part of marketing. Marketing executive management is not general management any more than production management, engineering management or financial management is general management. Production executives, engineers and accountants may consider production, engineering and finance respectively, to be the most important function in the business. Most specialists tend to believe that their activity is the crux of the business. Marketing men have been guilty of over-stating their case and general management has also been guilty of letting them do so. While it may be true, as Theodore Levitt[6] has said, that the marketing concept takes a *consolidating* view of the business process, this is not the same as saying that marketing is top dog and must always have the last word.

Many of the criticisms levelled against marketing and marketing managers specifically, would be better directed at general management who have uncritically jumped on the bandwagon in the belief that marketing was some kind of formula that would automatically solve all their business problems provided they hired members of the marketing priesthood who knew the right magical incantations. At the same time, marketing men have themselves been guilty of not taking much greater care in explaining and demonstrating in great detail exactly how their parent companies would be likely to benefit from their presence and from the concepts and policies they would apply.

Marketing men have possibly no-one but themselves to blame for this state of affairs. Either they have genuinely believed, or allowed themselves to believe, that marketing was a panacea for our industrial and managerial shortcomings. Company managements, forever in search of the philosophers' stone, which will turn base products

[6] *The Marketing Mode: Pathways to Corporate Growth*, McGraw Hill, New York, 1970.

into gold have turned with faith and hope but little charity to new concepts and techniques. Yesterday it was Corporate Planning and Management-by-Objectives; today it is Marketing and Technological Forecasting and tomorrow it will be the as yet unnamed and unnameable.

Both general and marketing management have been guilty of using the techniques of marketing with disregard for the spirit of the marketing concept. Blinded by the techniques of marketing which have conferred increased manipulative power in the market place, they have lost sight of the praiseworthy aims which inspired the early marketing philosophers. Moreover, technique management very often carries an implication of precision which is simply not inherent in a business situation. Those who doubt this may find it a salutary experience to reexamine their corporate 5-year marketing plan of five years ago (if such existed) and assess its value as a management aid today. Marketing is a great borrower of words from the more precise sciences and in a great many cases, these only serve to confuse the issue, to hide incompetence and to put up spurious smoke screens of apparent precision. In learning the words, many marketing men have forgotten the purpose of language which is to communicate and to be understood.

Why We Need the Marketing Concept

We need the marketing concept because it represents, despite all its operational shortcomings to date, a genuine attempt to orientate industry and commerce towards serving the community in its capacity as a customer for all the products and services it needs to survive and to enhance the quality of its life, both collectively and of the individuals of which it is comprised.

To this end society delegates to individual citizens in their capacities as commercial and business men, the right to own and use physical resources and to employ others to organise the production and marketing of goods and services in a socially responsible manner for a socially responsible reward. Marketing has a very important role to play in achieving the efficient performance of this task.

It was not so long ago that individual members of our society were more pre-occupied with where the next meal was coming from and where the next day's work was coming from to pay for it. There was less heard then about the bewildering choice of products and services to which the poor and unwary consumer was subjected. There was less heard then about pollution – the environmental crisis was of a different order and magnitude. It was about sheer survival of body and soul, about living long enough to begin to worry about what factory effluents and pollutants were doing to our air and rivers and about what waste products were doing to our countryside. Without these social costs we should in all likelihood have had none of the benefits which industry and commerce, in their single-minded search for ways of making money, have conferred, almost by default it seems, on our society, our material living standards, our schools, hospitals, universities and all the other things which go to make up our society. This is not to say that we should not look to the state of our souls. The fact that we can now feel so concerned about these higher and wider issues and about the quality of life itself may have something to do with the complementary fact that our basic bodily needs are better, if too profusely for some, catered for. For is not poverty the greatest social pollutant of all?

Nevertheless, it is right and proper that we should now have more regard to the social costs of what has been achieved, to minimising the social costs of what we want to achieve in the future and, in the process, to the re-ordering of our social priorities.

The case presented here is that industry and commerce, including the marketing aspect that we have been considering, must be indispensable partners in the endeavour to protect and enhance our environment and to put human and material resources to the most efficient use in pursuit of socially orientated goals. To fulfil their proper role in our post-industrial society, those in general and marketing management who have to implement the marketing concept must re-define the social responsibility of the free enterprise system, which seems likely to remain the prevailing mode of economic organisation for the rest of this century at least.

One definition of marketing which has gained fairly broad acceptance describes it as 'the management function which organises and directs the aggregate of business activities involved in converting customer purchasing power into effective demand for a specific product or service and in moving the product or service to the final customer or user so as to achieve company-set profit or other objectives'.[7]

[7] *Marketing in a Competitive Economy*, Hutchinson 1965. Third Edition Cassell/ Associated Business Programmes 1971, p. 47.

As a description of the marketing function encompassing the techniques and tools of marketing, i.e. selling, advertising, public relations, sales promotion, product planning, market and product research, market and sales forecasting, this definition would appear to have equal validity today. Within this definition the term 'customer' refers not only to the ultimate consumer or user but also the manufacturers' own customers – importers, retailers, wholesalers, processors, convertors, original equipment producers. Effective demand means demand at a price the customer is both able and willing to pay and at a profit that makes it worthwhile for the product or service which by virtue of its differentiation, can be readily distinguished from competitive or substitute products or services. The differentiation whether it resides in the product itself, its packaging, pricing, terms of sale or in its advertising and promotion, must be significant enough to form the basis for preference by the potential customer.[8]

Finally, the definition makes no assumption regarding the profit goals of the company. It does not presume that profit is the sole measure for judging a company's performance over a given period of time. Factors such as building up the company's prestige and status in the industry, the fear of attracting new entrants into the market, the fear of government intervention and regulation, the desire to steer an average-rate-of-profit course between the highest attainable short-run profits and the greatest risk of maximum losses, are other legitimate objectives or considerations. With the growing demand for greater social awareness and accountability of business, one would today add other less self-regarding considerations to the list. These would tend to have social implications such as maximising employment in a development area, keeping uneconomic plants open and uneconomic production going for social reasons, the desire to establish a reputation as a good employer by maximising employee conditions and benefits, concern for the environment which may show itself in investments in expensive plant and services to reduce or eliminate pollutants and to recycle waste products.

It is necessary to distinguish between the foregoing definition of the marketing function and the philosophy or concept of marketing. The former is concerned with the how and the when, the latter with the

[8] For a full examination of sources of differentiation in regard to industrial products, see Chapter 6 by Aubrey Wilson and Jeremy Fowler – *Marketing a Non-differentiated Industrial Product*.

what and the why. According to the Institute of Marketing,[9] 'The philosophy of marketing is a concept of business management which focuses the activities of all departments on the needs of the customer and organises the total resources of the company to the difficult task of identifying and satisfying those needs profitably. It stems from recognition of the fact that a business can only survive by providing profitably the goods or services which the customer wants to buy.' It goes on to state 'The concept of marketing is a corporate affair involving the whole company organisation. It is a generally shared management philosophy which should permeate top management thinking and influence company decisions and policies. It is not the special preserve of one department or one discipline. The concept actively involves in the marketing operation all those concerned with research, development, design, production, finance, distribution, after-sales service, as well as the labour force itself. Unless those responsible for all these areas of activity – and their staff also – are market-orientated it will not be possible to utilise the company's full resources to the best advantage.'

The main potential benefits to be derived from implementing this marketing concept are:

- reduced business risk as a result of systematic market research, the scientific acquisition and analysis of market data relevant to decision-making and better market and sales forecasting.

- improved business planning as a result of earlier identification and assessment of future market trends and opportunities and the acceptance of a planning discipline based on defined objectives with which all departments must gear their activities and integrate their programmes.

- greater competitiveness based on marketing skills – as more and more of our competitors achieve technological and manufacturing parity, the differences in the products from different countries and different companies will tend to narrow.[10]

Knowledge, it has been said, is power. Increased marketing knowledge and the acquisition of marketing skills brings greater marketing

[9] *Marketing – The Concept and Its Application.* A booklet prepared by the Institute at the request of the Confederation of British Industries Standing Committee on Marketing, January 1972.
[10] See Chapter 3 by Harry Sasson for a discussion of the major alternative marketing strategies open to technology-based enterprises.

power. But marketing power exists to be used or abused. How it is deployed depends on the motivation, the understanding, the ethic and the personal aims of those who wield it. There is only limited protection against the deliberate exploiter, the business man or firm who will consciously compromise product quality or safety in order to improve or maintain profits, who will use misleading promotion and who will use exploitative pricing methods. There are always those who will try to circumvent professional standards of conduct, who will find loopholes in and ways around the law. What is needed is a new ethical mode whereby the marketing concept can serve the best interests of society as a means to socially responsible rewards, i.e. profits arising from a necessary and worthwhile activity and from efficiently supplying customer satisfactions in the market place.

In this section we have been examining the need for the marketing concept in a business context. But a need exists also to persuade those not directly involved in business and those who may be antagonistic towards the conduct of commerce and industry to consider the validity and application of the marketing concept for social causes, social programmes and the solution of social problems. Education on what the marketing concept means and what it is capable of achieving is necessary on as broad a social front as possible, for in this author's view, the potential benefits of 'social marketing' are considerable.[11]

Confrontation or Reconciliation?

Much of the abuse of marketing power stems from the conflicts inherent in the way we organise and structure our business affairs. We are where we are because of the road we have travelled. A brief historical review of the development of the marketing concept and marketing organisation may help us to see the way ahead more clearly and certainly.

During the present century it is possible to suggest given points of time when a significant change in the marketing development of UK industry first became discernible resulting, in turn, in certain organisational changes. The changing orientation of business – from production to selling and then to fully-fledged marketing – has been reflected in organisation charts, in the nature of

[11] The concept of 'social marketing' is examined in Chapter 10 by Norman Marcus.

managements' main preoccupations and the changing emphasis given to the different key functions of the business, i.e. the relative ascendancy of manufacturing, sales and finance in the corporate hierarchy.

Table 1 attempts to relate the way marketing organisation has developed in British industry during this century to the changing problems and orientation of business management. Dates and periods cannot be too precise because by the time a new development or trend is discernible there has already been an indeterminate number of years of experimentation, of adaptation and missionary work by the pioneers.

I have adapted for my own purposes the configuration developed by Eugene J. Kelley[12] in relation to the American market and wish to acknowledge my debt to him for providing a model which I have applied to conditions in the United Kingdom.

Up until the outbreak of war in 1939 the main preoccupation of management was finding and organising the capital to develop manufacturing capability on an increasing, and eventually, mass scale. Production men, engineers and financial men tended to dominate general business management. The task of marketing was to dispose of the factory output as profitably as possible; this without benefit of market and product research for the most part and usually without a sales plan based on realistic market estimates.

After the war, manufacturing together with distribution developments were the primary business problems for management. The beginnings of a major revolution in retailing were to be seen – self-service, the first supermarkets, the development of powerful chains and buying groups. Big national companies serving mass markets with the aid of rapidly improving transport and communication systems put a greater emphasis on the selling role. This resulted in the development of more sophisticated sales organisations and selling, advertising, and sales promotion methods. It also led to the demand for more and better market research, better market estimation and sales forecasting and better sales planning. Sales management probably began to occupy a higher status within the company than hitherto and many more Sales Directors were appointed to board rooms.

[12] *Marketing: Strategy and Functions.* Foundations of Marketing Series, Prentice-Hall, 1965.

Table 1. THE PATTERN OF MARKETING DEVELOPMENT
IN THE UK FROM 1900

Approx. period	Major Pre-occupation of Business Management	Orientation of Business Management	Management view of the role of Marketing
Pre-1938	Manufacturing and Capital building	Production and Finance	Disposal of output
1945–1960	Manufacturing and Distribution	Production and Sales	Selling
1960's	Marketing	Customer	Integration of marketing functions-selling, sales promotion, distribution, advertising, PR, market research, market and sales forecasting
1970's	Marketing	Systems and Finance	Catalyst in integrated business system comprising technology, R&D, manufacture and finance. Developing total Company Plan
1980's	Social Integration – achieving an acceptable balance of company and social objectives and responsibilities	Social Awareness	Concern for the customer

The introduction of the marketing concept was still confined to a few large companies, mainly subsidiaries of US corporations. Typically, the chief commercial executive was the Sales Director who would frequently control the advertising and promotion functions as well as the sales organisation. There was little coordination and integration as yet with other marketing functions and integrated company planning was very much the exception. Some staff-functions

– economic and market intelligence, market research, corporate planning, and public relations – were beginning to emerge.

The 1960's probably saw the first real movement by some companies to develop a total marketing approach based on the marketing concept. The word 'marketing' began to appear in many company organisation charts but with not altogether happy results, as we have seen. This was also the decade of the Brand of Product Manager about whose success considerable reservation has to be made. It was also the period when physical distribution management began to be considered as a marketing function.

Factors which have had major impact on the development of marketing during this period must include the knowledge explosion in technology; the arrival of the commercial computer; the emergence of a more broadly educated and more discerning consumer with increasing discretionary spending power; the rise of shopping centres, discount stores and cash-and-carry wholesaling; containerisation; the internationalisation of business, i.e. the emergence of the modern multi-national company.

All of these factors required more and better market information, consumer and product research, industrial market research, as well as greatly enhanced numerate skills among businessmen as a basis for sophisticated marketing planning.

But still, at the end of the 1960's, there were probably fewer than a hundred companies who had developed real marketing skill in depth. The marketing concept, as opposed to the use of some or all of the various marketing tools on an *ad hoc* opportunistic basis, still remains to be adopted by the great majority of British business managements. Many more Marketing Directors have to make their appearance in boardrooms, putting the marketing view on basic questions of corporate policy.

The 1970's seem set to be a period of diffusion so far as the marketing concept is concerned. The prevailing mood is one of caution and experimentation in marketing since the application of the concept to date has been found wanting. As already stated some difficult problems at the marketing-technology interface are causing concern. The symbiosis of marketing and technology and the relationship between marketing and R&D are matters which will occupy many business managements until the end of the decade and beyond. The balance of power within a company between the technologists, the marketing men and the financial controllers has still to be resolved.

The 1970's will be characterised by a basic questioning of many precepts hitherto taken for granted and of established patterns of behaviour. These questionings, which will have profound implications for business operations in the 1980's and 1990's cover such topics as the nature and meaning of economic and social progress, the rates of scientific development and of technological change, the pressure for greater social responsibility among different sections of the community including the business sector, the rising expectations of consumers and the protection of their rights, the growing concern for the environment and its protection against further injury, the trend towards large-scale multi-national operations and bigness for bigness's sake.

These are some of the issues which will require business managements to radically rethink their role in society. Part of this rethinking must be a re-definition of the marketing concept. The main preoccupation of business management in the 1980's will be how to achieve a greater degree of social integration, how to strike a more acceptable balance between social and company objectives, how to regulate itself and become more responsive to the public interest. Business management must become increasingly concerned, in one direction, to learn how a company is influenced by and can be made more sensitive and responsive to changes in and the demands of the environment; and in the other direction, to learn how the environment is influenced by and responds to the various actions the company takes.

The function of general management will be to find appropriate profit-rewarding responses to the identified and anticipated needs of the environment and the role of marketing will be what it was always intended to be, namely, concern for the customer. It is time for marketing executive management to get back to doing the job it was intended it should do – representing the customers' interests at the corporate policy level – and to shed its misplaced zeal in its own ability to plan, cordinate and control a company's entire future independently and unaided by other functional interests. Marketing executive management is *not* general management. Marketing is part of an integrated stream of research – development – design – engineering – manufacturing – selling – profit-rewarding activity in which no single discipline or specialist function has primary importance over the others.

The proper instrument for achieving the necessary planning,

integration and control is not an all-powerful marketing department or chief marketing executive, but a closely-knit top management executive group in which Research and Development, Production, Engineering, Design, Finance, Industrial Relations – and Marketing – are represented. It is this group's task to build bridges between the different functions, to avoid inter-departmental confrontations and to constructively resolve the basic conflicts which will undoubtedly arise between company and social objectives and responsibilities, in order to create a new balance from which everybody gains – the company, its employees, its shareholders, its customers and society at large. This is the process by which the organisation approaches equilibrium within itself and with its environment.

It is precisely because the marketing concept recognises that the market is the only place where profits can be made and orientates the company towards its customers rather than towards its factories, laboratories and technologies that the marketing group within the company has a special obligation to do everything it possibly can to make this more mature approach to organising our business affairs, work successfully.

The root cause of many of the problems that have been highlighted in this chapter and the reason why negative attitudes have been allowed to develop until they are now approaching crisis proportions is that the business-society interface is one of 'adversary confrontation'.[13] By this is meant the process, already enshrined in our legal system, whereby one side seeks only to present the positive points of importance to its case, to withhold those facts that might be damaging to its case, to employ expressive emotive words to give a more desirable impression than the bare facts possibly warrant and to avoid explanations that might clarify a point that it would prefer to remain ambiguous or misunderstood. One might be forgiven for thinking that this is a description of commercial advocacy in advertising. Just as legal counsel leaves it to the opposing lawyer to draw out the potentially injurious points in the former's case or to support the latter's own predetermined conclusion, so the spokesmen for business and society stand in classic confrontation.

Such an analogy between legal and social-commercial adversaries is not altogether out of place. The very act of putting together a

---

[13] The business and social manifestations of this concept are elegantly described by Raymond M. Willmotte – *Engineering Truth in Competitive Environments.* I.E.E.E. Spectrum. (Institute of Electrical and Electronics Engineers), May 1970.

presentation or a case of any sort to 'sell' something to someone in what is essentially a competitive situation establishes an adversary confrontation and the ensuing controversy cannot lead to a constructive resolution of the two opposing views because the parties are not trying to reach the same conclusions or goals, e.g. company turnover or profit maximisation on the one hand and social welfare maximisation on the other. In the present selling environment, so the consumerists would have it, companies will tend to maximise their profit goals at the expense of the consumer by raising prices, lowering quality or reducing service.

What needs to be done is to get away from the confrontation mode and to find ways of reconciling the interests of society and business, buyer and seller, private profit and public benefit.

How can we create conditions favourable to reconciliation, that will allow business men, individually and collectively, to give the most effective service to society? An approach which commends itself to a growing body of opinion in both the business and consumer sectors, is the revitalisation of the marketing concept to take account of the new forces at work in society and the rising expectations of consumers.

Renewing the Marketing Concept

The need to review and renew the marketing concept is now urgent for the following reasons:

● The contrast between current philosophy and practice: relatively few companies seem able or willing, for whatever reason, to implement the concept at the day-to-day operational level. This has been reflected in organisational failures, high new product failure rates, disregard for the often harmful environmental consequences of marketing action, the deteriorating relations between business and the public. A basic cause of peoples' concern about marketing, which for many is synonymous with selling and advertising, is the very simple human emotion of suspicion, based on fear of being cheated, persuaded against their will, manipulated and exploited.

● The apparent inability of the present marketing concept to safeguard the interests of consumers as evidenced by the emergence of very articulate, increasingly strident consumer protection organisations and action groups. The Public Interest Research Centre already monitors and reports on misleading advertising and breaches in socially acceptable marketing conduct.

● The failure of management in general and marketing management in particular to realise the seriousness of or to react quickly enough or constructively enough to the changes taking place in the environment.

Society is changing and demanding different standards of behaviour from companies towards the community and towards their employees – the young, the disabled and the older executives. Society expects more than it is getting from businessmen.

People are changing. The young, especially, have different aspirations from the older generation – the so-called generation gap – and are looking for different things out of life; they have different attitudes towards work and employment and towards employer-employee relations. The situation of older people is changing and not always for the better; the social problems created by middle career malaise as reflected in executive obsolescence, redundancy, forced early retirement and feelings of personal insecurity, are becoming increasingly acute. It is no longer true, if it ever was, that if an executive is out of work it is his own fault. Yet the stigma still attaches to such people as is to be seen in the difficulties of re-employment, the absence of proper executive re-training schemes within companies as a means of avoiding redundancy, and the absence of humane properly phased, programmed retirement policies.

Where has the present marketing concept failed? Since most definitions of the marketing concept stress its responsibility for creating customer satisfactions, how is it that there is so much apparent customer dissatisfaction with the concept in practice? The answer to these questions are to be found in the way in which the basic philosophy of marketing has been interpreted and implemented at the day-to-day operations level. The reasons are to be found in the difference between the 'thought process' (the concept) and the 'doing process' (the practice).

The marketing concept as we have known it up to this point in time, rests on three propositions for successful business operation:

1. *Customer Orientation*. This puts the customer at the very centre

of the firm's activities and planning. Knowing the customer, identifying, anticipating and satisfying customer needs and desires, researching and analysing customer behaviour become the bases of all marketing decisions and actions. It will be apparent that this neither prevents the knowledge and understanding of the customer so acquired being used against him whenever necessary nor precludes the artificial stimulation of consumer's desires and the persuasion and manipulation of consumers to buy products and services for which the company believes a market can be created. Major criticisms levelled at marketing are that it creates demands for products and services that people don't really want or need, that it seeks to make people want more who have got everything already, and that it conspires with modern technology to develop innovations not needed by the market.

The answer of the marketing man is that if we have any faith in the system of free enterprise then people should be left to decide for themselves whether these innovations in the form of products and services are used. The point can also be made that, in practice, the usefulness and social value of innovation often cannot be judged very accurately in the short term. In any case, the one thing that the marketing concept is supposed to do is to get the company to produce things to sell at a worthwhile profit to markets which can be created, rather than merely disposing of whatever the company feels it would like to manufacture. The fallacy of this argument is, of course, that the pursuit of profit as opposed to the mere disposal of factory output does not automatically lead to the maximisation of customer satisfaction. It may do so but it is by no means axiomatic.

2. *Integration of Effort*. Almost every definition of marketing stresses the need for integrating related functions within the business – sales and distribution, advertising, sales promotion, product planning and market research – to achieve the company's marketing objectives.

3. *Profit Direction*. The whole point of the marketing concept is that its application will reduce the risk of loss due to inadequate market information and customer knowledge, misreading of the market, poor product planning and selection. Instead of salesmen having to unload on to the market at any price all that the

factory churns out, marketing is supposed to provide them with products which they know stand a much better chance of being sold at a profit because the market, the customer and the product have all been researched beforehand. The magic word is profit rather than sales turnover or market share.

The fact of the matter is that these three propositions – customer orientation, integration of effort and profit direction – do not add up to a philosophy. Customer orientation and integration of effort are merely operational means to an end – greater profitability. Customer orientation, if it results in greater customer satisfaction, is seen as a way of improving the profitability of the company's operations. Unfortunately, customer orientation has been interpreted too narrowly as turning to the customer for guidance on what can be sold at a profit.

It carries no firm implication that the company is dedicated to the customer's welfare or that it exists to serve the social interest. It may be argued that no individual or function within a profit-motivated organisation can have any claim to represent consumers and up to a point this must be true. But this does not mean that no one in the company should be personally committed to represent a point of view of relevance to consumer welfare. The marketing concept could be a potent instrument in protecting the customer's welfare and in serving and promoting the social interest. It is simply that the concept as at present conceived and implemented leaves it open to the individual companies or managers to interpret for themselves and to exercise their own degree of social reponsibility.

One thing seems highly probable. Unless business management finds a way of inculcating and exercising a much greater degree of social responsibility in its decisions and actions in line with the public's expectations then someone else will do it for them. Perhaps we shall reach a stage where a 'social responsibility audit' will be carried out by a government-appointed or socially accountable body in those areas where a company deals directly with society or in respect of its actions in specific social areas, in much the same way as a conventional audit is now carried out.

Having said all this, we have to recognise that we live in an imperfect world. One cannot expect one section of the community, be it businessmen, the trade unions, the government or the academics, to be wholly and consistently on the side of the angels. After all, Christianity has been trying for nearly 2,000 years!

There is much that is wrong in the way we order most of our affairs, but this does not mean that no good at all comes out of our puny endeavours. It ought to be said for the record, that much that is socially desirable, beneficial and worthwhile in business today is a direct consequence of the marketing concept which requires management to have more regard to consumer needs and desires and that our best hope for the future lies in the further development of the concept.

After all, the maximisation of social welfare, as a specific business goal, is a relatively new concept. Consumer orientation has been a means of achieving another business goal – more profitable sales – with consumer welfare as an added bonus but not a prime objective. If a product sells well and profitably in the market place, this has been taken as *prima facie* evidence that the company supplying the product is meeting a real consumer need, providing customer satisfaction and promoting the latter's welfare. But common sense and experience tells us that this is not a valid assumption.

Some of the major criticisms levelled against marketing relate to what happens *after* the sale has been made – bad after-sales service, indifference to customer's complaints, failure to assume responsibility for anything that happens as a result of using products bought in good faith but perhaps on the basis of inadequate information about the product, about how to get the best use out of it and how to avoid using it wrongly. In other words, the fact that a product sells well is no guarantee that it promotes consumer welfare. Consumers' judgments on products (and services) can only be made on the basis of what is known or made known to the buyers about the products, their experiences of them or some other products like them in the past and their understanding of what the products are capable of doing for them.

Granted then, that the present marketing concept is imperfect and inadequate, how can it be made more responsive to society's emerging requirements?

Professors Martin Bell and William Emory[14] have suggested that the achievement of a better business-society interface is to be found in a marketing concept based on the following three propositions:

[14] *The Faltering Marketing Concept*, Journal of Marketing. American Marketing Association, Vol. 35 (October 1971), pp. 37–42.

● CONSUMER CONCERN. A positive effort by the company to make the consumer the focus of all marketing decisions through service that delivers genuine consumer values. The authors cite a number of practical examples of ways in which companies can demonstrate a real concern for the consumer:

1. By supplying more and better product information to the buyer – nutritional information; product use and care instructions; content information; safety and health warnings.

2. By setting better criteria of acceptability for promotion in relation to: the selection and presentation of facts in advertisements; the substantiation of product performance and ingredient claims; the level of verbal extravagance.

3. By applying the strictest safeguards in respect of the exploitation of children in advertising and the use of advertising appeals directed at children; the use of misleading or obscurely phrased product and service guarantees; the promotion of lotteries, competitions, special price offers, coupons and premiums; the use of packaging to misrepresent value, e.g. slack-fill, disadvantageous price-weight and price-volume ratios in comparison with smaller or standard packs.

4. By providing better after-sales service, easily accessible complaint procedures and the efficient redressing of consumer grievances (a genuine consumer concern is needed in handling complaints).

5. By accepting greater responsibility for the effects of the use of their products and services. The customer does not always have the necessary knowledge or experience to get the best out of the things he buys. In many areas he is much less expert than the seller and does not always act in his own or society's safety or best interest. It is getting much harder for the market place – the customer, in other words – to analyse and evaluate what is being offered because of the complex technologies involved. Thus, unless the government or consumer organisations are to do the job for him, the seller must be prepared to accept a greater share of the responsibility for the protection of the users of

his products, e.g. detergent ingredients that may be harmful to the skin, drugs and medicines that may have deleterious side effects. Up till now, businesses have tended to react to situations as they have arisen and to *ad hoc* pressures from the government and public. What is now suggested is that companies should make a much more deliberate effort to promote product safety and the protection of the environment. 2

● INTEGRATED OPERATIONS. Greater emphasis on company integration will be achieved by abandoning the confrontation mode and by encouraging a more positive and direct approach, on an industry-wide basis if necessary, towards maximising consumer values and serving society better.

● PROFIT REWARD. This is the most difficult part. A greater concern for consumer welfare does not mean that businesses should not plan for profits. Concern for the environment and for consumer welfare should not be looked upon as constraints on profit-earning or as threats to the business but rather as new opportunities for creating satisfactions. The battle to protect and control the environment will not be won without the full resources of industry.[15] The reward for doing so efficiently should be profit.

But the community will demand that it be 'socially responsible' profit that does not exploit the consumer, damage the environment further, or incur unacceptable human and social costs.

These three propositions put forward by Bell and Emory would appear to offer a feasible alternative to the present marketing concept. The real crunch comes in relation to profit planning responsibility and it is at this point that they introduce some very contentious proposals. Instead of company managements setting profit targets and then devising means and methods of achieving them, it is suggested that they should approach planning in the following manner:

[15] An article by Arthur Conway, 'Where There's Muck There's Brass', *New Scientist*, 18 May 1972, p. 378, quoted figures from a Sira Institute report on 'Pollution and its Control: the role of instrumentation to 1980' showing that the estimated value of the market for air pollution meters alone would increase from £265 million in 1970 to £1,450 million in 1980.

1. 'What specific satisfactions *should* be provided to the consumer?'
2. 'What specific consumer satisfactions can my company provide?'
3. 'What is the most efficient way to provide these satisfactions?'
4. 'Is the rate of return expected from the venture sufficient to justify the investment?'
5. 'If the anticipated return is below the desired standard, what can still be done to supply the consumer need? For example:
   (a) Provide the services at less than normal profit?
   (b) Contribute know-how or other aid to others who might provide the services?
   (c) Pool interests with other businesses to provide the services cooperatively?
   (d) Assist government or other agencies to provide the services?'[16]

It seems unlikely, in my view, for the forseeable future and probably for as long as the private enterprise system remains the prevailing form of economic organisation, that the owners and professional managers of companies will surrender their freedom to plan their own social and profit goals and to earn a 'socially responsible' rate of return on their shareholders' investment. Professors Bell and Emory concede that within the planning constraints outlined above company executives will still be charged with achieving profit goals. But in order to achieve these goals, must they not be able to select those sources of business that will provide the levels of profit planned for?

Conclusion

Like it or not, companies will find it necessary to cultivate a much more serious concern for the consumer and a greater degree of social responsibility. We should not shirk our responsibilities to our fellow men by transferring them to the law makers and regulatory bodies. The modern business *must* achieve a socially acceptable balance in setting its objectives, with due regard to its conceived responsibilities to its shareholders, its own employees and to society.

[16] Op. cit.

In the long run a persistent loss-making company can be of no service to anyone. If it cannot employ its resources profitably then those resources ought to be transferred to others who can. What may appear to be a high rate of profit earned by one company compared to others in the same line of business may, in fact, reflect its more efficient use of resources. Whether or not they should be required to pass on this 'extra efficiency profit reward' in the form of some sort of social dividend or reduced prices is another matter. What certainly will happen, is that if such price reductions are enforced then the profitability of the other relatively less efficient companies in the industry will be lowered and bring about a transfer of resources used by those operating at the margin of profitability. But in a great many industries the normal pressures of competition, both domestic and international, already bring this about.

Concern for the consumer and the acceptance of a higher degree of social responsibility are already to be seen in the attitudes and policies of some companies. Perhaps the most explicit statement so far made is to be found in the list of basic principles which the Quaker Oats Company of Chicago has enunciated to guide its executives in achieving its corporate objectives.[17]

1. 'We apply the highest ethical and moral standards, and strive for excellence and leadership in everything we do.

2. 'We believe in a dual responsibility to shareholders: To earn a return on their investment that compares favourably with the return for other leading companies in our industries; To apply our corporate resources wherever practical to the solution of public problems in which the interests of shareholders, employees, customers and the general public are fundamentally inseparable.

3. 'We concentrate our efforts on products and services that are useful, of good quality and of genuine value to consumers.

4. 'We conduct our operations with respect for the intelligence and good taste of consumers.

5. 'We seek to provide an environment for personal development and advancement that attracts, stimulates and rewards

[17] Principles and Objectives (Chicago, Quaker Oats Company 1970) p. 2.

outstanding employees whose integrity, ability and ambition are essential to the Company's progress.'

A major company in the British retailing field, Marks and Spencer, has explicitly declared its concern for the consumer in a statement of marketing policy:[18]

'Our policy is based upon certain definite principles which have been responsible for the continuous growth of our business. They may be briefly stated as follows:

(a) to offer customers a selective range of high quality, well designed and attractive merchandise at reasonable prices;

(b) to encourage our suppliers to use the most modern and efficient techniques of production and quality control dictated by the latest discoveries in science and technology;

(c) with the co-operation of our suppliers, to enforce the highest standards of quality control;

(d) to plan the expansion of our stores for the better display of a widening range of goods and for the convenience of our customers;

(e) to simplify operating procedures so that our business is carried on in the most efficient manner;

(f) to foster good human relations with customers, suppliers and staff.'

As retailers of large quantities of merchandise, Marks and Spencer are an important link in the chain both of production and distribution in Great Britain. They go far in their desire to satisfy their customers by making it possible for them to exchange articles purchased from their stores and when necessary, to refund the price to the customer if she so desires. The growth of their business is based upon the principle of giving their customers whatever benefit they can obtain as large purchasers of relatively few selected articles. By the use of technical initiative and advice from their technological staff, they have upgraded their goods each year to reach their present high standards.

The approach illustrated by these two organisations requires future managers to think through the social implications of their decisions, control procedures and information feedback systems.

It would be foolish to underestimate the difficulty facing com-

18 Lord Sieff, Chairman's Annual Statement, 1966.

panies in making the renewed marketing concept work effectively with its clearly implied responsibility for the social consequences of their marketing decisions, operations, products and services. But to ignore the challenge and to condone the 'catch-me-if-you-can' philosophy of many of today's companies would be socially irresponsible.

It will not be easy to reconcile some company goals with social goals involving decisions about:

- making major investments to counter pollution and recycle waste products;

- keeping uneconomic plants in production in order to assist hard core unemployment;

- retaining labour surplus to requirements in times of economic recession;

- closing down plants in countries which apply measures of racial discrimination, which fail to establish minimum economic standards for their own people or whose social policies are oppressive;

- financing social causes and programmes, universities and colleges, research and social foundations;

- encouraging employee participation in community and social service organisations and providing time off for the purpose;

- full disclosure of financial and operating data about the company;

- allowing public interest and consumer representatives to sit on company boards;

- foregoing some of the profits on products and services that society really *needs*;

- foregoing all monopoly profits arising from technological or marketing breakthroughs.

Every advance in marketing has nearly always made great demands on management. The next proposed advance has probably never been more critical nor the demands on all of us more challenging.

CHAPTER 2

The Environment Revisited

BY RONALD HURST

Marketing practice is conditioned by the development and application of technologies, by the material and cultural levels of the community, and by the incessant flux of social development under the stress of these factors. This chapter examines the nature of these influences, considers their impact on current marketing thought, and the implications which are inherent for those working in this field, during the next decade and beyond.

The Work Environment

The Changing Industrial Background

It is beyond question that it is this sector of human preoccupation, above others, which must claim precedence among marketing considerations.

The scale of utilisation of national industrial and commercial resources, its levels of efficiency, and the distribution pattern of the wealth so generated, form the historical realities of the economy. And since it is these realities which basically determine the tempo of marketing activity, it is necessary that they should be brought into sharp focus.

Thus, in the first years of this decade, manufacturing industry – the core of the work effort – finds itself economically embattled by the saturation of existing markets and an inertial inability to penetrate into, or develop new outlets. In consequence, there is confusion as to the future and uncertainty as to the orientation necessary for a resumption of profitable operation. It is, too, an unpalatable feature of the period that this uncertainty extends, in many surprising cases (surprising in that these doubts have beset many companies hitherto regarded as immutably stable) to the very fact of survival.

The phenomenon of such a marked lack of assurance owes much to the inflation-without-growth trend evident during the opening years of the decade. To this must be added the physical and psychological effects of a level of unemployment approaching the figure of one million and the bankruptcy of productive units of the stature of Rolls-Royce, Handley Page, Upper Clyde Shipbuilders and others. Less spectacular, but no less conclusive, has been the demise of many smaller companies in the manufacturing field. Nor is the syndrome limited to manpower reductions announced by companies such as GEC, BSA, GKN, Burroughs and the National Cash Register Company, once front runners among the major employers of labour; both British Rail and the Post Office have announced their intention to run down 'thousands' of jobs within the next few years.

The Changing Pattern of Mergers

It is a reasonable assumption that productive capacity, bearing in mind the under-utilisation of existing plant, is now more than adequate to meet potential market demand during a period of economic recovery. It is unlikely, therefore, that such recovery can necessarily absorb the full total of those unemployed. Indeed, the effect of what has been euphemistically called 'the shakeout' of labour, whereby employers under pressure have pared manning requirements to the minimum, will be lasting in that an increasing number of sophisticated and machine or science-based industries will operate efficiently with smaller labour forces than before.

Where this lesson has communicated itself to the boardroom, it can be expected that consolidation and improved performance rather than outright expansion will be the main preoccupation in the years immediately ahead and there will be a keener involvement in more rational mergers wherein the resources can be seen to be complementary.

The Effect on Small Businesses

With consolidation will come product rationalisation, making it difficult for the smaller company to compete successfully in major sectors of the market. Inevitably fringe competitors, by virtue of a smaller scale of operation, will be eliminated from many of their traditional markets. The effects of such 'rationalisation', in fact, are already to be seen in the continuing contraction of Britain's aircraft industry, its shipbuilding industry and, inevitably, its automotive industry.

Other aspects of rationalisation must challenge the very existence of the small business which is dependent on the major companies. The latter, themselves threatened by the struggle to adjust to a buyer's market, will seek to rationalise their input of services, materials, components and assemblies. The survival capacity of many small companies, bedevilled by a chronic under-capitalisation, by escalating overheads in site rental or purchase, and in equipment, labour and power and fuel costs, etc., is likely to be limited and increasingly so. Where the small company's fortunes are entirely linked with those of a major manufacturer (e.g. Rolls-Royce) or project (e.g. Concorde), future profitability and survival, as past experience shows, can be at great risk.

The Future of Industrial Relations

In the classic spiral of wage and cost, the reflex action of the Trade Unions is predictable, and inevitable.

Given the purpose of protecting and furthering the interests of their members, largely tied to basic and hard-fought wage levels, it would be naive indeed to expect that they should, or could, dilute their traditional role – that of wage bargaining, with its implicit threat of sanction against employers.

This fact should be kept in mind in considering two features which will come into prominence during the next decade, namely the legislative harness on Union activity attempted by the Industrial Relations Act, and the growing strength of 'protectionist' professional bodies in many cases outside the frame of the Trade Union movement.

The dour and militant image of the Trade Unions will not, in essence, be changed by the application of the provisions of the Industrial Relations Act. The unions no less than management are, by history and circumstance, locked into an impossible posture, and make no secret of the fact that in their view 'control' is equated with contention, and that the sum effect will be to provide yet another arena for protest. Successive generations of organised labour have become hardened to the process of disputation on the shopfloor, in the factory yard, at boardroom, and at national levels, frequently stimulating Ministerial intervention. It is not likely that either their philosophy, or their powers of endurance, will be radically transformed by the threat, or even the act, of litigation in the courtroom.

Trade Unions will continue to exist in their present form for the foreseeable future for the simple reason that, given the elemental terms to which bargaining is reduced, no other form of representation exists which could satisfy the aspirations of their membership without adopting a similar approach to industrial negotiation. Professional bodies such as the Association of Scientific, Technical and Managerial Staffs, or the British Airline Pilots Association have demonstrated this in full measure, pursuing their various claims against employers with a tenacity and toughness unmatched by the most militant of Boilermakers.

If indeed there are suggestions or wistful hopes of logical social development, looking beyond the traditional Unionism of the craft and service vocations, there can be no misconceptions whatsoever as to the power of organised professionalism; nor as to the readiness with which this power will be used, should the occasion so demand. There are, of course, those who have looked on 'professional association' as a desirable, and perhaps more genteel substitute for the earthier atmosphere of classic Unionism; and with the diminution of poltical and emotional attachment to the Labour movement, professional associations offering an elitist platform may well attract substantial following. It is beyond doubt, however, that once committed to the material advancement of their membership, they will differ from the Unions only in the manner in which they will choose to apply their pressures. The weapon of professionalism will be the tourniquet, rather than the bludgeon.

The Problem of the Displaced Executive

The run-down of companies and the corollary of unemployment, does not, of course, spare the executive. The pattern of 'fall-out' among executives has, in general, hitherto reflected a primitive response to the financial pressures bearing on the company. It is not difficult, however, to isolate certain specific weaknesses in operating methods which have contributed to the present 'executive' crisis:

(a) Individual project planners or individual departmental managers have been permitted to generate demands for additional personnel without reference to real forward requirements.

(b) The failure of management to integrate the personnel function into any sophisticated planning mechanism able to deploy executive talent and experience at both the strategic and tactical levels.

(c) The failure of personnel management and 'operational' management to abandon 'standards' which effectively prevent the exercise of flexibility and ingenuity in the use of executive capacity.

It is obvious that the enforced 'streamlining' of manning levels referred to earlier will eventually stabilise in accordance with a demand, dictated in great degree by technological factors. These will be represented, not only by advanced methods of manufacture and processing – and the erosion of uneconomical methods – but also by marketing shifts set up by the social impact of these technologies.

Any hypothetical 'equilibrium' attained in terms of executive staffing may be threatened thereafter by these shifts unless a greater expertise is forthcoming from industry in the understanding and use of its human resources.

Positive steps must replace the traditional indifference to, or at best acceptance of, fluctuating 'executive needs'. The adoption of a professionalism in this area, according it the importance given to any manufacturing or marketing endeavour would be a logical beginning. Senior status deserves the assurance of reciprocal responsibility from the employing company in the form of the publicised provision of a career-path which is 'horizontal', satisfying, and implicit of continuity, rather than narrowly and hypothetically 'vertical' and frustrating in its inability to fulfil this promise. Planning for horizontal development will require an intelligent training and retraining policy, enabling the executive to acquire knowledge of and adapt himself usefully to a variety of company activities. No 'specialist' function should be regarded as automatically precluding its exponent from practising in the wider ranges of management responsibility.

Mature people outside the company may be of value as a pool from which temporary management needs can be filled, on a short-

term 'contract' rather than on a 'consultancy' basis. Single projects
requiring extra executive effort should be so staffed, rather than by
appointments which cannot be sustained in the long term. A list of
suitable contacts should be drawn up and retired or retiring executives, or those offered early retirement – again in a practical, generous,
and humane spirit calculated to eradicate any possibility of resent-
ment – should in particular be offered this type of association with
the company. And guidance, too, should be offered (the company
must enlist professional help in this) on the problems of adjustment
to retirement. This much can and must be done: Industry has not
in fact been spectacularly successful in making full use of the capacity,
energy and intellect so readily offered and so frequently and un-
profitably written off.

The loss to industry of talented and experienced executives is
patent. Yet there are signs that the pattern of 'rejection' is no longer
determined solely by the employing company. The redundant
executive, too, is now making a significant decision.

While the arrows of economic fortune wound all so affected, the
displaced manager faces a shock of traumatic intensity. Often the
possessor of specialist skills, or of knowledge no longer in demand,
invariably of mature years and almost certainly bearing the high
level of financial and social commitment associated with his status,
he is particularly vulnerable to long-term unemployment so long
as he retains the image of himself as a discard from a specific vocational field. The more so since opportunities in such fields may well
continue to contract.

It is, however, a fact that a significant number of executives in this
position will no longer attempt to contest the labour market in an
endeavour to reinstate themselves in some approximation to their
previous role. The established process of personnel-selection, to say
the least, does little to spare the feelings of the rejected applicant.
It is not surprising, therefore, that the reaction of many erstwhile
managers to the real or fancied humiliations of this prospect, is to
'opt out' – in fact, to abandon the hope of further employment in
industrial or commercial life, and to seek instead, suitable avenues
for their own capacities and resources.

For some these options may imply a turning to small business
opportunities, to the tenancies of public-houses or the purchase of
lock-up shops. Lacking the necessary resource, or resources, others
may find the answer in the acceptance of lesser posts, or in a

premature 'retirement' buttressed financially perhaps by the earnings of a wife who may herself be of professional standing. Greater stringency will therefore be imposed on this stratum of the public, which will impact not only on the labour market but also on the demand for a wide range of goods and services, on consumption and expenditure patterns and life styles.

The Educational Environment

Its influence on marketing practice

If marketing is accepted as a mechanism responding to human needs and aspirations, then clearly the educational level of the community can be seen as a major influence on marketing practice; for, if it is the facts of economics which determine purchasing capacity, it is unquestionably educational attainment which shapes not only tastes, i.e. the kind of goods which are manufactured and purchased, but also the *quality* of the demand and the receptivity of the public to the sales message and the product-standard offered. And while those in the educational field have faced and will continue to face their philosophical and organisational ordeals, it is plain that both as potential producers and potential consumers, the society of the seventies and beyond will be on the whole better educated and more articulate; more sceptical and more discerning; and perhaps given to a greater degree of experimentation than its predecessors.

Television, film and radio play their part in this process, in providing, beyond the range of normal (and inundatory) entertainment, specific 'educational' programmes offering direct visual and aural experience of geographic, historical, cultural or scientific themes. Visual aids, in fact, abound, as commonly accepted today as was the 'chalk and board' of yesteryear. Yet it is in the approach to the psychology of education that the greatest strides have been made.

Modern primary education, for instance, reflects the adoption of leadership rather than precept, the training of senses, the development of curiosity, and of an awareness of social interdependence. 'Academic' studies are in no wise neglected; but the approach to the respective disciplines is being increasingly influenced by liberal and uncommitted attitudes. Economic instability and factors such as the raised school-leaving age have done much to erode traditional ideas, and it is for example, unlikely that an engineering apprenticeship can still be regarded – as once was the case – as a guarantee of lifetime employment. Indeed, the decline of classic industries and the evolution of new technologies now face the educationalist with the problem of 'training' for vocations as yet unrevealed.

The factor of uncertainty, too, is evident at both secondary and university levels. In the former case there is controversy – as yet unresolved – as to the purpose and consequent orientation of the extra year of secondary education; and in the universities there is the growing tendency to take refuge from the raw options of the outside world in a first degree, generally in broad subjects (such as Oxford's 'Human Sciences'), rather than in vocation-linked professional studies.

People in Categories

In the truest sense, however, the educational environment of the seventies is, and will remain, formidable in its contribution to public affairs; and not only will this be evident in the advanced level of its formal teaching, or in the human product of the educational system.

Additional capabilities will reside in an enhanced awareness of international life and events, in the penetration and acceptance of the cosmopolitan idea, and in the consequent versatility of demand for a global variety of goods and services. This broadening of vision will be accompanied by enthusiastic public support for Adult Education, and by the saturation of applications for the late-education opportunities now offered by the Open University wherein places have been taken up by taxi-drivers, building labourers, clerks, and others hitherto excluded by occupation or circumstance from further educational development. To these developments must be added the excellence of news and publishing media, e.g. the explosion in paperback publishing which offers the human span of literature at a fraction of its historic cost. The speed with which marketing executives recognise how a more sophisticated, better educated, better informed public will affect company marketing policy and practice, is likely to be a major contributory factor to the success of their enterprises. Little further reliance, for instance, can be placed in the 'consumer categories' long cherished by advertising and media researchers. Such mechanistic identification in terms of occupation, geographical location, income and purchasing pattern may well have been relevant in the postwar period during which hard and fast behavioural differences were more readily observed.

Differentials in income, purchasing ability and inclination, and in educational and cultural standard are less evident today, and the erstwhile 'Grade B' consumer who watches his football league match on Saturday afternoon, may well spend the same evening in a 'Grade A' viewing of Shakespeare. It is this amalgam of cultures, this enhancement of appreciative capability which is increasingly becoming the social norm; thus, the traditional demarcations between consumer classes will become increasingly blurred beyond the point of useful significance.

This process will be aided by the general availability of credit and other methods of financing purchases of goods and services e.g. 'cash-by-budget' and revolving credit on the basis of 'repay as you wish, pay interest on the balance'. Personal convenience, too, will influence the further use of credit card purchases. A solid foundation has already been laid in the acceptance of the credit card (over a period of some years) as a ready token of payment for restaurant meals, petrol and, albeit slowly, for consumer goods and services. Particularly in the last two fields, the credit card will become a consolidated and general currency, to some extent masking for the uninitiated the true cost of the product or service offered. (Consumer protection bodies, however, can be expected to extend their vigilance in this direction.)

At the same time there will be further developments in consumer and industrial facilities. A prototype of the sort of financing arrangements that will become more common is the purchase and leasing schemes operated by Hawker Siddeley in respect of aircraft sales. The high cost of such products is recognised and unavoidable, and although outright purchase (of for instance, the HS125 Executive Jet aircraft) is by no means discouraged, alternatives are offered which are attractive in their own right. Thus, sales can be arranged by bank overdraft, by lease through merchant banks and finance houses, or by hire-purchase – all methods which are familiar. The departure from traditional practice however is the Hawker Siddeley concept of 'joint-jet operation'. In this concept a group of companies combine in joint-ownership of the aircraft, combining their travel requirements. This enables the 'first cost' and fixed annual costs to be spread over a high number of flying hours, proportionately reducing the cost per mile to each partner.

A rising generation of better educated and socially aware consumers will exercise a greater degree of control over the manufacturer by virtue of their developing tastes and standards and will not hesitate to resort to public criticism of inferior or sub-standard products or service. They will extract or be given gratuitously the maximum of publicity from the mass media, and pursue their appeals through the active consumer protection organisations. They will be no less vocal in their concern for the physical environment. The implications for marketing of both these socio-economic phenomena require further amplification.

The Consumer Protection Movement

The investigation and monitoring of standards by organisations set up to represent the interests of consumers is no longer a novelty to the manufacturer. Familiarity with the purpose and potential of alert consumer protection bodies, however, has done nothing to lessen his sensitivity to their pronouncements. Although latterly divested of Governmental standing, these bodies now exist on a regional and voluntarily-staffed basis, and invariably they have learned the lessons of their formative years to good effect. Product 'guarantees', for instance, have provided them with rich and fertile material for study, and it is largely through their efforts that the majority of such guarantees today are more intelligible to the consumer and protect the buyer as much as the seller.

For those claims which fail this test, however, as for other revealed shortcomings of product or service, there is the retribution of derogatory publicity on a massive and nation-wide scale. Established specialist publications wholly concerned with consumer protection – such as *Which?* – have built for themselves impressive reputations (and in the process have severely dented others) by means of 'comparative-value' surveys of products ranging from deaf-aids to contraceptives, from dishwashers to tape recorders, and from cars to electric blankets.

On a national scale, too, the news and magazine media have found the subject of consumer protection to be highly rewarding copy, and where the potential reader-interest is judged to be high, will readily depute their own staff to carry out investigations, frequently in the guise of 'disinterested' shoppers.

D

The harmful effects of adverse Press publicity have not gone unnoticed in marketing circles, since it has been seen to be effective in certain circumstances. For example, the campaign waged by Bernard Levin in the columns of the *Daily Mail* comes in this category since initially, at least, Levin, representing the consumer, was a puny David ranged against the Goliath of the Post Office. The latter's avowed intention was to splinter the existing London telephone directory into a larger number of volumes based on a suburban regional classification instead of the familiar alphabetical system. This elicited an immediate, firm, and public declaration of war from Mr. Levin. A single issue of this declaration was sufficient to recruit a vociferous and enthusiastic army of telephone users behind him; and it required only a short but intensive campaign distributed over some few issues of the newspaper to persuade the Post Office that the consumer interest would be better served by abandoning its original scheme.

The activities of Ralph Nader are perhaps better known, and it is more than possible that as 'quality' improves over the whole range of manufacture, that his task, and that of his world-wide associates will become increasingly contentious. The effects of Nader and of his predecessor, Vance Packard, with their exposures of engineering incompetence, of physical danger to the consumer, and of such peccadilloes as 'built-in obsolescence', may or may not have encouraged a change of philosophy in the boardrooms of America's manufacturing giants. What is certain, however, is that as a result, a considerable slice of life at General Motors, at Ford, and in many other large companies in a score of industries, is now devoted to heading off potential attack from the aspiring Packards and Naders, from the American Consumers Union, and from the consumer bulletins and reports which now circulate in their hundreds of thousands. Product testing in the consumer interest is now the province of engineers, chemists, physicists and technicians, and the indignation of manufacturers finding themselves assailed by such expertise rarely reaches the extreme of litigation. Manufacturers have come to regard even the prospect of a successfully contested issue involving their competence or integrity with some reserve. Most now recognise the fact that the only true refuge from the wrath of the consumer associations lies in the consistent exercise of those two qualities.

Concern for the Environment

Nothing is now likely to stem the tide of public concern and legislative vigilance for the protection of the environment.

Reaction against two hundred years of technology's indiscriminate development is fast approaching a state of panic as the wider implications are revealed for contemporary and future society. The deterioration of marine organisms, the fouling of seas and inland waters, blighted agriculture, occupational physiological disorders and the poisoning of local atmospheres, collectively represent the magnitude of this problem. The pressures mounted by active, environmental, special-interest, or other representative bodies seem likely to sustain (and increase) the tempo of public enquiry.

The manufacturer, inevitably, is the prime target of criticism for activities which appear to offend against the public interest. It is his processes which are threatened and attacked by legislation at source, and his products which suffer public contumely in the marketing sector.

It is true that many manufacturers, committed to now obsolete plant, have fought and are still fighting expensive rearguard actions, and particularly is this so in the vexed sphere of the treatment and disposal of industrial effluents. In general, however, the need to satisfy local authority and government requirements has been successful in changing the climate of the approach to manufacture and its residues. There are transgressors, certainly; but for the majority, the problems which exist are those of operating within the limits of public tolerance, and of balancing the public interest with commercial expediency.

An example can be found in the mass-production of articles in indestructible plastic and in consumer reaction to the now notorious 'one-trip' plastic bottle. Cheaper and simpler to produce than counterparts made in glass or ceramics, the criteria of manufacturing and servicing costs entirely favour the use of such plastics. Initially it was expected that enormous inroads could be made into markets once dominated entirely by glassware. For the dairy industry, for instance, the non-returnable bottle represented freedom from the need to install and operate re-washing plant, to administer the collection and scrutiny of 'empties' and to hire the associated labour. The concept of the plastic bottle appears less enticing, however, to a public now becoming more sensitive to real or potential environmental misdeeds; a public which has made clear its recognition of the fact that the use of non-returnables simply transfers the onus of disposal to the consumer.

The adverse reaction of one group of strong-minded consumers in setting up 'collection points' for soft-drink one-trip bottles and then dumping them in their thousands on the offending factory's doorstep, is hardly the relationship between company and customer which managements can desire. Such considerations now influence major marketing decisions. By way of example, it is possible to quote the proposal – intelligent and attractive in presentation – for the manufacture of disposable surgical scalpels in plastic, to be sealed in irradiated plastic packing. In every other way a viable manufacturing and marketing operation; yet in the light of the disposal problem, a source of potential public concern.

In the mass-consumer field, of course, public goodwill is vital. It is, however, only a fairly recent phenomenon that this 'goodwill', taken to include the environmental aspect, should seriously influence the planning of new industrial ventures.

The two factors – goodwill and environmental compatibility – are fundamental and inseparable, but there is a further factor which industry has been slow to comprehend, namely the economies which become possible as a direct result of efforts to control pollution from industrial sources.

In the process field, effluent, both gaseous and liquid, can be treated to extract not only atmospheric and biological contaminants, but also valuable constituents for re-cycling. It is open to manufacturing industries, in turn, to analyse the true cost of raw material as represented by actual product-content and by 'waste' in the form of residual materials and over-purchase etc. For the marketing executive who must act as agent between the manufacturer and the consumer, the lesson is plain. In the context of a world community now angrily responsive to every manifestation of industrial and commercial self-interest or indifference to social need, the product which he offers as well as its presentation, must, like Caesar's wife, be above suspicion. If a company's own marketing strategy does not ensure this, then competitors' strategies will.

The Leisure Environment

Subjective influences on leisure have been briefly referred to in the discussion of the broadened educational background and its attendant encouragement of exploration in the Arts.

These influences are evident too in the reaction to the machine-values of the 'sixties', and in consequence, in a growing return to non-passive recreational activity – to painting and writing, theatre-going, 'eating-out', do-it-yourself, travel, sailing, caravanning, etc. We have also seen some loosening of attachments to hitherto unquestioned values, and in many cases, their complete abandonment. The journey from the standard of absolute loyalty to one's employer to a condition of employment without even the pretence of security of tenure, has helped to create a climate in which, more and more, leisure has become the purpose of work, rather than its hard-earned sabbatical reward.

While it may not be correct to speak of hedonism as a prevalent outlook, there can be no doubt as to the potential of the lesiure market in this climate; nor of the potential for those who devise, operate, and purvey its facilities and requirements. The preoccupation with leisure as a more important and substantial element in the pattern of living creates its own wide range of marketing opportunities, influencing not only fashion and manufacture, e.g. the demand for 'casual' wear, but also hotel and catering management and investment, the purchase and utilisation of aircraft and sailing craft, as well as a whole new range of service industries associated with leisure and travel.

Leisure, of course, is but a slice of the economic cake. Translated into terms of shorter working hours, for instance, it may well appear to be a synonym for higher 'overtime' payment and it must remain so in those industries in which earnings are only marginally abreast of the cost of living. For the more fortunate, however, leisure pursuits will be explored on an unparalleled scale, providing a welcome market for a diversity of manufacturers ranging from boatbuilders to those engaged in electronics (for the seventies will see the continued decline of the local cinema and the introduction of film cassettes for home viewing).

Factors such as house-purchase and industrial recruitment will more accurately mirror the importance accorded to leisure; for whilst people in their thousands will continue to be attracted to specific firms and regions for family and economic reasons – although the escalating cost of housing must inevitably contain this movement – many more people, particularly among the executive and professional grades, will attach greater importance to the leisure and culture facilities offered, reflecting their belief that life is something to be lived 'in the round', rather than played out in the ordained role of worker ants.

Conclusion

This brief survey has reviewed and attempted to project some basic elements of the contemporary scene. It is possible now to place them in perspective and to consider their meaning for marketing in the immediate future.

It was remarked earlier that in the face of pressures and demands now unfolding, it will be necessary to revise marketing attitudes and to define new approaches to marketing problems.

In the boom years, for instance, it was too often the case that a modicum of rudimentary market research was considered sufficient, both to identify the customer, and to meet his demands. It may just be possible that, in the short-term, this level of operation will continue under a momentum which will progressively diminish as the effect of new marketing methods become evident.

It is these methods, however, which typically will offer not only machine tools but programmes for their utilisation, not only freight services but also promotion, penetration, and outlets for the products to be carried, not only appliances and vehicles but effective guarantees of performance.

Among the more alert companies, the beginnings of this process can already be observed. For management the challenge will be to educate themselves in the true value of properly planned and executed marketing research. For the executive, the task will be adapt to the role of entrepreneur; one who is capable not only of seeking out and exploiting marketing opportunity, but also, of creating it.

It will be necessary, too, for marketing executives to reject the passive acquiescence with which they have hitherto accepted the product delivered to them by design and engineering departments. The feedback of information from the point of contact with the customer, or potential customer, is now of critical importance to the sustained penetration of a given market and it will no longer suffice merely to identify the area of demand.

The full range of marketing research techniques and the knowledge which accrues therefrom must be brought to bear, not only on such identification, but also on such factors as comparative production cost and the use of new and more economical materials where these can in part or wholly replace existing ones.

Neither should the marketing executive be at all coy, should perception and the movement of events point the need, in guiding the very product-basis of his company. Mindful of the fact that an 'established' product offered to an historically declining market has undone many an industrial dinosaur, he will be alert, too, not only for the symptoms of decline, but for its causes.

The New Consumer

The comparative bleakness of the economic background described at the beginning of this chapter must inevitably leave its mark on consumer habits and life styles and a notable manifestation of this fact will be the newly perceptive shopper. Education and the cynicism of experience, too, will play their part in the creation of a demanding and highly critical consumer, and it is to be expected that this pattern will be sustained for long after some degree of prosperity is re-established. Brand loyalties will figure high among the casualties of critical shopping, since a primary yardstick, of necessity, will become best value for lowest price. And 'value' of course, will more and more be seen in terms of 'use-value' rather than of prestige, preference, or any of the traditional appellations now reduced to expensive irrelevance. A healthy cynicism, too, can be seen to be crystallising towards the brash advertising of TV commercials, and indeed, towards the less socially aware examples of media advertising. The Adman's world, in fact, once populated with exotic and improbably slender models ('A' people, of course) may approach more closely to fact as diminishing returns emphasise the lack of appeal such unreality carries for an educated public case-hardened by its own vastly different experience.

Response, therefore, to pricing, to standards of service and advertising will provide avenues through which the consumer will exercise his influence over the manufacturer and supplier, and in all but degree this situation is orthodox enough. In the context of the seventies, however, the degree will represent a crucially important advance on previous experience.

*   *   *

This, then is the marketing environment of the decade, and the challenges it poses for its practitioners.

In the space of a chapter it is possible only to comment on some of the salient facets. Those which have been picked out for discussion, however, must be considered among the most significant for future marketing policies and practices. The alternative is stark. Either these policies and practices will reflect a more realistic understanding of modern society and its circumstances or the marketing organisation will fall victim to the cumulative onslaughts of changes in the cultural and social fabric which have gone unremarked, or worse, failed to elicit a timely response.

The new policing and regulatory bodies inaugurated by the Government in 1972 have only proved necessary because of a clear failure by business to take the initiative in responding actively and constructively to changing social and cultural patterns and attitudes.

The full impact of the decision to appoint a consumer 'supremo' within the Government and the style of the new Director of Fair Trading's management of consumer affairs remains to be seen, as do the policies to be adopted towards mergers, monopolies and business and commercial practices in restraint of competition.

One thing is certain. Life for the marketing man is never going to be quite the same again.

CHAPTER 3

Marketing Strategy for Technology-based Enterprises

BY HARRY SASSON

The effect of technological change on markets is as pronounced as its effect on design, materials, processes, systems and products. With product life cycles becoming shorter and shorter as a result of competition, obsolescence and substitution, there is a very real problem of maintaining steady growth. The problem is magnified when the effect of superimposing life cycles is considered, or the need to match the appropriate marketing strategies to successive stages of each product's life cycle.

Profitable life cycles cannot be generated or exploited without successful innovation, but what is the appropriate amount to spend on researching and developing these new products? And how can one ensure that they are selected on the basis of perception, not extrapolation, of market needs?

In order to achieve perception and innovation, a four-stage approach is necessary: to scan the environment, logically analyse the data obtained, generate ideas from the data, and finally to set the objectives and determine the strategy. Arrived at in this manner, strategy can be the means of rejuvenating a company in terms of its own life cycle. It needs a follow-through, however, of key marketing activities in an overall corporate planning context.

Relevance of Technology to Marketing Strategy

In technology-based fields, perhaps more than in any other, the battle may already be lost on the very same day a new product is launched. If that is the case, then from that point on, no amount of marketing skill can redress the situation. In technology-based fields, perhaps more than in any other, the chances of coming up with the wrong product are greater because:

● a dominant R&D function can generate products that are 'wrong' in marketing terms;

● high development and launching costs are irrecoverable if the size of the market does not live up to expectations, or if product substitution abruptly cuts short the expected payback period;

● prices often decline dramatically as complex production technologies are mastered, making the early product unprofitable.

The arena of technology is littered with commercial failures that could have been avoided had chief executives ensured that new projects satisfied real market needs and opportunities, that they were matched by appropriate financial and production capabilities, that marketing men were alerted to new technical means of satisfying long-standing needs, and conversely that scientists and technologists appreciated the realities of commercial facts of life. The list reads like a recipe for corporate planning – and it is just that. Its relevance to the development of a marketing strategy for a technology-based enterprise is that the same list is equally a recipe for the successful marketing of advanced industrial products. Successful marketing begins at the top, and corporate strategy is more inextricably intertwined with marketing strategy than with any other function. The trigger that starts the expensive process of technological innovation leading to the marketing of new products which will shape a company's character and to the commercial uses of new technological processes and equipment is market awareness. There is thus a strong case for marketing strategy being very closely concerned with the selection of new product projects, and the specification of research and development briefs.

There are very few products or services left today that are unaffected by technological change. To narrow the field for this chapter, a distinction of degree rather than of kind has been adopted, but the chapter is nevertheless relevant to the technology-based enterprise providing either products or services or both.

The impact of technology may be felt at one or more points in the 'pipeline'. The areas of greatest opportunity or vulnerability will be found amongst the following:

Design: With a mastery of current technology, technical

design is not a problem and firms can 'innovate to order'. If current technology is displaced by a new or unfamiliar technology, then a completely new approach to design may be necessary, but the lead-time may be too short in which to complete it.

Materials: The development of new alloys and additives, synthetics and very pure materials, together with changes in price levels may increase the substitution of one material for another in many products – displacing whole process industries.

Processes: New protective treatments and manufacturing processes may be cheaper, more accurate, faster or use less material than current processes.

Systems: Developments in methods of controlling machines, processing information, solving problems, improving communications, transportation, distribution, energy generation and control have far-reaching implications.

Products: It may become feasible to fill existing or newly identified needs with entirely new products, as a result of technological advance in design, materials, processes or systems applications. Such substitution can make existing products obsolete overnight.

Maintaining Growth

The problem of maintaining a high growth rate in a technology-based enterprise is acute; as new products are successfully introduced, others have to be discontinued because they have reached the end of their useful product life cycles or are no longer profitable.

The effect of introducing products having identical life cycles at regular intervals is not one of indefinite growth but for the overall value of sales to reach a plateau. This may sound surprising but it will be clear from the somewhat simplified case illustrated in Fig. 1 and Table 1. If the annual value in successive years of the initial product 'a' is 0, 1, 3, 4, 4, 3, 1, 0 and if additional products b, c, d, e, etc. of equal potential are introduced, at yearly intervals, the overall growth pattern is established by simple addition.

But, because the 'layers of the cake' under the envelope curve (i.e. the contributions from successive new products) get more and

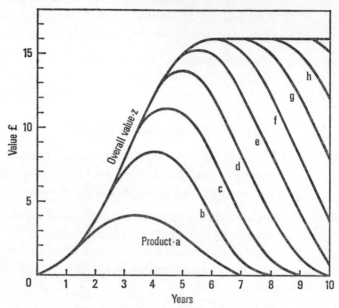

Figure 1 The Envelope Curve. The overall value of new products with a 0.1.3.4.4.3.1.0. life cycle, introduced at yearly intervals.

Product	0	1	2	3	4	5	6	7	8	9	10
a	0	1	3	4	4	3	1	0			
b		0	1	3	4	4	3	1	0		
c			0	1	3	4	4	3	1	0	
d				0	1	3	4	4	3	1	0
e					0	1	3	4	4	3	1
f						0	1	3	4	4	3
g							0	1	3	4	4
h								0	1	3	4
i									0	1	3
j										0	1
Overall value·z	0	1	4	8	12	15	16	16	16	16	16

Table 1 Overall Growth Pattern. Reproduced from *Why more new products may not mean growth* H. Sasson, Financial Times, 5th March 1971.

more inclined, the risk of disaster if a new product is late or not up to the mark becomes progressively more serious. This risk is very real in the absence of an adequate bread-and-butter business, a common condition in high-technology and similar fast-moving fields.

The only ways open to a company in this situation wishing to maintain its initial high growth rate and avoid stagnation are for it to introduce, at regular intervals, products of greater and greater total value, or alternatively for it to reduce progressively the interval between new product introductions.

Both strategies are potentially unstable. The first would aggravate the extent of the disaster that would result if anything went wrong, particularly in view of the generally higher and higher minimum threshold levels of development cost. The second would inexorably draw the company into an ever-increasing number of different products, services, markets and technologies, leading to organisational complexity and problems. The conclusion is clear: the forward planning of a technology-based enterprise cannot be done as an extension of research and development or marketing or manufacture or finance alone. The implications of a growth strategy must be recognised and clearly thought out in terms of an overall corporate strategy.

Applying a Marketing Strategy to the Product Life Cycle

The concept of product life cycles is now fairly widely understood, but it is not often put to use in a strategic manner. Most firms tend to react tactically to the factors that predominate at different stages in the life cycle; they are the victims of their own products' life cycles.

By predicting the shape and duration of each stage in the life cycle of proposed new products, and by determining the stage existing products are in, one can more realistically adopt active rather than reactive product policies. This is increasingly important because product life cycles are shortening. There is less time to learn by trial and error, and there is a high premium on organisational speed of response.

The four stages of the typical product's life cycle are shown in Figure 2. They are, successively, market development, growth, maturity and decline. The characteristics of each stage are different, and this must be taken into account in developing an appropriate marketing strategy.

In the market development stage, sales are low and unprofitable. There is not yet a proved demand for the product, which in many respects is still untried and untested. The strategic requirement at this stage, where one is trying to create customer demand, or even to get them to try the new product, is to overcome resistance to change. The reasons for such resistance may be foolish or wise, logical or illogical, obvious or unsuspected, but they must be anticipated and allowed for.

In the market growth stage, customer demand 'takes off', distribution pipelines are being filled and there is a rapid increase in profitability. This attracts other firms to the field, and to anticipate this,

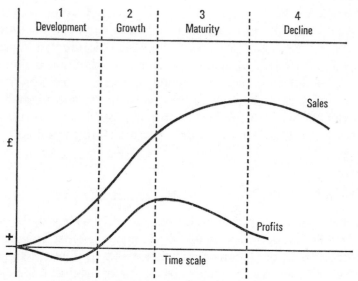

Figure 2 The Four Stages of a Product Life Cycle.

strategic emphasis must shift to creating product preference through advertising, better distribution channels, and more effective pricing. However, with increasing competition the market moves towards saturation.

In the market maturity stage, growth tails off and profitability declines. Strategic emphasis moves to market stretching devices, to identifying and satisfying special market segments.

In the market decline stage, all will admit that there is no further growth to be had. Attempts are made to arrest the decline in profitability by better cost control. The decline is sometimes long drawn out if some firms withdraw from the field, leaving their customers to those who remain.

That is the life cycle in full. In technological fields perhaps more than in others, products are vulnerable to being superseded long before their final decline. The need may disappear; a better, cheaper or more convenient substitute may appear; or a competitive product may gain a decisive advantage through superior marketing strategy. Product obsolescence arising from technological substitution of design materials, processes, systems, or applications is a regularly occurring fact of life that must be reckoned with. A patent, for example, is no longer a guarantee of sales and profits for a number of years ahead. Strategically, the risk of product substitution is guarded against by scanning the environment and logically analysing the data thus obtained, as a prelude to one's own innovative thinking.

Successful Innovation

Technological innovation can be defined in a number of ways. One, adopted by the Central Advisory Council on Science and Technology, is that it denotes the technical, industrial and commercial steps which lead to the marketing of new manufactured products and to the commercial use of new technical processes and equipment.

Successful technological innovation is a complex process involving the interaction of many factors, all of which need to be got right. The 'product arrogance' and the 'solution in search of a problem' arising from strong research and development alone is no longer credible or profitable – however fashionable it may have been in the 1950's and 1960's.

Since we are concerned with marketing strategies for technology-based enterprises, the criterion for success must be commercial rather than technical. Failure must therefore be defined as an attempted innovation which does not establish a market and make a profit, even though it may 'work' in a technical sense. Apart from product defects, failure may arise as a result of inadequate market analysis, higher costs than anticipated, poor entry timing, competition, an insufficient marketing effort, an inadequate sales force, weaknesses in distribution, or low product acceptance because of resistance to change that has not been overcome. Failure is usually clear-cut: the product is withdrawn; the plant is closed; a receiver is appointed; or the firm is wound up. Success on the other hand is not as quickly evident. It may take a long time for the innovation to show a profit on the original investment. Where success is clearly evident, however, it will generally provide pointers to the kinds of factors on which it depends.

Recent studies of successful innovating companies have indicated that the characteristics they tend to possess which less successful companies do not are the following:

- they make more use of market forecasting;

- they are more familiar with the market concerned;

- they understand user requirements better;

- they concern themselves only with projects whose launching costs are in balance with the size of the market and the scale of their production capacity;

- they have better coupling with the outside scientific and technical community in the specialised areas concerned with the innovation – e.g., they take licences, embark on joint ventures, and generally tend to 'look outside';

- they have better external communications;

- they seek the innovation more deliberately;

- they encounter less opposition to the innovation within the organisation on commercial grounds;

- they employ larger teams at the peak of development activity and achieve a shorter lead time from the start of a new project to the marketing of the initial product;

- they benefit more from dependence on outside technology during production;

- they give more publicity to the innovation;

- they tend to drop products as a result of innovating others;

- they devote more effort to educating users;

- they employ greater sales efforts.

These characteristics are either inputs to a successful marketing strategy, or are a part of the strategy itself. Together they reflect the outward-looking, non-extrapolative approach that is the hallmark of successful innovation.

Implications for R & D Policy

A marketing strategy for a technology-based enterprise cannot succeed for long without a continuing innovative input emanating from an appropriate research and development effort.

Even if appropriate marketing strategies are applied at each stage of a product's life cycle from growth to maturity to decline, total profits will fall to zero unless new generations of products are introduced, in line with market opportunities and needs.

New products, whether developed in-house or acquired through licensing agreements, are the result of research and development. Expenditure on research and development has been increasing at an accelerating rate, particularly in the last 20 or 30 years, as Figure 3 shows.

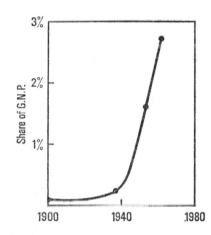

Figure 3 U.K. Research and Development Expenditure as percentage of G.N.P.

Sources:

1900: D. W. Hill, Analyst, 1962, 87, 337; W. W. Rostow, British Economy of the Nineteenth Century, 1948, 105, Oxford: Clarendon Press;

1938: Ministry of Aviation, Central Statistics estimation; Annual Abstract of Statistics, 1958, No. 95 HMSO;

1954: Annual Abstract of Statistics, 1958, No. 95 HMSO; Chambers Encyclopaedia, 1959, 284 London: George Newnes Ltd;

1962: Economist, January 1963, 333.

Although it is now a major item in the budget of all technology-based enterprises, and is likely to increase still further, R&D is a difficult item to plan and control. If a company is spending £100,000 a year on R&D, the question of whether it ought instead to be spending £50,000 or £200,000 or nothing at all is far from theoretical.

The first parameter to establish is whether the scale of the research and development effort is of a sufficient size to be productive within a time scale that will allow the products developed to arrive onto the market before they are obsolete. The second parameter to establish is whether the production resources and markets potentially available are large enough to make it possible to show an adequate return on the investment being made in research and development.

E

With these provisos satisfied, the short-term and long-term effects on profit of changing the level of research and development expenditure are shown in Figure 4.

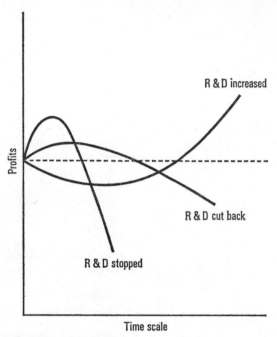

Figure 4 Effect of changing the level of R & D expenditure.

Reducing or eliminating expenditure has a short-term benefit and a long-term cost; increasing expenditure (but not beyond the optimum level determined by the two parameters discussed above) has a short-term cost and a long-term benefit. The time scale that applies to what is meant by short-term and long-term depends on the rate of product obsolescence. This in turn depends on the extent of competition and the nature of the raw materials, the process and the product itself. The existence of a time dimension in the relationship of expenditure and profit has led to the development of a Discounted Profit Forecast technique for calculating the maximum amount a firm or an industry is justified in spending on research and development. The main criteria on which the calculations are based are the rate of obsolescence and the profit potential of the products of the firm or industry, and the economic evaluation of its research and development projects.

The following simplified example will serve to illustrate the technique, which has been more fully described in a paper by A. Hart, published by permission of Morganite Research and Development Ltd.:[1]

1. Leaving aside the question of growth, continuation of R&D investment at an economic rate must ensure a steady state *A*, which represents the level of net profit plus R&D expenditure, in Figure 5. The chart has been constructed for a hypothetical company with £12 million capital employed, £12 million annual turnover, £200,000 annual R&D expenditure, £1·8 million annual net profit before tax (15 per cent on capital or turnover), and an interest discounting rate of 5 per cent.

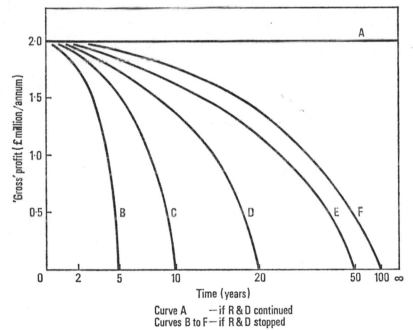

Curve A — if R & D continued
Curves B to F — if R & D stopped

Figure 5 Forecast 'gross' profit curves (net profit + R & D expenditure). The area under each cuve is proportional to the present worth of the profit at an interest rate of 5 per cent compounded continuously.

2. Discontinuing R&D, will cause net profit to jump to £2 million and then decline to zero – along line *E* for the data

[1] *Planning for increased research productivity*. Symposium on Productivity in Research, 1963 (London: Institution of Chemical Engineers). Charts reproduced by permission.

quoted. In other cases the life of the company might be variously estimated at 1, 5, 10, 20, 40 or 100 years.

3. The present worth, at an interest rate of 5 per cent, of the area under line *A*, i.e. if R&D is continued, is £41 million. The present worth, at an interest rate of 5 per cent, of the area under line *E*, i.e. if R&D is stopped, is £24·6 million.

4. The value to the company of its future R&D expenditure is therefore a present sum of £16·4 million, which is equivalent to an annual expenditure of £800,000 (say nearly 7 per cent of turnover). This is the maximum amount the company is justified in spending on R&D in order to achieve its 'gross' profit (net profit+R&D expenditure) of £2 million every year.

5. If the maximum justifiable R&D expenditure of our hypothetical company is calculated on the assumption that it would otherwise have a 'life' of 5, 10, 20 and 100 years if R&D were stopped (as represented by curves *B*, *C*, *D* and *F* in Figure 5), and the results are expressed as a percentage of turnover, a graph of maximum R&D expenditure against

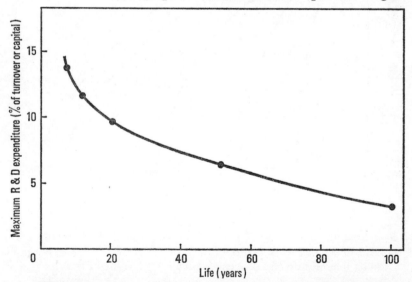

Figure 6 This chart expresses the relationship between the 'life' of a company if R & D is topped and maximum justifiable expenditure on R & D, if present turnover and earning rate are to be maintained. Based on a company having a capital/turnover ratio of unity, and earning a net profit on capital before tax of 15 per cent.

'life' may be plotted. This is shown in Figure 6. The graph quantifies the greater pressure to spend more on R&D to which are subjected companies (or industries or product units) whose products have a higher than average rate of obsolescence.

6. The Discounted Profit Forecast technique is then applied to each product or product group made by the company. As a hypothetical example, three products A, B and C might each be yielding a present 'gross' profit (net profit + R&D expenditure) of £600,000 on a turnover of £4 million. Present annual R&D expenditure is £300,000. Profit forecasts with continuing R&D are shown as curves A, B and C on Figure 7, and A', B' and C' are the forecasts if R&D is stopped.

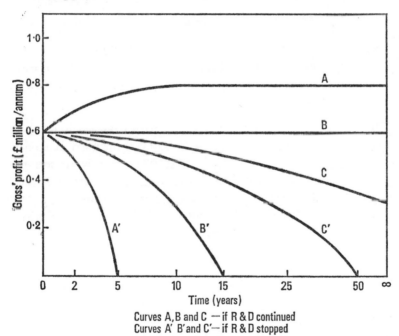

Curves A, B and C — if R & D continued
Curves A' B' and C'— if R & D stopped

Figure 7 Forecast 'gross' profit curves (net profit + R & D expenditure) for a company's three products A, B and C. The area under each curve is proportional to the present worth of the profit at an interest rate of 5 per cent compounded continuously.

7. Calculation of maximum justifiable R&D expenditure, as in 3 above, gives the following results:

Product *A*: maximum R&D expenditure £690,000 p.a.
Product *B*: maximum R&D expenditure £400,000 p.a.
Product *C*: maximum R&D expenditure £150,000 p.a.

Total £1,240,000 p.a.

The company would thus be justified in spending up to 69 per cent of its 'gross' profit (net profit + R&D expenditure) on R&D – four times its present rate.

8. On product *A*, which has a high rate of obsolescence, and is expected to yield increasing profits in the future, the company is justified in spending £690,000 – 115 per cent of 'gross' profit. In 10 years' time, however, if the forecasts prove to be correct this figure will have fallen to £670,000 – 83 per cent of 'gross' profit.

9. On product *C*, which has a low obsolescence rate and is expected to yield decreasing profits in the future, the company is justified in spending only £150,000 – 25 per cent of 'gross' profit.

10. The company has a long way to go before it is likely to reach its limiting figure of £1,240,000 on R&D expenditure: its present figure is only £300,000. If it is reasonable to assume that R&D expenditure should be proportional to the calculated limits, then the present annual expenditure of £300,000 should be allocated £167,000 to product *A*, £97,000 to product *B* and £36,000 to product *C*.

A more empirical method of determining research and development expenditure is a comparative approach which relates industry growth rates to expenditure expressed as a percentage of net output. This is the basis on which Figure 8 has been prepared.

It is interesting to note for example that in the period under review, the US aircraft industry grew at twice the annual compound growth rate achieved by the UK aircraft industry, even though both industries spent on research and development a sum equivalent to about 30–35 per cent of their net output. In the case of other technology-based industries, such as electronics, other electrical, instruments, and chemicals, US firms spent more on research and develop-

Double logarithmic scale

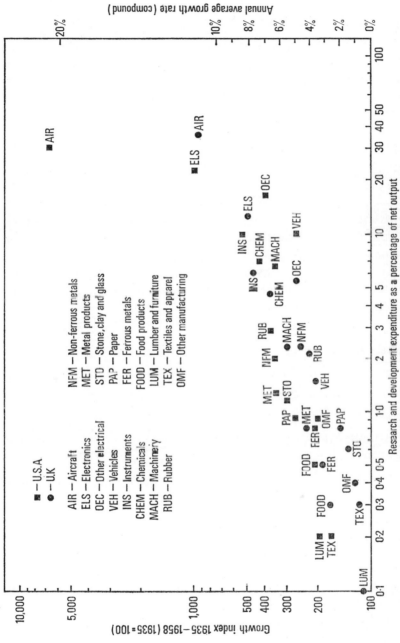

Annual average growth rate (compound)

Research and development expenditure as a percentage of net output

Figure 8 Research and development as a percentage of net output in 1958, and growth of industries, 1935–1958.
Source: National Institute Economic Review No. 20, May 1962.

■ — U.S.A
● — U.K

AIR — Aircraft
ELS — Electronics
OEC — Other electrical
VEH — Vehicles
INS — Instruments
CHEM — Chemicals
MACH — Machinery
RUB — Rubber

NFM — Non-ferrous metals
MET — Metal products
STD — Stone, clay and glass
PAP — Paper
FER — Ferrous metals
FOOD — Food products
LUM — Lumber and furniture
TEX — Textiles and apparel
OMF — Other manufacturing

Growth index 1935–1958 (1935 = 100)

ment (as a percentage of net output) and achieved a higher annual compound growth rate than UK firms.

A third approach to determining the appropriate level of research and development expenditure is to build up to the total by deciding what is the appropriate expenditure justified by the availability of, and return on, capital in relation to cost saving and product improvement programmes, new products and processes, and fundamental research.

In practice, decision-making would be aided by looking at the results of all three approaches, as they are not mutually exclusive.

Clearly, apart from planning research and development expenditure, there is also the question of controlling its productivity, and the follow-through to profitable commercial exploitation. Both requirements will be met by ensuring very close working relationships between the marketing function and the research and development function, by the use of interfunctional appointments such as venture project managers, and by making sure both the marketing effort and the research effort are an integral part of an overall corporate strategy that is both innovative and perceptive.

A Four-stage Approach

To develop a successful marketing strategy for a technology-based enterprise requires an approach that will successfully fulfil three fundamental requirements:

- it must overcome management preoccupation with day-to-day problems;

- it must get away from straight line projections in an age of increasing change;

- it must recognise the need to innovate despite the problem of predicting the future.

Preoccupation with day-to-day problems can occur for a variety of reasons, such as reliance on operational rather than strategic information systems, a traditional operational management background and promotion ladder to top decision-making roles, insufficient attention to environmental scanning, and emphasis on the recent past rather than the future. A manager in this situation will react to adverse results but his options will be very limited. He is like a man driving a car with his eyes shut, and relying on the seat of his pants for contact with the world around him. His behaviour is an example of 'Management by Crisis'.

The danger of straight line projections is that the extrapolative approach (last year + 5 per cent) focuses management attention on tactical matters and methods rather than on strategic opportunities. Those who adopt the extrapolative approach are captives of their products' life cycles and characteristically have a 'reactive' posture. They are very vulnerable because product or service substitution can bring a product's life cycle to an early and untimely end. With improvements in management information systems and techniques our manager will now react to adverse trends, and thus anticipate adverse results. His options will be less limited. He is now driving the car with his eyes on his rear-view mirror, or his side window at best. His behaviour is now an example of 'Management by Exception'.

To produce and manage innovation is difficult. It is doubly difficult within organisations because these are usually structured to routinise the accomplishment of essentially repetitive tasks. The mastery of routine, which is a central purpose of organisation, is not conducive to creativity or innovation. Yet it is through innovation that our manager can best react to his environment, and thus anticipate adverse trends. His options would be much wider, and would include the possibility of anticipating strategic opportunities. He would then be driving with his eyes on the road and the signposts ahead, and his behaviour would be an example of 'Management by Perception'.

How can this perceptiveness best be introduced into the process of developing a marketing strategy?

The traditional approach has been first to appraise internal strengths and weaknesses and external threats and opportunities, and then to set objectives. It is an approach doomed to failure because it inevitably results in extrapolation, and extrapolation cannot resolve the conflict between the need to exploit profitably the firm's existing products and markets, and the need to innovate continuously to ensure the firm's survival and success. The two needs compete for resources and management attention, but they represent altogether different systems and cultures. Within an operationally-structured organisation extrapolation may be accepted, but innovation is a low-priority need.

If the appraisal stage of the traditional approach described above is replaced by four distinct activities described below, an approach to developing a marketing strategy will result which will prevent extrapolation and provide greatly increased scope for innovation. In adopting this approach, the sequence of activities leading up to setting objectives is:

1. scanning the environment

2. logical analysis of data

3. generating ideas from data

4. setting objectives

These activities are best performed separately, as they rely on quite different human qualities to be successful. The first activity requires drive and inquisitiveness, the second insight, the third creativity and the fourth judgment.

Each of these activities will now be considered in turn.

Scanning the Environment

Acquiring information and analysing it are the two closely interacting halves of a loop or continuous cycle. It is necessary, however, to distinguish between scanning an organisation's environment for information, and the subsequent analysis to find out why what is happening *is* happening, because by separating the two stages, one reduces the risk of the conditioned responses symptomatic of an extrapolative approach.

For an innovative decision the task of scanning typically involves information requirements that cannot be precisely defined, data that is not readily available, and subjects that are unfamiliar to the scanner. Any piece of information or bit of data encountered, regardless of the purpose or lack of purpose in acquiring it, *could* possibly bear on a strategic problem, yet no type or class of information is intrinsically strategic.

This is in sharp contrast to the solution of a routine problem, where the full range of relevant information can often be identified, acquired and understood; it is programmable, and one can usually specify exactly what information is needed as a stimulus to trigger a suitable corrective response.

A senior manager must participate in the scanning process firstly to seek information for himself and second, to make sure his subordinates are getting the right quality and quantity of information in line with what is needed as a basis for innovation, and what is available. He must make sure his subordinates are able to grasp the significance of information to which they are exposed. He should do this by ensuring they are aware of the issues of actual or potential importance to them or to the company, and are familiar with the subject matter.

For managers in any given industry, conditions and trends in that industry determine in large measure what areas of external information will be relatively most important. Any given set of industry conditions and trends will, through cause-and-effect relationships, have implications and consequences. These in turn will define areas of attention that should be scanned and receive management attention. A formal definition of all such areas is useful, because it may serve to alert managers to important areas of scanning attention that had previously been overlooked. Important categories of external information that must always be scanned include:

- market information on market potential, structural change, competitors, customers and prices;

- technical information on new products, processes and technology, product problems, costs, licences and patents;

- broad issues; events of a political or social nature, and government actions and policies;

- leads for joint ventures, acquisitions and mergers, and similar possibilities;

- resources possibly available, including persons; and purchasing considerations for products of current or potential interest.

A manager obtains external information in one of two ways: he either asks for it, or it reaches him unsolicited. Information which he asks for is either explicitly requested or it may be organisationally solicited, when a standing responsibility exists to inform him. Unsolicited information may be directed at a manager if there is a potential benefit in this to him or the source. Alternatively it may be undirected information, such as something important noted in the course of general conversation or in a publication.

His sources of information may be internal or external, and they may be personal or impersonal. Typically, they include customers, suppliers, bankers, consultants, licensees, business and professional associates, neighbours and social contacts, trade publications, newspapers, conferences, exhibitions, special reports, subordinate, superior and other internal organisational contacts, internal reports and notices and meetings.

When a company as a whole is considered, almost all external information originates from outside sources. This does not apply to the individual manager; usually, much of the external information he secures comes from other individuals in the same organisation.

Scanning methods range from the superficial and informal to the very detailed and formal. Table 2, which amplifies a concept first described by F. Aguilar,[2] indicates the characteristics of the types of scanning that are available.

Table 2. SCANNING METHODS

	less structured less costly ⟵		⟶ more structured more costly	
	Undirected viewing	*Conditioned viewing*	*Informal search*	*Formal search*
Description	General exposure to information	Directed exposure to a more or less clearly defined area or type of information	Relatively limited effort to obtain specific information, or information for a specific purpose	Deliberate, methodical approach to obtain specific information, or information for a specific purpose
Purpose	To alert to the fact that something has changed	To ensure sensitivity to particular kinds of data	To increase emphasis on relevant sources	To place maximum emphasis on relevant sources
Result	Focus on something more to be learned	Readiness to assess significance	Significant data monitored	Maximum possible information acquired

[2] *Scanning the Business Environment*, F. J. Aguilar, Collier Macmillan, 1967.

Information is boundless and scanning is costly. For the process to be economic, it must be limited to what is efficient in cost-benefit terms. The level of resources to allocate to acquiring information about an issue may be established by rating the check list in Table 3.

Table 3. RATING AN ISSUE TO DETERMINE
SCANNING METHOD TO USE

	Score				
	Low				*High*
	0	1	2	3	4
Magnitude of the issue					
Urgency of the issue					
Extent to which it constitutes a problem					
Extent to which the issue and its information needs can be defined					
Relevance of the issue to long range plans					
Inadequacy of existing information					
Availability of additional data					
Predictability or regularity with which information might appear					
Time, energy and other resources that can be devoted to scanning					
Predominance of this issue over other issues competing for information					

Summating the score will yield a total of between 0 and 40 points for each issue that is rated. In general terms, with a score of below 10, an issue should not warrant anything more than undirected viewing, bearing in mind that the expense of scanning increases progressively as one moves from undirected viewing to conditioned viewing, to informal search, to formal search. Conditioned viewing may be appropriate to an issue scoring 10–20, an informal search to an issue scoring 20–30, and a formal search to an issue scoring 30–40.

For example, technical innovations as an area of attention might, in the case of a technology based enterprise, rate $4+3+2+2+4+1+3+3+2+3 = 27$, so justifying a basic state of informal search, whereas in a case of an enterprise that is not technology-based the rating might be $1+1+0+1+2+3+1+1+2+0 = 12$, thus requiring no more than conditioned viewing.

In both cases, however, registering something of potentially greater significance would alter the ratings and would trigger a move to a higher order, more structured, and more costly method of scanning.

Logical Analysis of Data

This is the next stage in which a manager attempts to find out why what is happening *is* happening. The object is to understand, interpret, and correlate data acquired at the scanning stage.

Where the data is quantifiable and reasonably complete, it lends itself in part to the use of sophisticated quantitative management techniques of appraisal. These include the use of models, statistical methods, operations research, decision theory and probability theory which will yield useful results, but in the final analysis much reliance will always have to be placed on specialist knowledge of the particular field of activity.

There are many techniques that are an integral part of the process of analysing environmental data, which are useful in identifying and forecasting possible business opportunities. A representative cross section is included in Table 4.

Table 4. TECHNIQUES FOR ANALYSING DATA

Technique	*Application*
Demographic and sociological analysis	Forecasting and assessing demand in areas such as waste disposal, air pollution, communications.
Conditional demand analysis	Assessing conditions under which new technologies will be needed, and the probability of such events occurring.
Opportunity identification	Identifying alternative ways of providing properties possessed by present products.

Technique	Application
Trend plotting	Comparing the technical-economic performance trends of rival products, systems or services.
Theoretical limits test	Probing known phenomena to their limits, and studying the implications.
Parameter analysis	Predicting technological crossover points and substitution growth curves.
Systems analysis	Identifying weaknesses in present product/service systems.
Diffusion studies	Assessing applications in some fields of innovations in other fields.
Impact studies	Assessing the implications of technological advance – actual, probable and hypothetical.
Scientific surveys	Reviewing inventions and current research programmes.
Life cycle model studies	Anticipating future substitution of competitors' products.
Technological mapping	Assessing future performance by analysing competitors' capacities.
Strategic analysis	Assessing competitors' actions, e.g. mergers and acquisitions to anticipate where they will be placing their technological emphasis.
Delphi	Establishing earliest, latest and most likely time estimates to desirable and realisable breakthroughs, using a poll-with-feedback approach.
Morphological research	Mapping out all possible alternative solutions by considering all the variables.
Normative relevance analysis	Working back to the present from an actual or assumed future requirement to see what needs to be done to make it attainable.

Generating Ideas from Data

Having logically analysed the data obtained by scanning the environment, one is then in a position to generate ideas—the first step in innovation.

Some company environments are more conducive to creativity and innovation than others, and it is important to ensure that creativity is not stifled in the company's structure. This may happen, and usually does, in organisations designed primarily for the mastery of routine and not for the provocation of constructive dissatisfaction with an established order. It should be recognised that the ability to generate ideas does not increase hand-in-hand with general experience, but sometimes goes in the opposite direction. Equally, a general exhortation to be creative is useless without a basic understanding of the process, and of practical techniques for applying it.

Specific techniques of 'lateral thinking', synectics, brainstorming, bionics and other methods have been developed and refined. Some are appropriate to individual thinking and others to group situations. Their aim is to aid the definite process of escaping from a fixed way of looking at a problem in order to move to a more effective way. Often they involve a structured approach to creativity as the means of innovation.

Lateral thinking is the term introduced by Dr. Edward de Bono to indicate the definite process involved in escaping from a fixed way of looking at things, in order to move to a more effective way. It recognises that the mind is organised as a biological processing system which is fundamentally different from computer processing systems. Dr. de Bono has developed many techniques making use of the lateral thinking process for introducing creativity into thought and language.

Synectics is a nine-step method developed by W. J. J. Gordon for creative problem-solving. It makes use of psychological mechanisms (personal, direct, symbolic and fantasy analogies) to move information that has been stored in the subconscious mind to a conscious level. The nine steps in the synectics process are:

1. Brief explanation of the problem as given;
2. Analysis and explanation by an expert;
3. Purge, to get the more usual solutions aired and out of the way;

4. Generation of problems as understood, i.e. restatements;
5. Choice of problem as understood – momentary agreement on an understanding of the problem;
6. Use of evocative questions to trigger the use of analogies to discover possible solutions;
7. Examination of possible solutions;
8. Force-fit of solutions to problem as originally posed;
9. New viewpoint of problem is reached, and many potential solutions may arise.

Brainstorming is probably the best known approach to generating creative ideas. It was developed by Alex F. Osborn and first achieved prominence in 1950. Three phases are involved in the brainstorming process: a fact-finding phase, an idea-finding phase, and a solution-finding phase. In the fact-finding phase the problem is properly identified, questioned and revised to produce the specific problem to be worked on. In the idea-finding phase ideas are produced, then re-processed by such means as modification and combination: criticism is ruled out and reserved for a later screening session; wild ideas are encouraged as they may trigger practical suggestions that might not otherwise occur; quantity is encouraged. In the third, solution-finding, phase tentative solutions are verified, criteria are developed for judging ideas, a final solution is adapted and its implementation worked out.

Bionics is one of a number of less structured approaches to creativity and innovation. It has been defined as the art of applying the knowledge of living systems to solve technical problems. Living systems are not copied in detail, but are used as models to understand the principle of why things work in nature. This knowledge is then applied to designing and making things. A ground speed/altitude indicator for aircraft was based on the way the beetle's eye functions. Study of the bat's echo-sounding mechanism and its relationship to radar is well-known. Less well-known are the continuing studies of how the bat prevents jamming from other bats and how certain insects jam the bat's detection system. The dolphin's skin is known to defeat turbulence. Certain fish can detect electric potential gradients as low as a millionth of a volt per foot. These and very many other living systems can provide useful and sometimes spectacular clues to the solution of technical problems.

In using these techniques, an essential requirement is the provision

F

of an appropriate 'climate' in the internal environment of organisation:

● 'Sacred cows' should be got rid of – gradually, in order to avoid setting up a counter-reaction;
● the rigid control of vertical thought should be relaxed. Ideas should be tentatively accepted even if they seem wrong, in order to explore what they lead to;
● stimulation should be sought from the interaction of ideas, as in brainstorming, or from an unfamiliar or inappropriate setting.

There is more to creativity than keeping one or two ideas men in a research department, consulted whenever a problem arises. Professional managers who, like lawyers and doctors, tend to think vertically along rigidly defined orthodox lines should seek to adapt to their world some of the techniques used intuitively by lateral thinkers such as journalists, advertising men and artists – the openness to ideas and influences, the seeking to develop awareness, and the deliberate use of unreason.

According to one eminent business commentator:[3]

'In too many companies the young men with the bright ideas have been kept firmly bottled up, ideas and all. In one typical case, a well staffed management services department was asked to tackle a basic problem. In a complex company, no clear decision had been taken on who made what where. The bright young men worked out a simple, elegant solution of which they were rather proud. However, they had direct access only to the production board – not to the engineering side, which dominated the company and had the ultimate say. The engineering people threw out the new idea, and said they would come up with their own solution, which was duly produced. It was the system which already existed. This basic situation crops up again and again with endless variations. The men are there: the ideas are there: but those who have the power to let the men and ideas break through insistently obstruct. The problem is to a large extent social. But until it is resolved, promise and performance will continue to be miles apart. You can teach an old dog new tricks: but he won't perform them as well as a

[3] *Management in Britain – The Real Challenge*, Robert Heller, Ashridge Management College Paper in Management Studies, 1971.

young dog – or as the young dog would perform them if the old one would stop barking at him.'

How does one go about setting up an appropriate climate? Clearly, in the example quoted, the chances of acceptance would have been greater if the engineering department had been brought into the situation at an earlier stage.

Resistance to change is a fascinating if sometimes infuriating trait. Long before a company's staff join forces to overcome potential customers' resistance to change and get them to buy a new product, internal resistances to change within the company must be overcome in order to make the new product policy a reality in the first place.

A number of steps can be taken to reduce internal resistance to change. The more heavily structured the situation, the more important these steps are to the future well-being of the company, and by the same token, the more difficult they are to implement:

● More use must be made of management processes that run across organisation charts rather than up and down: these include venture management, project management, formal corporate long range planning, short-term operations planning, etc. More frequent transfers, travel and horizontal communication are also valuable. The move is from hierarchical flows to decision flows.

● Strategic information sources and systems must be developed and they must be separated from operational and logistical management information systems. The emphasis must move from cost to cost effectiveness.

● The focus of management attention must move from the past to the future, from inward-looking to outward-looking, and from product, geographical, functional or departmental consciousness to total profit consciousness.

● People's ideas, whether they result from individual creativity or group creativity must break through communications barriers, whether up and down or across and into a company. For this to be possible, the company's internal environment must become outward-looking, and constant change must become acceptable as the normal state of things. This will result in a greater receptivity to ideas and an improved likelihood of their successful implementation.

Developing practical approaches to achieving innovation by means of 'group think' methods including the following:

(a) Subdividing the problem; when isolated, the essential problem may be easier to solve.

(b) Assuming the problem is solved; from the consequences, work back to the essential problem.

(c) Trying every logical and apparent procedure.

(d) Using analogies that provide a new axis of reference; these could be biological, metaphorical, personal or direct analogies, fantasy analogies or simply physical models.

● Making wild or random guesses, avoiding immediate criticism.

● Assuming a plausible solution, which is known not to be right, and challenging others to attack it.

● Assuming an impossible solution and challenging others to attack it.

● Letting the opposition have its way, but only as an intermediate stage to eliminate polemics.

● Denying that the problem exists.

● Breaking off if all else has failed; participants' minds will incubate the problem and an effortless solution may appear on re-convening.

● Producing as many solutions as possible; not only will this indicate the best solution, but it may indicate possible competitive approaches and suggest lines of defence.

Creative persons tend to be independent, enthusiastic, determined and dissatisfied – and also disruptive and difficult to manage. They can be managed, however, if their personality, their intellectual and motivational characteristics and their needs and attitudes are recognised and if managers accept the implications.

Managers must also learn to recognise unhealthy environments for group activity and acquire the skill and insight needed to counteract the negative influences by which ideas are killed before they have a chance to develop. Their role in a creative environment is not so much the traditional one of planning, controlling and evaluating, as that of skilfully managing individual differences, creating healthy groups, managing social power and resolving conflicts.

Setting Objectives

The fourth stage in evolving a marketing strategy is the conversion of the ideas that have been generated and accepted into objectives.

It is necessary to plan and set objectives because markets develop neither entirely at random, nor with complete certainty, and because the long lead time of most manufacturing investment makes it impossible for a company to respond instantly to profitable opportunities. If this were not the case, there would be no need to plan and set objectives. Yet although the need to plan and to set objectives is universally acknowledged, there has not been a corresponding success in their implementation and achievement.

Most company plans are the outcome of an annual budgeting and forecasting exercise, in which the management of each part of the company say what they are going to achieve in the planning period, and, basing themselves on this, set out their justification for resources they would like allocated to them. The results of this exercise are aggregated into 'The Plan'.

This 'bottom-up' approach does not produce a strategically-based plan at all, but a budget which is no more than an extrapolative control device through which performance is monitored during the planning period. This remains true however elaborate the profit planning undertaken, however detailed the projections calculated for contribution, return on assets, cash flows, or other indices. The reason the 'bottom-up' approach does not produce a strategically-based plan is because at no stage does it ask strategic questions or seek to answer them.

Strategic Planning

Strategy is an attempt to maintain a better long-term match between a company and its environment than that achieved by competitors. Since companies, like products, have life cycles, strategy must take into account the stage in the life cycle at which the company finds itself. As a company grows, matures and perhaps inevitably declines, it goes through five stages where, successively, the most important considerations are in turn survival, rapid growth and prestige, profitability, stability and security, and self-preservation and survival.

Strategy is the means to rejuvenation, since by consciously and creatively planning its own destiny, a company can move across industry, product, market and geographical boundaries and contrive to stay – perhaps perpetually? – on the growth and profitability 'shoulder' of its life cycle curve. To do this, a company must undertake a 'top-down' approach to its strategic planning.

Earlier in this chapter we have shown how it must compare its performance with that of other companies, and against economic trends, and how it must learn to see what is happening and be prepared to innovate, even if this only refers to things new to the company or its industry.

By following the sequence described up to this point, it can now define the amount of growth, the area of growth, and the direction for growth in line with leading strengths and a profitability target. As statements, these can be translated in an operational form that is usable for guiding management decisions and actions. Together they constitute the objectives and strategy that give expression to the concept of a firm's business.

The 'Top Down' approach

In a 'top down' approach financial objectives are worked back from the continuing level of dividends that would satisfy shareholders and investment requirements, after likely future inflation is taken into account. A target rate of growth in dividends, and historical retention policy will together determine a net profit target. This and estimated tax will enable required pretax income in turn to be determined and, with depreciation added in, cash flow.

The need to generate these earnings has implications for capital investment, and objectives must be set for a target rate of return on existing investment and for a minimum cut-off rate for new investment.

In the final analysis it is people, not companies, that have objectives, and consequently the process of setting these objectives should be accompanied by changes in attitudes of mind, reflected in a 'raising of sights' and in a subtle evolution of a company's fundamental purpose and beliefs.

If these changes are achieved, then the corporate strategy which will be developed will reflect, in its imaginativeness and calculated risk-taking, the entrepreneurial thinking synthesised by the approach that has been described.

Alternative marketing strategies

The innovative firm can adopt one of four alternative marketing strategies in respect of each area of opportunity:[4]

1. *First to market*

    Characteristically this strategy requires a research-intensive effort and outstanding technical leadership, with a high risk of failure for individual products because of large investments in technical and market development made without the prospect of any immediate return. In order to be successful it requires the ability to absorb mistakes, withdraw and recoup, without loss of position in other product lines. It requires first-rate long-range planning and the ability to make important judgments of timing, balancing the improved product development stemming from a delayed introduction against the risk of being second into the market. Examples include De Havilland (the Comet 1 jet airliner), Rolls-Royce (successive generations of jet aero engines), Du Pont (Nylon, Corfam), the Beecham Group (semi-synthetic penicillins – ampicillins), Pilkington Brothers (float glass), and Berger Jenson Nicholson (Magicote thixotropic paint in 1959).

2. *Follow the leader*

    Characteristically this requires an organisation that gets things done, and first-rate competitive intelligence. The company environment is often that of a perpetual fire drill. Many interfunctional techniques are used, and top management is constantly concerned with maintaining the right balance of strengths between the technical, manufacturing and marketing functions. Examples include Boeing (the commercial jet airliner), Armstrong Cork (vinyl floor tiles), IBM (computers), Texas Instruments (transistors), and Walpamur (Crown Plus Two thixotropic paint in 1967).

[4] *Strategies for a Technology-based Business*, H. Igor Ansoff and J. M. Stewart, Harvard Business Review, November–December 1967.

3. *Applications engineering*

> This strategy requires strong product design and engineering resources, ready access to product users within customer companies, technically perceptive salesmen and sales engineers working closely with product designers, and an emphasis on cost control and cost effectiveness. New technologies are cautiously introduced, and management is profit-oriented. An example is Saunders Valve (diaphragm valves).

4. *Me too*

> Characteristically, this strategy reflects a strong manufacturing function dominating product design, and a strong price and delivery performance. Manufacturing and administration overheads are kept low and a direct hard sell is maintained on price and delivery. An example is Black & Decker (home user power tools).

A particular company's choice will largely depend on the type of internal skills and resources it possesses or which it is in the process of acquiring. It will, however, tend to develop a consistent style in its approach to opportunities and tend to restrict itself to only one of the four alternative marketing strategies.

Although it would seem that only the first two strategies are innovative, this is not necessarily so. The scope for innovation in design, materials, manufacturing processes and marketing is equally wide in the third and fourth alternatives.

Key marketing activities

A number of activities are involved in implementing a marketing strategy for a technologically-based enterprise. These are market research, product and market planning, selling, sales promotion and sales service. The effectiveness of the overall marketing strategy depends entirely on the effectiveness with which each activity is implemented. The checklist which follows will enable a top manager to assess the extent to which adequate attention is being paid to each activity, and to ensure that each contributes to the overall success of the whole strategy. Successful innovative firms characteristically respond with a high proportion of affirmative answers to the check-list questions.

CHECKLIST OF KEY ACTIVITIES IN
DEVELOPING SUCCESSFUL MARKETING STRATEGY

Market Research

	Yes	No
Is the effort adequate, and showing a return?	☐	☐
Are the results used by senior management?	☐	☐
Is demand forecasting undertaken?	☐	☐
Are overseas markets researched?	☐	☐
Is performance assessed against customer requirements?	☐	☐
Is performance assessed against competitors' performance?	☐	☐

Product Planning

	Yes	No
Is product policy clearly defined?	☐	☐
Are product designs in line with what the customer wants, particularly overseas?	☐	☐
Do design briefs for R&D include data on user needs and price-volume needs?	☐	☐
Are R&D costs controlled to establish R&D cost-effectiveness?	☐	☐
Is the approach to pricing flexible?	☐	☐
Is close attention paid to the profit mix of the product range?	☐	☐

Market Planning

	Yes	No
Is market policy clearly defined?	☐	☐
Are alternative distribution methods reviewed in terms of effect on sales and profits, as well as on costs?	☐	☐
Is sales forecasting undertaken, and for overseas markets?	☐	☐
Are overseas agents adequately motivated through personal contact, pricing freedom, market feedback being welcomed?	☐	☐
Are markets carefully selected and is the market mix periodically reviewed?	☐	☐
Are marketing resources planned as part of long term business planning?	☐	☐

Selling

	Yes	No
Do sales engineers have specialised product knowledge and is this made available to customers?	☐	☐
Does senior management participate in selling?	☐	☐
Is multi-level selling aimed at all customer decision making units?	☐	☐
Are sales force activities planned and controlled in detail?	☐	☐
Is outside recruitment of sales staff used as a means of avoiding an inbred inward-looking approach?	☐	☐
Is the sales force motivated with appropriate individual incentives?	☐	☐

Sales Promotion

	Yes	No
Are records of promotional expenditure kept and analysed?	☐	☐
Are shared promotions used, in preference to none?	☐	☐
Are catalogues regularly updated, and for overseas are they printed in local languages?	☐	☐
Are films and direct mail used as well as exhibitions and advertising?	☐	☐
Is as much use as possible made of public relations and technical press editorials?	☐	☐
Are demonstrations used as a convincing form of promotion?	☐	☐

Sales Service

	Yes	No
Are there standards for product servicing, including breakdowns and repairs, and is performance monitored?	☐	☐
Are there standards for customer servicing, including training, installation and demonstration, and is performance monitored?	☐	☐
Are service engineers decentralised, and does sales service report to sales or marketing?	☐	☐
Do users know whom to contact when in difficulty?	☐	☐
Is stock policy appropriate, particularly for spares availability and delivery?	☐	☐

Are overseas agents self-sufficient for stocks, spares
and trained staff, and are their manuals in local
languages?   □   □

These key success factors have been set out in terms of the characteristics displayed by successful innovating companies. They are
stated in terms of the detailed activities whose effective performance
is vital to a successful marketing strategy.

Planning and Follow-through

In more general management terms, there exists another key
success factor, which is the ability of a company to evolve a corporate
marketing plan, and successfully to implement it. This requires an
effective overall planning process to make sure that marketing
objectives relate properly to relevant corporate objectives, and that
the strategies developed conform to these company objectives.

This is ensured by adopting the following format for a corporate
marketing plan, which will involve a company's entire top management team in its preparation:

Format for Corporate Marketing Plan

● Summary of assumptions, results of environmental scanning and
  market forecasts on which the plan is based:

  (a) Political, social, fiscal, economic and business environment
       for the next five or more years;

  (b) Competitive environment and market forecasts for the
       next five or more years:

       — user needs
       — products and services offered
       — sales trends and market shares
       — marketing capabilities and methods
       — plant locations and capacities
       — technological capabilities
       — earnings records and returns on investment
       — key factors in success (location, outlets, quality,
         service, price, cost, performance, etc.)
       — competitors' actions and reactions

- Analysis:

  — assessment of performance vs the industry
  — assessment of performance vs major competitors
  — priorities for resolution of problems identified
  — priorities for exploitation of opportunities identified

- Basic commercial policies to be followed:

  — statement of fundamental purposes and beliefs
  — corporate objectives: financial, physical and non-economic

- The Product/Market Strategy:

  — objectives
  — plans for growth products/markets
  — plans for products/markets that are static
  — plans for products/markets that are declining
  — new products/markets envisaged
  — new product/market gap

- Marketing Strategy:

  — product development
  — distribution methods
  — pricing
  — promotion
  — profitability
  — share of market

- Detailed marketing plans:

  — market research
  — product planning
  — market planning
  — selling
  — sales promotion
  — sales service

- Functional Support Programmes:

  — research and development
  — manufacturing
  — physical distribution

- — systems and accounting
- — organisation and personnel

● Financial Summary:

- — contributions by product, area, market segment, period
- — functional programme costs
- — profit plans
- — cash flow
- — source and use of funds
- — analyses of alternative sources of capital
- — analyses of discounted cash flows
- — analyses of returns on investment

This approach to planning is the one most likely to fulfil the three fundamental requirements stipulated earlier, of overcoming management preoccupation with day-to-day problems, of getting away from straight line projections in an age of increasing change, and of recognising the need to innovate despite the problem of predicting the future.

It is the approach that is best suited to developing a successful marketing strategy for a technology-based enterprise.

CHAPTER 4

Planning a Diversification Strategy*

BY JEREMY FOWLER

Introduction

Most companies are now finding that in order to increase their
profits they have to seek new business outside present operations.
In doing so, they rapidly learn that the decision to diversify is one of
the most difficult which can face a management team. Not only is
the range of apparent alternatives wide and the factors in favour and
against many of them complex, but even the basic decision whether
a diversification move is desirable at all is usually subject to much
internal difference of view. Why should a successful company
change its winning formula? If times are bad, should not the company prune costs and wait until an upturn in business occurs? The
argument is powerful and emotional, and usually results in the
decision to diversify being put off until the right opportunity (whatever that may be) is found. Because business is a human and not a
mechanical activity, this lack of commitment usually leads to a
failure to locate the right opportunity until a drastic decline in
profits obviates the need for formal commitment – the company
now must take some positive action if it is to survive.

It is clear that before a company can embark upon a diversification strategy the senior management must recognise the need for
new sources of earnings well in advance of any downturn in the
company's business.

Recognising the Need for New Sources of Earnings

A diversification strategy is imperative if any one or a combination
of the following conditions is present:

* A monograph prepared by Industrial Market Research Limited, 1970.

1. *The present markets will not support the growth needed by the company.* Assuming that the company has set targets for future growth or at least has a good idea of what these should be, then an examination of the markets the company is in should be carried out to see if the targets are feasible. The market analysis could show that they are only growing slowly or even declining. In making the market examination, it is vital to place the emphasis on the prospects for the end-use markets and not simply on a projection of the present product's performance.

In short, this examination is asking the question: where are the markets currently served placed on the product life cycle of *introduction, growth, maturity, saturation and decline*? Figure 1 shows these stages in the life of a typical product.

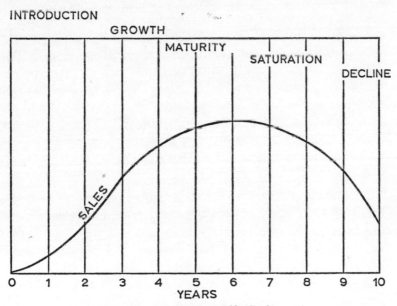

Figure 1 Product Life Cycle

A further question that needs to be answered is: how does the product's performance compare with that of the market itself? It may be that the present sales and profits of the company can be improved by the introduction of new products, services or marketing techniques.

Possibly the best products are rapidly approaching a market saturation point and diversification is most needed there, while a weak product in an otherwise good market simply needs re-organisation within its own market area. Whatever the result of this market analysis, it is the ability of the existing markets to react favourably to improved performance that must be assessed. If the present markets cannot offer the scope no matter how operations are improved, then the company needs to diversify.

2. *Profitable operation in the present markets becomes difficult.* There are many threats which can emerge and destroy profitability in a business which is otherwise attractive. The changing technology of the electronic components industry is threatening the capital structure of some companies. Monopoly buying of government and quasi-government agencies is destroying earning power in markets ranging from concrete road bridges and drugs and medicines to communication equipment. Change can also take place in the character of business. The development of domestic central heating products from a slow moving market with mainly industrial purchasing characteristics to a fast growth, consumer orientated market badly affected the profit of many companies in this field. Many found themselves quite unable to adjust to the new conditions of operation. Almost any move these companies made inside or outside the central heating products business was a form of diversification since they had no experience of fast moving consumer operations upon which to build.

3. *The existence or long term stability of the company is threatened.* Political, economic, competitive, social or technological changes can threaten the continued existence of a company in its current business. For example, the nationalisation of the steel industry in the United Kingdom has raised considerable doubts in other industries, such as transport and pharmaceuticals, about how long independence can be maintained. The changing social attitudes towards cigarette smoking combined with the actions of the Ministry of Health have been strong factors motivating the tobacco companies to diversify into other businesses, such as convenience foods and cash-and-carry purchasing.

Setting Objectives – The Gap Analysis

Having recognised the need for a diversification strategy and evaluated the prospects for the company's existing business it is then necessary to measure the size of the need. This is a two stage process. The first step is a setting of long term objectives which may be in terms of sales, profits, return on investment or the growth rate of earnings. Secondly, a comparison of the forecast for the existing business must be made against the objectives. The comparison of the two is termed a 'gap' analysis. Figure 2 shows this evaluation.

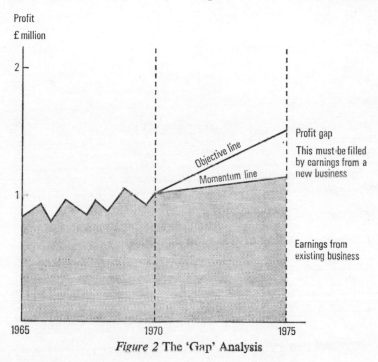

Figure 2 The 'Gap' Analysis

The size of the need can now be expressed in terms of sales, profit or investment but at this stage the means to fill the 'gap' are unclear. Furthermore, the direction of search for the best alternative new business opportunity must also be decided. Therefore, this becomes the next step in the planning process.

Which Types of Diversification Moves Are Most Successful?

The basic characteristics of successful diversification moves are reasonably well known. Studies conducted by Stanford Research Institute's Long Range Planning Service shows that moves which are *related* to a company's present business are more successful than those which are not. Whereas closely related moves yielded average

G

or above average profits for companies concerned in 70 per cent of cases, unrelated moves only did so in 38 per cent of cases. The higher profitability of related moves is perhaps to be expected. Companies earn profits on proprietary positions or strengths, and it is the essence of related diversification to seek new businesses where the existing company strengths can be used. These are identified below:

Product and manufacturing:

● product and process patent protection

● unique process know-how

● unique machinery, parts, supplies, rentals

● unique efficient manufacturing control.

Marketing:

● pioneering a major position

● capture of leading distribution channels

● unique customer services, personal selling, executive selling, applications engineering

● unique marketing techniques.

Research and development:

● unique research and development skills

● consistently successful new product development.

Thus, a company has a starting point in its search for new opportunities. By determining its strengths, it can define in some detail the new business it wants even though it has not yet been found.

Additionally, the company will have some other essential needs that it demands from the new business if it is to be compatible with present and future abilities and plans. These will at least outline basic ideas on: the size of new business needed; the type of business (such as research or quality manufacturing based); what new strengths should the new business bring?

Precisely how a company defines its strengths and needs for a new business to be compatible determines to a large extent the type of business into which it will diversify. These steps are, therefore, critical.

To Find New Businesses, Research The Market Requiring Your Strengths

Today, it is taken for granted, and rightly so, that the markets for products and services can be studied in a comprehensive and orderly way. However, recognition that the markets for a *strength* can also be studied in a logical way is a new concept.

In the past, once a company identified its strengths and the need for new business to be compatible, it used these to screen ideas derived on a random basis by such methods as brainstorming, new product committees, and the qualitative screening process. It is vital that this approach should be avoided. *Screening ideas from all sources is a selection process and at this stage it is the generation of alternatives that is important – not their selection.*

Thus, to be creative the strengths of the company need themselves to be used to generate the whole range of related opportunities open to the company.

The location and definition of a company's strengths is a matter of judgment. Primarily, the existence of a strength should be reflected in above average profits; that is, the company should have some form of proprietary position in its present markets. It is an important first step in isolating strengths to examine the ways in which customers are willing to pay the company a little more than average. To have a proprietary position means that in some superior and perhaps intangible way, the firm's products are linked to their markets better than those of competitors.

The difficulties of analysing 'plusses' result from companies being mixtures of profit and loss-making products, and strengths and weaknesses. Thus, the analysis of a company's strengths becomes a subjective judgment. This does not diminish the need for the exercise or its importance.

It is often difficult for executives of a company proposing a diversification to identify their organisation's real strengths, as opposed to those that are solely relevant to the efficient running of the existing business. The following guidelines will be of help in this identification.

Strengths are almost always intangible. For example, companies never make above average profits from such factors as the ownership of a machine, a product or a distribution method. However, they may be made, say, from a *unique* production machine which incorporates know-how, skills, and expertise on the part of those who developed it. If, however, the machine can be purchased by anyone, profits will tend to become average. Similarly, a product may be patented which represents some form of development know-how.

A distinction should also be made between strengths that enable above average profits to be made by providing value to the customer (prices will be above those of most competitors) and strengths in management or cost control (these enable a company to make higher than average profits at similar prices to competitors). While both types of strengths are important to a company, attention must be given to the former, value oriented strengths as a source of new business alternatives. There is an important danger in creating alternatives from cost oriented strengths in that businesses with inherently low profit yields are almost always located where such skills are needed just to survive.

A situation quite common among businesses which have deteriorated or operated for a long time in a non-competitive situation is to find that they have no real strengths. In these cases, the first priority is to build the company's strengths through senior manpower development. New business areas can still be derived using the methods to be described in this chapter but entry will be harder, profits lower and the risk of failure greater than for other companies. Having settled on a particular business direction for future development, a company without strengths should place first priority on recruiting the skilled staff that are needed in the important management areas.

The time required for a strength analysis is small – often one week for a small company, or two or three weeks for the complete analysis of a large company. Data is obtained in two main ways:

i.   Single and group discussions – both unstructured and using specially developed forms
ii. Interviews with customers in key areas.

The second step – interviews with customers in key areas – provides an important check to the in-company interviews and discussions.

Listed below are the results of a strength analysis of a large electronic equipment manufacturer:

1. R&D skills in microwave technology
2. Divisional strengths in electronic laboratory instruments
3. Group capabilities in providing technical and managerial training and in the preparation of instruction aids such as courses, manuals, films and slides
4. Market leaders in video tape recording equipment
5. Proven success in obtaining and completing local and national government contracts.

Defining the Product-Market Scope

The strength profile indicates areas in which the company would be able to compete effectively. These strengths can then be redefined as product and market limits within which the company should seek new businesses – the end result is a number of 'product-market scopes' encompassing the alternative directions available for diversification.

It is not difficult to see that as an example the first strength listed above could mean, in terms of the product-market scope, 'short-wave communications equipment' whereas the second strength could indicate, 'measuring and test equipment'.

Because a small company is likely to possess fewer strengths than a large organisation it can best capitalise upon its limited skills and reduce the area for research by combining its strengths in the definition of the product-market scope. For example, as listed, strengths two and five could be combined to form the product-market scope 'specialised instruments for government research stations'.

Alternatively, a large company possessing a wider skill base can fully exploit its breadth of skills by combining a number of strengths to form a broadly defined product-market scope. Thus, strengths three, four and five in the list indicate the product-market scope 'educational products'.

The example of the electronic equipment manufacturer shows that having analysed the company's strengths and defined the potential sources of new earnings the senior management may be left with a number of product-market scopes as alternative opportunities. It is therefore necessary to evaluate each alternative on the basis of the advantages and disadvantages to the company of proceeding in each direction and the chances of a successful diversification, or more pertinently, the *risks* of failure.

As has been stated earlier, this evaluation must, to an extent, be subjective as all the information on the alternative product-market scopes will not be available to senior management at this stage of the diversification plan. However, previous experience has shown that a rudimentary examination of each alternative, on the basis already outlined, is normally sufficient to narrow down the possibilities to a single product-market scope.

If depth examination of the selected area shows this not to offer any diversification possibilities then the second alternative can be selected and so on. In practice however, the examination of a second area is not normally found to be necessary.

Finding New Businesses

The product-market scope that is selected by the company's senior management must now be evaluated in some depth to determine whether suitable profit opportunities do exist.

To illustrate the next steps in this process, the third, fourth and fifth strengths of the electronics equipment manufacturer listed earlier will be used. This yielded a product-market scope of 'educational products'. The actions needed to locate the opportunities within this scope are shown in Figure 3.

The first stage is to identify the nature and types of all the products, markets and technologies involved. These are then grouped into 'businesses' so that the structure of the market becomes apparent. Then each segment is evaluated from five major aspects.

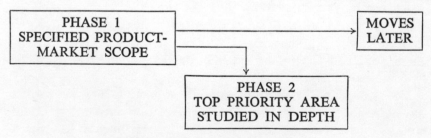

Figure 3 Finding New Businesses

FINDING NEW BUSINESSES

PRODUCT MARKET SCOPE: EDUCATIONAL PRODUCTS

Phase 1 Identifies and Structures the Demand for Educational Products

● develops information on market size and growth of each product/ market segment

● eliminates obvious misfits and small low growth areas

● places a priority from the resulting information on each type of product group

● isolates participating companies

Interim meeting selects from the priority list the product or product groups for further detailed research

Phase 2 Provides Information for Market and Product Entry and Strategy Development of the Selected Products

● conclusions and recommendations

● priority acquisition candidates

● market size breakdowns

● user industry purchases, methods of distribution

● user requirements and buying practices

● competitor company evaluation

Market Size

The size of each market in value is determined in order of magnitude (such as £2 million to £3 million). While only broad estimates are used, the figures should nevertheless be reliable. The detail required and how far the markets should be sub-divided depends on the size of the new business needed by the company concerned. There is little point in generating detail on markets which are too small to provide the profits required by the company. Businesses should not be sub-divided to the point at which they cease to be viable businesses on their own; that is, at this stage, segments of a range of sizes, by-products, or division of customer needs for which a 'package' is demanded should not be studied separately. The rule is that the analysis must be sufficiently detailed to show all the businesses that can be operated viably on their own. Such a structure for the product-market scope of educational products is shown in Figure 4.

MARKETS	BOOKS £130m	COMPUTERS £85m	FURNITURE £20m	AUDIO VISUAL £19m	MUSICAL £8m	SPORTS EQUIPMENT £3m
GROWTH RATE % per annum	2	15	4	8	1	3
MARKET SEGMENTS	Textbooks £m 70 Reference books 30 Library books 20 Other books 10	Hardware £m 50 Software 35	Desks £m 8 Chairs 5 Laboratory 4 Other 3	Movie projectors £m 9 Overhead projectors 5 Language laboratories 2 Teaching machines 2 Other 1	Instruments £m 6 Sheet music 2	Gymnasium £m 1·5 Other 1·5
MAJOR USERS	Secondary schools 50 Primary schools 35 Universities 25 Colleges 10 Other industry 10	Universities 70 Colleges 10 Schools 5	Secondary schools 10 Primary schools 6 Universities 4	Secondary schools 10 Industry 4 Primary schools 3 Universities 2	Secondary schools 5 Primary schools 3	Secondary schools 2 Primary schools 1
MAJOR SUPPLIERS	O.U.P. Collins Pergamon Macmillan	I.C.L. I.B.M. Honeywell	Gallenkamp Morgan and Grundy Midland Educational	Rank I.T.M. E.S.L. Grundig	E.M.I. Boosey and Hawkes Schotts	Dunlop Slazenger Grey

Figure 4 United Kingdom Educational Products Market 1970 (all figures adjusted to preserve proprietory data)

Market Growth

The future growth expected is a vital factor which requires careful evaluation. Growth is needed to provide a continuously attractive environment for future corporate development (in terms of favourable markets and in attracting the best employees, customers, suppliers and shareholders). The characteristics of growth markets are very different from static or declining markets. The pressures on prices and profits are lower, the opportunities for business entry are higher, and often the rate of technical and market change provides continuing opportunities for product or service development.

Compatibility

The basic compatibility of each business area considered with the existing business is also vital. Failure to understand that the underlying characteristics of a new business may be very different from those of the present business is more frequently a cause of failure in entering new markets than any other reason. This is especially true where entry is by acquisition. Many 'parents' tend to make their acquisition conform to operational procedures which conflict with the basic business needs of the new business. At this stage, an assessment is needed of compatibility with:

● existing markets

● company image

● technologies

● production

● management

● sales and marketing

Throughout a diversification study, compatibility needs to be considered. A diversification study starts by examining the company's strengths, then moves to the markets requiring these strengths, and now, in considering compatibility, moves back to the company again. The study can be thought of as a continuous search for opportunity and compatibility.

Climate of Competition

The existing competition requires analysis to determine the degree of interest and participation of each important company. Many of the companies will be well known in other fields and their methods of operation will be familiar. The participating companies are also a simple guide to some of the underlying characteristics of the business. A small or medium sized company would, perhaps, have greater interest in markets where the existing competition is of the same order. If several opportunities are found, an order of market entry can be established so that as the company grows it can meet larger competitors.

Opportunity for Profit

The opportunity for profit requires a qualitative assessment. Examination of the profits of companies already in a business area is not generally a good reflection of potential. First, it is difficult, if not impossible, to locate published data on companies solely in the area under consideration. Second, most companies carry out various forms of 'window dressing' and published figures are misleading. Third, within a large company, profit margins on specific products or services vary greatly and taking the total as a representation of the part of the business being studied is highly unreliable. Fourth, data that can be identified may not be a good guide to profit opportunity since the participating companies may have outlooks, objectives and methods of operation which are not in line with market requirements.

To show profit potential, research should concentrate on identifying factors in the markets which could be used creatively to produce above average profits. These could be:

● unsatisfied user needs

● specialised and needed know-how of any type

● proprietary situations, e.g. patents, raw material sources, captive distribution

● changing technology

The quantitative data assembled on each segment of the market is shown in Figure 4. The company is now in a position to consider its

basic future development. This is best done by grafting the accumulated experience of the firm onto the assembled market and business
data so that the executives can decide on the priority order of the
opportunities which have been revealed.

At this stage, only *existing* markets are considered. New products,
services or research, or new ways of looking at the markets themselves
are all *methods of entry;* that is, with the markets it has been decided
to penetrate located then, under 'methods of entry', new products can
be considered.

Methods of Entry

Once a priority order is established among the good areas emerging
from the initial analysis, this is studied in greater detail to establish
both market data and the most suitable methods of market entry.
For example, both audio visual and computers (heavily outlined
in Figure 4) emerged from the initial analysis as diversification
opportunities. These are the two areas which would be examined in
depth to provide information for making tactical marketing decisions.

There are four primary methods of business entry and to be sure
of success, all will need to be considered. (Clearly, by this stage
one or more methods of entry may have been excluded as being
impractical. However, for completeness, all are discussed.)

New Product Research and Development

This is the slowest, highest risk and probably most profitable form
of market penetration. Here the aim is simply to obsolesce the
products produced by the existing competition. The main question
is not 'can it be done?' but 'is there time?' Few companies possess
R&D facilities capable of operating outside their present area. Most
organisations spend over 80 per cent of their R&D budget on improving their existing products, their production process for existing
products, and maintaining library, data banks and advanced test-
and problem-solving facilities – again for the existing products. Thus,
it is unlikely that a 'team' having this background could obsolesce
the products of companies in markets outside their own area. This
form of entry is most likely to be used when the new business under
study is directly in the area of the existing physical research ability
of the company. The creative talents of the R&D team must be

directed to the best market areas. In fact, the type of study described in this chapter is becoming more and more accepted for this purpose. These studies will not increase the chances of innovation occurring but they do mean that when it does occur it will be of real significance to the company.

The areas for new product development should always be of importance to users. The developments must help the user to do a better job as he, the user, sees it. It should seek an obvious outcome but the results of many research projects show how often this objective is forgotten. The sequence is:

● decide the markets to serve from the analysis of markets defined by the company strengths

● identify user needs in these markets

● direct the research programme to meeting these needs.

Thus R&D is usually the best form of market entry when the opportunity lies very close to the present business and where time is available for development.

Licensing

Licensing is the pure acquisition of know-how. Its drawback is simple: licence fees can quickly turn above average profits into average, or average profits into below average. To be successful, licensing should be combined with considerable product development to reduce the dependence of the company on the originator in future years.

Personnel Acquisition

The characteristics of many businesses are such that above average profits result from know-how rather than from any more tangible form of investment. In many of the educational products markets shown in Figure 4 it is detailed know-how and feel of the business that makes for success. Several of the high technology electronics markets are the same. In these cases, personnel having these skills need to be employed. This almost always means attracting them from the existing competitors in the new business. The acquisition of key personnel is likely to expand as a method of market entry as firms begin to analyse the real requirements for successful operation and realise that R&D or company acquisition are sometimes very expensive alternatives to offering a high salary.

Company Acquisition

When a company has approached diversification from an analysis of where it wants to go, followed by a determination of how it is to get there, acquisition is always an attractive method of entry. The speed of market entry is fast compared with the R&D method of entry; the usual risks attendant to entering a new business are very much reduced. The acquisition can be expected to pay from day one.

There are, however, two important drawbacks. If the acquisition candidate is aware that he is situated in a good market, he is likely to be expensive. The business world is gradually learning that fast growth companies are not as expensive as they first appear, but nevertheless the initial return on capital can be low. Top priority acquisition candidates in any good area are likely to be few and the target of many approaches already. Thus, it is usually necessary to purchase a 'second choice' company which has a weakness of some kind. It is here that acquisitions may start to fail. To make up for the weakness, the acquiring company has to take a direct operational part in the new business and may suffocate it. The strengths and weaknesses of each candidate need careful assessment when 'second choice' companies are being considered.

Conducting the Research

The procedures which have been used most successfully for generating the data needed by a diversification study are shown in Figure 5. The size of the boxes in the diagram are proportional to the amount of data contributed to each part of the research programme.

Thus, under 'these methods', the first step is a comprehensive search for all published data on the subject areas, including companies' annual reports. However, for most subjects, official statistics are inadequate and published articles tend to be descriptive and in broad terms. The major method of obtaining data is personal interviews. Here data is generated during discussions with individuals selected because of their knowledge of a particular aspect of the problem. These interviews are not to be compared in any way with

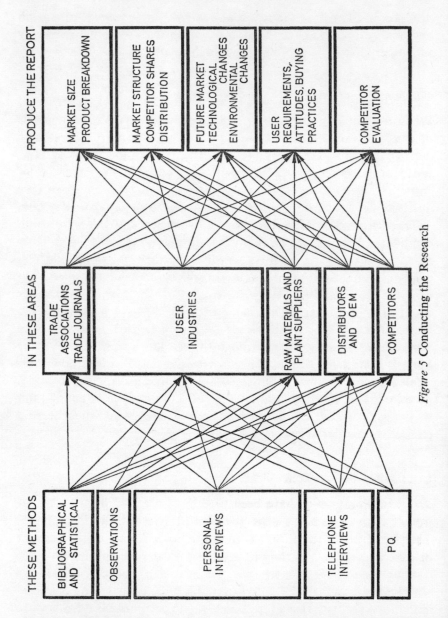

Figure 5 Conducting the Research

the type of interview common in consumer research which are usually structured questions answered by respondents in a statistically controlled sample. In a diversification study, the analyst is seeking experts whether they are technically or commercially knowledgeable and recognised as such in the industry, or whether they are simply knowledgeable through their own experience of a particular process. The analyst is essentially looking for business understanding within a framework for comparative data. Telephone interviews, postal questionnaires and observations are used to generate limited but specific data over a wider area than that covered by the personal interviews.

The second column in Figure 5 shows the areas where the research is conducted. Trade associations and journals, in addition to their normal functions, are often able to contribute data that is directly useful in selecting the various experts who form the first part of the personal interviewing. Thus, they form an important stage in the fieldwork. However, the majority of the required information will come from interviews with respondents in the user industries. Additional data will come from all other areas of the business: raw material suppliers, original equipment manufacturers, distributors, consultants, architects, and others.

Finally, it is important to interview the present participants – the competitors. Here the research companies have an advantage over analysts employed in the company undertaking the diversification study since they can interview competitors without disclosing the name of the sponsor. Competitor interviews are always conducted openly at the end of the study on the basis of exchanging information. The analysts having just completed a major study of the competitor's own business, the competitor should be interested in learning some of the results and in most cases they are. The key to success in competitor interviews is to know the answers before going to the interview. In other words, they should provide confirmation rather than new data.

The cross mesh of interconnecting lines in Figure 5 illustrates the extent of cross-validation which must be obtained and highlights the importance of not placing too great a weight on any one technique or information source. The total effect of the cross-validation is to provide a patterning of response at a high level of confidence.

Summary

It is an old saying that 'if you don't know where you're going, any road will take you there'. Yet the most cursory glance at many new products of diversification moves shows them to be the result of technical development with no market objective. In short, they are products in search of markets. The key to success is to choose the markets to be served first from a consideration of strengths and the opportunities offered, and then to concentrate all the company's creative talent on the problems of market entry.

Increasingly, the ability of a company to survive and to grow will depend upon developing a total sensitivity to changes and the impacts which will stem from them. The threats and opportunities which will open up will provide both the conditions for corporate profitability and for corporate disaster unless a methodology is adopted and adhered to for deciding on new profit opportunities through diversification. The old methods of serendipity and brainstorming are techniques for more leisurely times. The diversification steps illustrated and which have been proved practical are geared to environments in which change can be sudden and violent.

CHAPTER 5

Patterns and Development in Multi-national Enterprise

By Philippe E. Bieler

Introduction

Since multi-national enterprise will play an important role during the seventies and will to a certain extent influence the total business environment in general, and the total marketing environment in particular, it is pertinent to examine its makeup, and its place in the international business scene. Certain patterns will emerge, indicating those assets which enhance its performance and conversely those liabilities which detract from its success. From these patterns some conclusions can be drawn with regard to the optimal paths to be taken by multi-national enterprise during the next decade.

First, the function of the multi-national enterprise will be looked at. Second, its advantages and disadvantages will be examined. Finally and more specifically a set of hypothetical strategies will be developed for a multi national consumer product firm operating in the developed world.

The Multi-national Enterprise

Definition

A multi-national enterprise can most simply be defined as one that has activities in more than one nation. Such a definition is broad and would include many minor businesses which only have incidental activities of a multi-national nature. For the sake of this discussion the emphasis will be on industrial firms of a certain size, probably having a turnover in excess of £1,000,000 per annum, and having manufacturing facilities and/or marketing operations in several foreign markets. This is not to say that multi-national enterprise is

H

necessarily always 'big business'. There have been precision equipment manufacturers in Switzerland for many years who for the most part operated from a few craftsmen's homes and yet marketed recognised brands in diverse foreign markets. Multi-national enterprise will therefore include giants like Unilever and Shell, or smaller firms such as Baxters of Scotland. The difference in their field of activity is often more important when analysing these firms than the difference in their size.

It may be pertinent to also emphasise that there is considerable difference between the export oriented company and the truly multi-national company. The former is involved to a much lesser extent in the range of multi-national operating problems but neither is it in the position to obtain the full range of operating opportunities. Operating problems include such items as tax, currencies, management, transfer pricing, etc., whereas the benefits can accrue from optimal multi-national sourcing and marketing strategies.

The History

Multi-national enterprise is the product of the multi-national environment. Today, the increasing mobility offered by modern transportation and communication methods is a catalyst promoting such enterprise. It is, however, by no means the only force as successful multi-national firms, on a scale which relatively speaking was as important as it is today, existed long before efficient modes of transportation and communication had been invented. It is often said that there is a danger that some firms will become so large and so important that they will, or already are, threatening Government action. General Motors is often included in this category as its resources are as sizeable as those of important European countries. There can be little doubt that the influence of General Motors has been more positive than negative for the United States. General Motors is in many ways only a modern phenomenon because of its product and perhaps also because of its product contribution to world pollution. The Hudson Bay Company, several centuries ago, had a much more determining effect on the future course of the Government of Canada than General Motors would likely ever have on the American Congress. It may be said that despite the sometimes questionable policies of the Hudson Bay Company it was a principal contributor to the development of Canada.

It is more difficult to draw specific examples from the Egyptian, Greek or Roman empires, but it is probably safe to say that multi-national enterprise existed then and played an important role in the advancement of those civilisations and hence eventually of our own.

One of the main differences in the developing pattern of modern multi-national enterprise is the increased opportunity for the smaller firm. Several hundred years ago it was undoubtedly only the very powerful who could commandeer a ship and send it to America. Using today's transportation and communication media, a relatively small firm can successfully be multi-national.

As the world becomes increasingly multi-national there is a growing opportunity for multi-national enterprise. This is not to say, however, that success is more easily attained in the multi-national arena. Firms such as Rolls-Royce and Lines Brothers were large and once-powerful, and yet they failed. Their reasons for failure were most probably independent of this multi-national dimension, but for them and for all those in this sector it is nevertheless important to recognise that the multi-national environment is a complex one. Change is as rapid and unpredictable as in the national environment, but the variables one has to contend with are much more numerous.

In the following pages an examination is made of the opportunities for multi-national enterprise during the next decade. The discussion will point out that success will be largely dependent on the multi-national executive team. In turn, their success will inevitably result from an enlightened appreciation of the dynamics of environmental change, and hence an intelligent isolation of key business strategies. The business environment is never stagnant. The policy of today's Hudson Bay Company bears little resemblance to that which it originated so successfully several hundred years ago – it changed with the times and is still therefore a successful merchant. It is unlikely that multi-national firms will completely overwhelm their national counterpart nor that these firms will overwhelm government, but it is most unlikely that the dynamics of environmental change will diminish in the years to come.

The Advantages

In the following section is presented a number of marketing advantages offered to the multi-national enterprise. This book is mainly concerned with marketing, but as it is almost impossible to completely separate the marketing function from all others a certain amount of discussion will involve non-marketing areas. Often a successful marketing programme will be very dependent not only on the manufacturing function but also on the financial and personnel functions.

Changing Pattern

As outlined earlier, one of the principal criteria for success in business is the ability to correctly forecast environmental change. This becomes particularly true in the multi-national context where the variables are infinitely more numerous. One hundred years ago, a firm was usually correct in emphasising technical innovation over marketing or cost analysis. It was necessary for the multi-national firm to keep abreast of the technical innovations of its competitors in those markets where it was present. Today, technical innovation has not by any means been cast aside but it is as important, and by no means easier, to consider the dynamics of marketing change within the business environment. As time progresses, change appears to be for ever accelerating, so that it is necessary to be more and more resourceful and flexible. As these trends are not likely to change, they will tend both to jeopardise the future success of the less flexible giants and give opportunities for the imaginative smaller firm. The multi-national firm should, therefore, by its very existence, be even more aware of the dynamics of change than its average national counterpart. Although in a sense this could be considered a disadvantage, it is an opportunity for the dynamic young firm, and a positive stimulus for the training and development of the management team.

Size

A multi-national firm, by its very definition, is interested in more diverse markets than a national firm. In any particular field, therefore, those who venture into the multi-national sector successfully should be able to become larger than their national counterparts. It would be erroneous to dwell on this point as there are many examples to prove the contrary, but there are few small national firms who would not welcome the opportunity to distribute their fixed costs to their foreign subsidiaries. However, the advantages of cost distribution can well be outweighed by the need for more complicated organisation and communication facilities. On balance, a well-run firm should be able to capitalise on its size and the opportunities of foreign markets are clearly one of the more plausible growth routes. It is unlikely, for example, whether any of the automobile or aircraft companies in the UK could have developed or now survive were they not multi-national.

Research

Technical innovation and leadership continues to be one of the prime factors for business success and is becoming more and more linked to the marketing function. In the case of IBM, for example, they do not hide the fact that they are basically a marketing company and that their prime marketing strength is technical superiority and innovation. Technical superiority alone is not sufficient. A good example of this involved a French surgical instrument company which attempted to gain a position in the American market with a unique product. It failed dramatically because it had not considered how to establish successful distribution nor how it would produce the product in sufficient quantity and at reasonable delivery dates.

The multi-national firm has potentially an edge in the research area. Product requirements and skills vary from country to country. The UK has been a leader in electronic testing equipment, the USA in data processing hardware. An electronic company such as Hewlett Packard has a decided advantage in having decentralised its research and development in such a way as to develop those products in those countries where the skills, cost, and marketing factors are optimal. The cross-fertilisation of developmental ideas from various parts of the world is also usually beneficial.

The research and development advantage is not restricted to high technology firms. Companies in the toy industry, for example, benefit from obtaining ideas from different sources. Products produced for the Italian market may be suitable in America if some minor changes are made. A multi-national firm is therefore more likely to know of, and react correctly to, ideas and innovations produced in many parts of the world.

Marketing

To the same extent that marketing is at the heart of the modern corporate hierarchy, it is also becoming the most complex function.

For a multi-national enterprise it is rendered considerably more complicated by the diversity of market and environmental conditions.

The multi-national firm has the opportunity to choose the most favourable markets for its product line. The Singer Company, for example, knows that its sewing machine products can bring an optimum return in a lower-middle income economy with sufficient population concentration. In its worldwide marketing strategies it can therefore conclude that it is better to concentrate in Spain than in Scandinavia. The national firm does not have this leeway.

A multi-national firm should be very conscious of the changes in environmental conditions affecting the success of its product sales. It follows, therefore, that it should be able to predict more accurately than a national firm the changes in market conditions. Useful parallels may often be drawn based on environmental criteria between two markets at different stages in their evolution.

For those firms involved in consumer marketing it is usually advantageous to have a complete product line. Distributors are becoming larger and prefer to deal with fewer larger accounts. The multi-national firm has an advantage in selling a complete product line to these distributors. Furthermore, the distributors themselves may often now be multi-national and will therefore prefer to deal with an international source.

The multi-national firm will often produce products for its line in various countries. The market demands and perhaps other conditions in one country may be such that one product is better and less expensively produced there and exported in part to other markets. This allows for a relative degree of product flexibility. A small market can have, for example, products produced in volume for another at competitive prices. Conversely, in the event of a national decline at the market place the factory is 'hedged' by its foreign sales. The multi-national firm must avoid problems associated with 'dumping' but there are nevertheless many pricing permutations and combinations open to it as it produces and markets in more and more diverse countries.

In marketing, not unlike research and development, there is an advantage in the cross-fertilisation of marketing techniques between one country and other. General meetings of multi-national marketing organisations are a fruitful source for the exchange of ideas and techniques. Often certain patterns emerge between techniques and environmental parameters. In the case of the Singer Company, for example, it was found that the American experience of selling fabric and related soft goods in sewing machine stores was a much better tactic than selling miscellaneous consumer hardgoods. Tests in a number of highly-developed European markets proved this fact. It took national competition about two years to realise that they too should follow the Singer example.

The 'brand image' of a multi-national concern is normally more effectively promoted. The increased mobility of the consumer has an inherent effect. The Englishman moving to the US may prefer to buy a Jaguar there rather than an American Motors sportscar. There is furthermore a growing awareness about foreign products brought about by the communication media for which the frontier is of less and less importance. For example, French television must have a tangible influence in French Switzerland for the sale of Killy skis. Magazines, radio, improved language education, are contributing factors which tend to enhance the image of a multi-national firm at the expense of its national competitor. As the cost of advertising, particularly television, increases at a considerably faster rate than other costs, there is likely to be a growing disparity between multi-national and national opportunity in the projection of corporate and product image.

Manufacturing

As inferred earlier, manufacturing can be defined as that function which produces the products to be marketed. The multi-national enterprise usually has a distinct advantage in the manufacturing context.

The quality, reliability and cost of manufacturing can, to a great extent, be related to environmental factors. For the most part, these environmental factors deal with skilled labour and raw material. The Ford Motor Company has produced engines in the UK because this country afforded an availability of skilled labour at competitive wage rates. The raw material factor in this case was secondary. Recent developments in the labour front, including strikes, unsatisfactory productivity and rising wage rates, have upset the balance and the Ford Motor Company announced that it would probably move one of its engine plants to one of its Continental factories. British Leyland unfortunately cannot be as flexible and may well be at an increasing competitive disadvantage.

British toy manufacturers are perhaps finding that the cost of wood in the UK is reducing their competitiveness for wooden toys as other materials replace wood and the relative price difference with imports declines. A multi-national enterprise will have a growing advantage in this case to make wooden toys in a country where wood is more plentiful and hence cheaper. In this case, skilled labour is not the primary consideration.

A further advantage parallels those discussed in the section on research and development where the multi-national enterprise may normally have an advantage of scale resulting from the production of specific products for diverse markets in specialised factories. The toy company, for example, may have advantages in producing its entire worldwide demand for musical toys in Switzerland, its demand for injection-moulded plastic products in the UK, and its dolls in the Far East.

Objectivity

The multi-national enterprise should have an advantage in being more aware of environmental change than its national counterpart. For the most part, this reflects a generally more objective opinion by the management team. The Singer Company's European operations, some years ago, were almost entirely autonomous and operated more or less as several national firms. Reorganisation, including the establishment of a European head office, curtailed this autonomous attitude and enabled the management to look more objectively at both marketing and manufacturing techniques. It was an opportunity to force local management to test new techniques which, mostly by force of habit, they would not have encouraged. The German market had been eroded over the years and it was felt by the new management that their technique of selling through agents and distributors might be improved by establishing wholly owned distribution outlets in suburban shopping centres. Initial pessimism and even poor early test results were reversed and the country management recognised that their market was not necessarily a unique one. There is often a tendency in a national firm to take this attitude, to the ultimate disadvantage of the performance of the company.

Financial

The industrial strategies taken by a company are normally aimed to maximise the return on the capital it has invested. There is no relationship between multi-national enterprise versus national enterprise which would indicate that one or the other has the better return. If there were, it would most certainly indicate that there are more national concerns having returns over 25 per cent than multi-national ones. This would only show, however, that special situations are obviously more frequent amongst smaller businesses and that multi-national business is generally bigger. Therefore, the financial justifications for moving to the multi-national arena must be looked at in absolute terms. In other words, the multi-national firm should be able to grow larger and produce more profit than its national counterpart even though its overall percentage return might be reduced.

There are some further financial advantages for the multi-national concern beyond those of a strictly operating nature. Historical evidence points out that any national economy suffers from cyclical trends and that barring international disaster these cycles are not therefore concurrent from one country to the next. A multi-national operation may therefore suffer from a lower percentage return on equity than a national one but it should be more stable over the years. The firm's French operation, for example, may more than offset the current difficulties in Germany.

Multi-national industrial enterprise has its counterpart in the banking world. Assuming that national regulations permit, a multi-national firm can borrow money where interest rates are lowest, and invest them directly or indirectly in operations where local interest rates are higher. Such an approach can be accomplished by reinvesting local profits in the latter and repatriating an excess amount from the former.

In somewhat the same way, a multi-national enterprise has greater opportunity and flexibility in raising money via stock or bond issues. It may also choose between different markets more easily than a national concern. Its stock might, for instance, warrant a higher P E ratio if introduced on the New York Stock Exchange as opposed to the London Stock Exchange.

The Disadvantages

Multi-national and national industry have historically lived side by side. It is unlikely that national business will ever be replaced by its multi-national competitor. One obvious reason is that there are many business sectors, particularly in service areas, that would not sensibly be expanded to multi-national dimensions. The local doctor has very little incentive to become multi-national nor do the majority of hospitals in which he works. In the more classical industrial sectors there is also good reason that national business will operate very successfully. This could be in part due to their infancy at any given stage, but more importantly is due to the fact that there are also many disadvantages to multi-national enterprise.

National Controls and Prejudices

For the most part, the same forces motivating corporate executives are responsible for motivating the government policy-makers. These latter desire to be re-elected and as their main measurable contribution is a better economic climate for the electorate, they will do their utmost to influence the national economy accordingly.

One could immediately conclude that the destinies of the corporate entities within specified national boundaries is therefore overwhelmingly influenced by government. Historical evidence will prove, however, that this is not the case and that there is a great deal of interaction between the two bodies and that each can outwit the other depending on how resourceful and determined they are. Labour legislation in the US in the last half of this century may have been difficult to accept by business, but it was one of the more important forces pushing American business toward automation. American business might not have become nearly so competitive internationally had this labour legislation not gone into effect. Tariff barriers established by most governments almost since the inception of world trade have often forced the foreigner to merge with a national firm. The results are usually a stronger unit which is more competitive internationally and repatriates profits as opposed to paying duty. However, such positive developments are not always the rule, particularly if viewed over the shorter term.

Multi-national business constantly faces the more classic governmental barriers. In response to declining balance of payments, legislation is often passed to introduce some form of trade barrier. The 10 per cent surcharge imposed by the United States in the autumn of 1971 is an example of this. The result is obvious: many firms are faced with a decline in margins which makes it no longer equitable to carry on trade, which in the past may have been an important profit contributor. The Japanese electronics industry and the UK automobile industry have been hit hard and the consequences for lesser firms can be drastic. In this instance, the firm whose market is mostly national is both secure and given an increased opportunity.

Another type of government barrier is exchange controls such as those presently in existence in the UK. These controls have their reason for being, but one of their effects is to make it more difficult for national firms to implant themselves overseas. In France, a national business forms manufacturer is presently attempting to expand throughout western Europe. It wishes to do this by means of merging with some known entities in the same field in Switzerland, Holland and Italy. Industrially and financially speaking, the concept is viable but the French Government is reluctant to allow the creation of a suitable foreign holding company. In the view of the industrialists in question, such a holding company is a pre-requisite for the success of the group. Thus this first step towards multi-nationalism may be thwarted by exchange control regulations even though in an instance such as this France would likely benefit financially over the long term.

There are many barriers which governments implement with an outward design of safeguarding the consumer but often with hidden powers affecting the international competitor. Ralph Nader in America stirred up considerable controversy with regard to the safety of American automobiles. Legislation has followed, which to a certain extent is biased against the foreign competitor. Some firms may lose months if not years in order to adjust. Electric consumer goods sold in the US must be approved by a central authority. This authority invariably is slower with foreign applications than local ones. The lag in time can sometimes make the difference between a market breakthrough in America by the foreign multi-national firm or its failure in face of local competition.

Prejudice against foreign competition is not easily analysed but is often an important factor affecting the performance of the multi-national enterprise. To counteract it many of the more well-established multi-national firms combine a centralising policy on the one hand with the fostering of the national entity of their subsidiary on the other. In some instances the consumer is not aware that the firm is multi-national. An example of this is the Singer Company where every step is taken not to disrupt the national image which is so strong that most Frenchmen believe this firm to be French and

Englishmen that it is English. It must be added that in certain markets foreign brand image is an advantage. It appears to be true, generally speaking, in the less well-developed countries. In Europe, Spain is an example. It has taken Japan 30 years for its poor quality image to be forgotten by the American consumer: it has not yet won in Europe. The Japanese firm introducing a product in Europe will necessarily have to be more astute and probably spend more in promoting and servicing the product than a national competitor. The recent wave of anti-American feeling following the introduction of the ten per cent surcharge has been detrimental for the American multi-national firm. A certain electronic company felt the impact immediately and had to lower its prices to meet local competition.

Such prejudice goes beyond the spectrum of client relationships. It also has an impact within the organisation. Recently in Europe there has been a growing determination by business executives, probably in part as a result of Servan Schreiber's remarks some years ago, to work for nationally based firms even though financial rewards are often less attractive.

It goes without saying that the ultimate 'governmental risk' is the nationalising of industry. In Chile, the American copper producers were nationalised and in British Guyana Alcan Aluminium lost its mining operation. The rate of such nationalisation has increased in certain developing countries in recent years. The multi-national concern must face greater hazards in this respect than its national counterpart.

Organisation and Controls

When the small private firm reaches a certain critical size, it almost invariably runs into difficulties in making the transition to a larger corporation, sometimes it fails. Usually the major problem that is encountered is of an organisational/control nature. These same potential problems face the multi-national firm. The permutations and combinations involving foreign government legislation, language, communications, transportation, etc. are much more complicated for the multi-national firm. The success of the firm is therefore very dependent on a good organisation structure and meaningful accounting controls. There is no ideal organisation structure for the multi-national enterprise. Some executives believe that a strong head-quarters group and autonomous subsidiaries are best. Others that the operation should be much more decentralised. Neither is completely right and it is usually better to choose some in-between solution. The autonomous body has advantages in terms of reduced administrative expense and often better human relations. The more centralised operation causes greater friction and can be more expensive; however, if the advantages of multi-nationalism discussed in the preceding pages are to be realised, a certain measure of centralisation is imperative. Centralisation is always a problem.

Controls are less subjective than organisation charts and should be easier to introduce and maintain but this is not always the case. Multi-national controls are inherently more complicated than those employed in a national enterprise. Problems include difference of standards in transmitting equipment, hours of work, language and of operating techniques between head office and subsidiaries. Controls are therefore more difficult to introduce and monitor for the multi-national company. It goes without saying that operating without adequate controls cannot be a recommended procedure in today's business environment.

Distance

Beyond the communication problems that arise between head office and its foreign subsidiaries, there invariably also exist many problems associated with distance for the multi-national company. Distance almost invariably means cost.

In attempting to maximise its advantages, the multi-national company will normally ship goods from many different sources to many others. This is a classic operations research problem as the several variables are continually changing. However, in addition to the direct transportation costs, there are numerous intangible liabilities. An obvious one is shipping damage. For the high volume low price consumer goods manufacturer, this is not a terribly significant one but for a manufacturer of large precision equipment this problem can be very serious, eventually resulting in large expenses and the potential loss of clients. Dock strikes, unreliable freight handling in trans-shipment, make for less reliability than the product manufactured in the same country. The reliability factor can be improved by increasing inventory and hence once again increasing costs, but in the case of custom products this is of course not possible. Electronic devices have tended to simplify the solution for these problems but that cost must also be added to the disadvantage of being far removed from your markets.

One must also consider the reaction of the consumer or buyer of the product. The latter may choose a national product if it is equal to foreign competition for no other reason than delivery reliability and better after-sale servicing. Delivery dates for goods shipped from foreign countries cannot be as reliable as those from a national producer and it is not always, but usually, a correct corollary to say that the servicing will also be less prompt and good.

Currency

During the recent monetary crisis, a number of industrial firms have made as much profit from astute currency speculation as they did from their industrial operation. One multi-national company operating in the UK made several million pounds subsequent to the devaluation in 1967. However, for every 'windfall' such as this, there are probably hundreds of major and minor disturbances caused by the fluctuation in the value of currency.

In Brazil, inflation has been rampant for many years in proportions far exceeding even the recent European examples. As a direct result, foreign firms operating in Brazil are forced to invest a minimum of their funds and borrow the maximum. Borrowing rates are high and unpredictable. This is not to say that Brazil is typical. A much more serious overall problem is currently facing the multi-national firm as a result of the unpredictable currency fluctuations. 'Source' planning, i.e. the planning for the manufacturing of the product, has become almost impossible in some instances. The Swiss watch industry had been hit hard by Japanese technical developments and the 1971 US surcharge, however, the speculation in the Swiss Franc, which resulted in its upward revaluation by 7 per cent, was more serious as it affected their margins at once in all foreign markets. Market forecasts made by Swiss watchmakers a year ago must now look very much out of date.

Therefore, despite better management training and bigger and better electronic hardware, it would not necessarily be safe to say that 'sourcing' and market forecasting is any better today than it was several decades ago. A substantial contributor to this is the unpredictable currency situation. A national company, although also to a certain extent affected, is in a less vulnerable position.

Environmental Differences

A more tangible advantage for a national firm, and yet in some cases an important one, is its intimate historical involvement with its environment. Both employees and the customer should inherently be well acquainted with the environment. This translates itself into a more accurate appraisal of markets, or of motivating factors, which in turn should allow for better long-range planning and strategy determination. Management will better understand their customers and employees and should therefore tend to make less mistakes than the foreign firm. A subsidiary of Lines Brothers reputedly built a 'standard plant' in Canada from British drawings. The drawings called for a bicycle rack for several hundred bicycles but no parking lot – it is understandable that some friction was created subsequent to the official opening of their new factory.

The bicycle rack example was not a serious one, however, it does point with certainty to the fact that equally naive decisions can be made by people not familiar with the particular environment, which can have a serious long-term impact. In France, for example, an American company restructured the remuneration system for their newly-acquired subsidiary along the lines of the one they used in America. Fixed pay was decreased and commission opportunity increased. They were surprised to see over a period of months that a number of their best salesmen left. These salesmen had felt insulted although the American management had intended that these better salesmen receive a higher reward. What motivates the American salesman is therefore not necessarily what motivates the French one.

Marketing Strategies for the Multi-national Enterprise

In this section a synopsis is made of some of the strategies which a multi-national enterprise could employ. Their success will ultimately be mainly the result of the good judgment of the firm's management in both identifying the most appropriate strategies and implementing them successfully.

General Karl von Clausewitz, the brilliant military strategist, defined strategy as, 'the combination of individual engagements to attain the goal of the campaign or war'. It may perhaps be an unfortunate parallel but a good deal of the same logic and action can be used in the successful waging of war as in the successful management of business.

If corporate strategies are to have the necessary impact, they must be few in number and chosen so that the strengths of the firm, the opportunities of the business environment, and the weakness of competition, are maximised. For a multi-national enterprise the variables are almost infinite on the one hand, and the rate of change of these same variables unpredictable on the other hand. All this emphasises that although the multi-national firm may generally have greater opportunity it also faces a much more complex planning exercise than the national firm. The relative strengths of the firm must be weighed against the strengths of the much more numerous competitors. Furthermore, the economic and political considerations are different for each market.

A treatise on planning methods for multi-national enterprise will not be undertaken. It suffices to say that as planning is one of the key functions of the chief executive its complexity in the multi-national arena is a relatively more demanding and important task for both the chief executive and his staff than it is for the national firm.

The process of formulating marketing strategy will be different depending on the particular organisational pattern of the enterprise. Four basic patterns can be identified:

1. international grouping, e.g.: home and overseas

2. geographical grouping, e.g.: EEC, or by Continent or country

3. product, business or market grouping, e.g.: automotive, leisure

4. functional grouping, e.g.: R&D, Production, Sales.

The first pattern is the one most usually implemented by the company entering the multi-national arena. It permits a useful identification and therefore hopefully an organisation to deal with that part of its business which is of a non-domestic nature. Such an organisation should normally be more capable of coping with the peculiarities of the multi-national business scene. As the company expands internationally, this structure is usually insufficient as problems in the Far East have really no relationship with those of Canada.

A 'geographical' grouping is probably the most common overall structure used by the large multi-national firm. It allows for a grouping of businesses in like environments. A common disadvantage, however, is that the knowledge with regard to an important product of the parent company may be disseminated with difficulty to a far-flung subsidiary.

The third grouping is used by some multi-national firms as a primary organisational pattern. In some firms this is a wise choice where product emphasis is clearly more important than most other business characteristics. In most large successful multi-national firms such a group is of a secondary form and functions only to supplement the basic line structure. This reflects the most usual circumstance where specific local market and manufacturing expertise is of a more critical nature than product design and development.

Not unlike the former, the functional grouping is also usually a secondary organisational form for the multi-national enterprise. Such a structure may make sense for a domestic operation where adequate communication exists between the various functional departments but as adequate communication between functional organisations in a multi-national arena are more difficult to achieve this form is not usually recommended. The success of the business after all is very dependent on effective inter-communication between marketing and manufacturing. Large multi-national firms, particularly the conglomerates, however, often superimpose a secondary product and/or functional group in order to improve both strategy determination and control.

In order to illustrate more specifically some of the programmes open to the multi-national firm, a variety of strategies are itemised in the following pages. They are not necessarily complete as the emphasis is on multi-national marketing tactics. A multi-national consumer marketing firm operating on the Continent will be used as a hypothetical example. In the latter part of the section these remarks will be supplemented by some of the variations which exist for consumer firms operating in under-developed countries or for industrial firms in general.

Some Strategies for Multi-national Enterprise in the Consumer Products Field and Operating in Developed Countries

I *Develop a More Effective Organisation*

(As mentioned earlier, the organisation structure and its successful role is particularly relevant for the multi-national enterprise.)

ı

(a)   Establish a Continental Headquarters located at a geographically convenient place which would provide:

● Accounting consolidation of all Continental financial activities and production of pertinent control data.

● A centre for regular operational meetings for all key Continental Managers with their 'staff' counterparts.

● A 'staff' team which would help to control programme priorities and the interchange of ideas.

● The opportunity for reducing three Continental Management teams.

● A rapport between the various manufacturing and marketing operations.

(b)   Reduce the functions of the Corporate Head Office to that of overall planning, financing, research and development and new business development policy determination.

II   *Substantially Increase the Penetration of Product R in the Total Continental Market*

(This type of strategy would identify the goals by national market so that the appropriate management is made accountable.)

(a)   PRODUCT

● Identify product *RA* made in Germany factory as 'high end' product for all markets.

● Curtail marketing of product *RE* in the UK and alter it for use in Scandinavian line.

● Strengthen 'middle-of-the-line' by importing product *RN* from the US

● 'Strip down' (i.e., remove all appendages that are not strictly functional) existing product *RO* manufactured in Italy so as to reach a maximum transfer price of *X* and use it for promotions.

● Promote development of product *RY* at firm's R&D headquarters.

● Purchase 'off-brand' product from Italian competition for a maximum price of Y and use it in sales channel B.

(b) PRICING

● Establish pricing of product line in all markets so that maximum price is 20 per cent higher than competitor X's top model, and that lowest price is equal to competitor Y's price.

● Despite the widening disparities in margins between these markets, increase average price in market A by 5 per cent and reduce it by 7 per cent in market B.

(c) *Promotion*

● Establish promotion programmes market by market emphasising local advertising for sales in channel B and Continental-wide image advertising for 'high end' product.

● Undertake regular consumer market surveys market by market and revaluate product and advertising tactics accordingly.

III *Develop an Effective Retail Store Programme*

(There are numerous sales channel alternatives, of which the following is only one.)

● Establish a central research group at the Continental Head-quarters to develop an overall plan for the optimum location of new distribution outlets and the closing of others.

● Establish a retail store committee in each market to alter plans in accordance with their specific judgment. Implement the programme, emphasising the overall corporate image and all benefits of standardisation.

● In conjunction with the Continental Headquarters, country management will review the field selling organisation in order to determine optimal staffing. Subsequently, a pro-gramme will be introduced to gradually merge the field selling organisation with the retail organisation.

- Country management will submit, and subsequently implement, a programme of centralising the services and repair operation which will result in reducing the number of outlets by 60 per cent and enlarging some of the remaining.

IV *Enter a New Field of Activity*

(Despite the main activities of an already well-established firm, it is often to its advantage to consider entirely new business that for manufacturing or marketing reasons might well complement its operation and add to its overall return. For a multi-national firm wishing to enter a new market, the acquisition of a competitor can sometimes be particularly attractive. The detailed strategy for such an approach is variable but could include the following headings):

- Undertake an acquisition search in countries A and B for firms having criteria X, Y and Z. Study and implement in accordance with conclusions of field analysis.

- Examine the prospect of extending existing factory to produce new product R. Establish costing and develop a marketing programme for the product in markets C, D and F. Implement in accordance with manufacturing and marketing conclusions.

- Identify manufacturers of products G, H and J from Continental, UK and American sources and sort out those firms producing these products most closely to criteria M, N and O. Make an analysis of the most likely firms and attempt to establish licensing arrangements or purchasing contracts with any one.

- Make an analysis of operation T to establish its current and long-term prospects. If such an analysis indicates that criteria B and Y are likely to be below acceptable standards, take steps to dispose of business and find a new source of supply for product S, preferably in that country where the raw material is abundant and inexpensive.

V *Improve Cost Controls*

(Few strategic programmes are complete without assuring that costs are adequately controlled. This is particularly relevant as strategies tend to be developmental in nature and hence vulnerable to 'cost creep'.)

(a) Establish a centralised administration and data processing activity which will concentrate on reducing 'fixed' selling and administration costs and provide more pertinent, accurate and timely management information.

- Centralise systems on a total division basis.

- Establish accounting systems for each sales distribution outlet and inventory and accounts receivable systems for each of the principal markets.

- Establish a central data centre located in country *B*.

(b) Instruct chief accountant to be responsible for taking all necessary measures to protect the firm from any 'downfalls' resulting from variations in currency market.

(c) Increase inventory turnover by 15 per cent per annum (this involves improving control reports and improving sales forecasting).

(d) Improve the trans-shipment of merchandise (this involves an evaluation of optimal transportation methods, the establishment of the optimal number of distribution points, the analysis of improved materials handling methods and the establishing of more pertinent control reporting).

(e) Review purchasing in order to establish a centralised purchasing function for the entire Continental operation.

Multi-national Enterprise in Other Geographic Locations and in Other Business Sectors

The strategies outlined above were for the most part applicable to a Continental operation in the consumer goods field. Generally speaking, consumer marketing in a developed environment is more complicated, though not necessarily easier, than other categories of marketing. Industrial firms in other geographic locations obviously do not have identical problems or opportunities. A brief review of the differences existing between the Continental operation in the consumer goods field and firms of a different category follows:

A. *Consumer Product Firms in Developing Countries*

Developing countries present difficulties arising from less reliable communication, transportation and distribution facilities. On the other hand, the increased costs that these may impose are largely compensated by lower labour rates and a less demanding consumer. In fact, if one casts aside major political upheaval, the margin opportunities in developing countries are usually better than in developed countries. The major pitfall is often the difficulty of controlling a relatively small operation in a distant country.

'Organisation' is most important and strategies in this area have to take into account the peculiarities of each market. Product line distribution strategies are less demanding. Assuming that there is demand for the product, the consumer is usually less difficult and the methods of promotion also less sophisticated. More emphasis must usually be given to 'sourcing' as distance, government import regulations and currency instability are problematical. The labour/raw material equation can sometimes allow for small runs and hence more economical local manufacturing or assembly. Cost controls may not have to be detailed in the same way as in the developed country but as the operations are often more distant, a simplified version is mandatory.

A multi-national enterprise faces greater risk in an under-developed country, but in return should reap higher profits. Furthermore, the long-term growth prospects offered by these countries in many instances are considerably higher than those in developed countries.

B. *Industrial Product Firms*

There is not necessarily a clear distinction between the consumer and industrial sectors and in most aspects they resemble each other. The basic difference is the classification of the 'end user'.

The purchasing department of an industrial firm is normally much more demanding than that of a consumer firm. Buyers usually know exactly what they need and the price they should pay for it. In some senses, therefore, it is easier for the industrial producer as he need not be as concerned about stocking a wide range of products. Marketing is much less complicated as advertising does not usually play an important role, sales channels are more limited and the number of clients are usually fewer. On the other hand, technical innovation and technical standards, e.g. quality and reliability, must be higher, and very often margins are squeezed as a result of competitive bidding. Furthermore, during an unfavourable industrial 'climate' firms can usually do little to stimulate demand.

Industrial firms have usually been more prominent in the multi-national sector than consumer firms, particularly in the developing markets. Consumer products tend to be less technically advanced and have lower capital demands so that they are more likely to be produced locally. As capital investment is higher and national demand lower, advantages of 'scale' are more important and often force industrial firms to seek sales growth in overseas markets. This is particularly true where technological superiority and costs for a given product make it competitive on world markets. Furthermore, as an industrial firm is very often more dependent on raw materials than its consumer counterpart, it is also forced to seek international sources.

It would be somewhat redundant to deal with the potential strategies for a multi-national firm in the field of industrial products. In the marketing area, as mentioned above, they would be less complex, with a greater emphasis on a higher calibre sales team having adequate technical knowledge and proficiency in the preparation of sometimes complicated quotations. On the manufacturing side, although inventory problems would be less, technical development, quality and critical path techniques for minimising delivery delays are more important than for the consumer firm.

The return on investment of a good industrial firm will tend to be less than those for a good consumer firm. This reflects, generally speaking, lower asset requirements and often higher margin opportunities for consumer firms. On the other hand, except in certain specific fields, there tends to be more long-term stability in dealing with industrial products and industrial clients rather than the 'fickle' consumer product and consumer himself. The multi-national firm can 'hedge' against the inevitable industrial cyclical downturns by being involved in many countries. This is of considerable advantage.

A brief review of some of the major names in the industrial sector would indicate that there are few which are not multi-national. For the consumer sector this is not necessarily true. In the future this pattern should not change.

Conclusions

This chapter has dealt with 'Patterns and Developments in Multi-national Enterprise'. Put in another way – what characterises multi-national enterprise? What are its opportunities and liabilities? What methods should be implemented to stimulate its advance in the decade to come?

The first section defined multi-national enterprise: the second and third dealt with its advantages and disadvantages relative to its national counterpart: the final section dealt with the type of strategies required for it to develop during the seventies.

This chapter would be incomplete if it did not attempt to isolate those factors which lead to success. What then are the elements of success for multi-national enterprise?

Is it its emphasis and success in a particular function? This book deals with marketing and in several instances it has been suggested that marketing can be considered the 'lead function'. It might therefore be concluded that the success of a multi-national firm in particular is primarily dependent on marketing. This would be a great over-simplification. IBM would be a weak marketer if it were not a first-class developer and manufacturer. The same comment could be made for Hewlett Packard, or many other firms.

Is it its presence in a particular field of activity? One of the fastest-growing consumer hard goods products in the last decade was motorcycles, but despite this, BSA failed. One of the most fiercely competitive fields of activity is the synthetic fibre business. ICI has grown and flourished in this field.

Is it the nationality of the firm? Unilever competes against the American soap and detergent giants who have the reputation of being second to none in the area of high-pressure consumer promotion: it too has flourished. Brown Boveri in Switzerland has competed successfully in world markets against General Electric and other international giants.

Is it its size and financial strength? The small French firm manufacturing and merchandising 'Camping Gaz' is increasing its already important penetration of world markets. Dymo, a small US firm, has built in a little over ten years a sizeable international business, which is now larger and more profitable than its domestic operations.

Of the many remaining factors categorising business which one could question, none is more important than 'management'. No business can succeed through management alone, but over the longer term few businesses could succeed without enlightened management. Any one of the successful firms that have been mentioned in the last few pages owes its success to excellent top management. For the multi-national giant the single individual has usually long been replaced by the effective executive team. However, it is interesting to remember that in a majority of cases the success of these huge firms was largely the success of individuals. These included Sloane of General Motors, Davis of Alcoa, Watson of IBM, or Sarnoff of RCA. Today's dynamic smaller firms to a great extent are still influenced by individuals.

The one inevitable success factor for the multi-national or the national firm is the excellence of the chief executive and his management team. For the multi-national enterprise, therefore, the key ingredient for success is an excellent multi-national executive team which realises and deliberately sets out to exploit the fact that national boundaries are not natural boundaries to making, distributing and selling a product.

At the beginning of the chapter, it was pointed out that multi-national business was not new, and that its place in the world economy was not necessarily more influential today than it was centuries ago. Multi-national enterprise will probably grow at an accelerating pace in the next decade as smaller and smaller firms join in but it is still unlikely that their influence will increase. This is not to say that there has not been an increase in the number of multi-national firms nor a trend towards multi-national business agglomeration of the type of General Motors or Shell. However, their size and influence in the context of the enormously powerful modern economic empires of America, Russia, Europe or China is not more overwhelming than the Hudson Bay Company was to the British Empire of several hundred years ago. If there is an aspect of our modern industrial and political development which is overwhelming, it is its influence on the human being. The UK's entry into the EEC cannot be anything less than positive for the country and its citizens for economic considerations, but the question that remains is whether the result is as positive in terms of the psychic well-being of mankind.

CHAPTER 6

Marketing a Non-differentiated Industrial Product

By Aubrey Wilson and Jeremy Fowler

Introduction

What are non-differentiated industrial products? In essence they are industrial products produced to a standard or fixed specification, bought only in response to basic and essential needs, and used in markets where purchasing decisions are governed in the main by rational factors. Computer reels and cases, electro-mechanical relays, electric wire fittings, cables, drills, ball valves, plastic tubing, hand tools, plywood and laboratory glassware are, in a marketing sense, similar to sugar or detergents. These are examples of non-differentiated industrial products. This chapter sets out to explore the problems facing manufacturers of non-differentiated industrial products and to show that at least some consumer goods marketing techniques may be appropriate in the very different area which constitutes industrial marketing.

The increasing similarity of products and services which are purchased by consumers is frequently bemoaned by sociologists and commentators on the domestic scene. It is of course the principal difficulty facing marketers of consumer goods and services seeking to differentiate their offerings from many with characteristics and appearance closely resembling their own. The consumer goods marketing answer has been to build into products of this type perceptual rather than fundamental physical differences, for example by virtue of unusual design, by packaging, by endowing the product with psychological rather than physical attributes or, most important of all, by branding.

The improved knowledge of the domestic consumer – one outcome of the increasingly vocal and militant consumer movement – has injected a healthy dose of cynicism towards detergents that wash whiter, aspirins which banish headaches quicker, and margarine which cannot be distinguished from butter. Nevertheless there is little evidence of slackening of manufacturers' interests in brand loyalties and a marked preference continues to be exhibited for selected goods, even though they are essentially similar in price, performance and appearance to others. Thus it would appear that marketers of many types of consumer goods have at least partially solved the problem of differentiation.

However far fitted hose may be from hose fittings and cheese-spread from chipboard there appears to be good reasons to examine if there are some techniques used in the raucous consumer goods markets which might be applied, with profit, to the more restrained industrial markets. The reluctance of industrial goods manufacturers to consider consumer marketing techniques is well-known. But in rapidly changing markets where the conditions of market leadership are shaped either by firms which do common things uncommonly well or else do uncommon things, no avenue of marketing development can safely be ignored.

Pipes and hose fittings are typical of a large number of non-differentiated industrial goods in that they are almost all indistinguishable from other products of the same type either because of competitive pressure to manufacture to a given level of performance or appearance for example, or because of the adoption of national or international standards. Either way, the situation appears to leave little room for product adjustment. But there are in fact many means which can be used by a manufacturing company to distinguish its goods and services from all others in a positive way which will encourage favourable consideration of its offering.

Characteristics of Non-differentiated Products

The approaches for marketing non-differentiated products are numerous but none can be selected nor implemented unless the basic characteristics of these types of products and their markets are understood.

These are products where:

● users prefer and seek lower prices rather than improved products

● no significant financial or technical benefits can be obtained from the use of the product as against the use of any other of the genus

● there are no corporate or personal prestige factors involved in purchases.

No benefits accrue from the introduction of product 'plusses' which in fact lead to a downward pressure on prices. The majority of chipboard buyers would not pay one penny more for twice the quality since they use the minimum specification compatible with their needs. Thus if a producer offered a better quality at the same price as the current product, the customer would seek a lower price on the unmodified product.

Similarly while a particular hand power tool may be demonstrably superior in some respects to competitive products, it is extremely difficult to distinguish a standard bit from any other bit.

Finally a computer, a new factory or a new communication system may endow the firm with a more favourable image of promotional advantage; a concrete pipe or a standard valve fulfils a utilitarian function and nothing else. There are no corporate or personal prestige factors involved in purchase.

The situation is in fact the closest to the cloud cuckoo state of 'pure competition' beloved by theoretical economists and which rarely exists in reality in the industrial world. But if the condition caused by non-differentiation is not one of 'pure competition', it is certainly as close to it as is likely to be found. A comparable situation can be found in many hundreds of consumer products where differentials are more illusory than real, but still the competitive position changes almost daily in response to the effort of the marketers.

Perhaps there is a lesson to be learnt from cornflakes marketing than can be applied to computer tape reels. Only the most naive accept that there is any radical difference between similar grades of petrol and lubricants. (Indeed research has shown that many consumers believe that different brands of petrol come out of the same hole in the ground and are pumped into the ship and then into the same refinery and finally stored in the same underground tank at the filling station!) Nevertheless in consumer petroleum products, product differentiation and with it product preferences are well-developed. This is not because of observable product differences but because of the intangible differentiation created by various forms of promotion – some brutally obvious and some subliminally devious. The fact that a differentiation can occur in a non-differentiated consumer product naturally prompts the question as to why such a position cannot be achieved in an industrial product. In marketing terms, how different is a solvent from a premium grade petrol? The consumer only buys petrol when he needs it and the oil company only buys solvents when it needs them.

Buyers of Non-differentiated Products

How then can a manufacturer of an industrial product produced to a standard specification in a market that buys only when it must, obtain a competitive lead? The answer, since price collusion became illegal, has most frequently been 'price cutting' or price cutting in its very worst commercial and social form – bribery. Such policies are as injurious as they are unnecessary, and often destructive for the purchaser as well as for the seller. Price cutting is a philosophy of desperation based on an ignorance of marketing and of market forces.

It is a constant jibe that every industrial buyer seeks to purchase at half the price, twice the quality and delivery from stock. All three propositions have been shown on serious investigation not to be true.

How British Industry Buys and its American and Canadian[1] equivalents clearly demonstrated that:

- a significant number of buyers would not switch from their best supplier for a price drop often as high as 10 per cent, because buyers not only buy products, they buy security,

- value analysis could not have achieved the huge (and quantified) successes it has if products were not frequently over-designed (i.e. too high a quality) for the purpose they are required,

- study after study has shown the buyers most frequently want *assured* delivery, not *quick* delivery.

These factors should be recognised since they open up the way

[1] Industrial Market Research Limited/Institute of Marketing, *How British Industry Buys*, Hutchinson (London, 1967); D. E. Thain, *How Industry Buys*, School of Business Administration, University of Western Ontario (Canada, 1959); John H. Platten, *How Industry Buys*, Scientific American (New York, 1955).

for developing techniques to establish market leadership by removing some aspects of buyer – seller folklore which inhibit creativity in industrial marketing.

The widely held view that buying in most markets, not just those involving non-differentiated products, is a simple mechanistic, moment-of-truth decision, is totally incorrect and is one which leads to 'saturation' calling and selling and 'probability' call cycles (i.e.: a given number of orders as a percentage of all sales calls). This is a hit and miss method of selling and as expensive as any known technique. A knowledge of the buying processes avoids the need to use this approach, makes sales calls more effective, and at least partly protects the supplying firm from competition.

The study of purchasing attitudes can be broken down into three major areas: deciding *who* buys, *how* do they buy, and *why* they buy.

With non-differentiated products the buyer tends to be the Purchasing Officer since the purchasing takes on the characteristics of repeat purchases or straight re-buys where information requirements are low and consideration of alternatives is also low. Because there is no innovation content in the purchase, the purchasing decision is a fairly simple one involving lower levels of management only. David Rowe and Ivan Alexander in their book *Selling Industrial Products* first illustrated this as reproduced in Figure 1 (p. 144) showing clearly how a buying situation can be disturbed and manipulated by the introduction of innovation.[2] If the seller can introduce an aspect of innovation into his offer, which will in any way change the *status quo* in the buying firm, he can force the consideration of alternatives and perhaps move the decision into the responsibility area of others who may favour the company. 'Innovation' in this context can be related to commercial terms, product applications, reciprocal trading and other non-product aspects of the transaction.

Similarly, if there is knowledge of the buyphases of the purchasing process it is possible to influence the specification and the search for suppliers.[3]

Finally, given that buyers (particularly in non-differentiated product markets), do not buy the products but the cluster of satisfactions with which they are surrounded, a knowledge of buyer motiva-

[2] David Rowe and Ivan Alexander. *Selling Industrial Products*. Hutchinson. (London, 1968)
[3] P. J. Robinson, C. Faris and Y. Wind, *Industrial Buying and Creative Marketing*, Alleyn & Bacon (Boston Mass.), 1967.

tions makes it feasible to present the offering in a manner which most closely accords with what they seek to purchase.

The knowledge of the buying processes dovetails with the need for executive selling discussed later, since the sooner the selling company is involved in the buyphases, the greater becomes the need to work with senior management on the buying side, and thus to engage in executive selling.

The buying processes are complex and sometimes difficult to understand, but knowledge of them places the marketing company in an infinitely better posture for completing a sale than their more pedestrian rivals.

Search for Uniqueness and the Innovative Content

A manufacturer of industrial products which cannot be differentiated from similar products in a physical sense can usefully consider a number of different approaches which will help him distinguish his offerings, to the industrial buyer, from all others. However, any attempt at product differentiation, to be successful, requires consideration of two important factors. The first of these is the concept of uniqueness and the innovative content of any offer, and second, the product and its market fit.

An essential primary requirement is to develop some aspect of uniqueness, if not in the product itself (which by definition cannot be differentiated), then in its surrounding services, commercial characteristics or any other activity which impinges on the successful operations of the customer firm or its wellbeing.

It is the factor of uniqueness which opens up the prospect of exceptional profits even for non-differentiated products, *not* the latest tool (which any competitor can buy and operate), *not* large sums of money available (because finance can be acquired at a price), *not* cheap labour, *not* good procurement practices. All these, alone or together, might ensure what could seem to pass for a respectable performance but, introduce the element of uniqueness and that resource or skill can be transmuted to gold by its creative exploitation. A unique operating skill makes a workaday machine exceptional, a unique way of manipulating funds, of purchasing, or of utilising labour separates profit earners in the top quartile from all the others.

The development or use of uniqueness, of course, places a firm at risk which means that it can make both high profits or high losses, since in a risk situation both results are possible. What is certain is that while losses can always occur, profits are only likely to be exceptional if a degree of uniqueness can be achieved and the firm is willing to embrace risk in its exploitation.[4]

The greater the number of unique elements or the degree of innovation which can be introduced in an offer, the greater the value sensitivity of buyers becomes. This situation often eliminates and always reduces price pressure. The marketing implications of introducing innovation or an element of uniqueness in an offer is illustrated below.

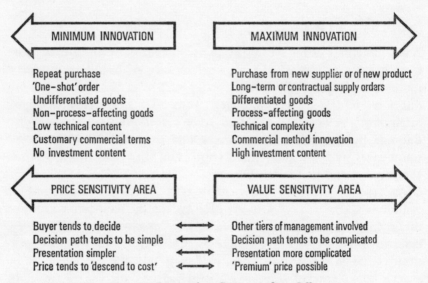

Figure 1 Innovation Content of an Offer

It is obvious that the opportunity for applying uniqueness to skills and resources even in risk situations is limited, and increasingly limited in most activities of a company. However, there remains one area where opportunities for uniqueness are myriad, where pay-off can be quick, and where rewards of leadership can be high.

[4] The development of uniqueness in an offer and the risk attached to this marketing strategy is perhaps seen in its most dramatic form in the field of highly differentiated capital goods. Chapter 7 by David Rowe on *Marketing Purpose Made Capital Goods* provides further insights into this whole aspect of innovative content and uniqueness as well as some interesting comparisons with the marketing of non-differentiated industrial products.

This area is marketing, for in non-differentiated industrial products it is marketing that has been least practised, least understood and least appreciated, because it has been thought inapplicable in a situation where everyone is selling the same product. Competition, as has already been pointed out, tends to centre round price which is the least flexible, the most destructive and non-creative use of an important marketing weapon. By the use of the full range of marketing tools which are available to the producer of industrial goods it becomes possible to invest the firm and the product with a 'plus' which cannot easily be followed by competitors.

Product and Market Fit

Every firm must consider precisely how the existing standard product meets the market's real requirements. But although the market may have accepted the standard this does not necessarily mean that it prefers it to other alternatives. It has been commented with some truth that product development and marketing orientation ceases when a BSI committee or an ISO specification is accepted. These standards however, often represent no more than minimal guidance and protection to the buyer and reflect a consensus of committee opinion designed to satisfy the least exacting member of the committee. Any manufacturer of good quality locks will confirm this.

The position is perhaps understandable since, although BSI committees are supposed to be composed of representatives of firms making the product, of user companies and sometimes trade organisations, user companies frequently take such little interest that in practice manufacturing companies dominate the committees. One result of this is that some users will purchase to the appropriate British Standard with regard to test methods but fix their own acceptance limits. For example, while electric light bulbs are made to a standard of 1,000 hours it is recognised that there is no difficulty and with an insignificant increase in costs, in making 2,000 hour bulbs and there are now claims for unlimited life.[5]

Opportunities for differentiating standard products without inducing price changes abound if the manufacturers do not assume the standard is preferred as opposed to *accepted*. Marketing research will provide a profile of user needs, both tangible and intangible, which at least enable a supplier to direct his R&D, his manufacturing

[5] *Financial Times*, 18th September 1971.

K

processes and his marketing towards meeting something more than an acceptable minimum. Marketing research often reveals that products are over-designed for their intended use. Indeed the success of the technique of value analysis often proves this.

Application Engineering and Second Use

A tendency exists in non-differentiated product markets to assume that the applications for the product are limited to its major and conventional use. In fact, although concrete pipes are used largely for drainage and water movement, a limited study showed a further 23 uses, some of which have been successfully exploited. A spring balancer for spot welding guns was found to command a substantial market within abbatoirs and tanneries.

Plastic-lined paper sacks, biscuit tins and other forms of packaging frequently have a second life for purposes other than those they were intended for. The second-life features can be made part of the product, or at the very least provide a useful advertising medium.

Product arrogance, prejudice and history all tend to make companies manufacturing non-differentiated products assume that all known uses have been exploited. There is ample evidence to show that this view is often incorrect. The fecundity of the human mind is truly surprising, and it takes only one person to devise a new use or modification for an old product to open up whole new market segments.

The study of new uses for a product should be one of the major and continuing activities for all firms in non-differentiated product markets, since the rewards of open-minded searching are considerable.

But to manufacture not so much a 'better' product (with its perjorative sound) as a product more suited to the market needs is not just a question of redesign, nor of the search for extended applications of the product. It may also be a question of production and engineering know-how and skills, the possession of some special and unique machinery, or ways of using machinery. It can be – and this is rarely considered – the brilliant manipulation of buying skills by the purchasing team. In short, the firm must find out how close to the ideal product profile it can go and then direct its efforts to achieving this, leaving the standard only as a benchmark against which the superior product will be assessed by the buyers.

Thus it is in marketing, and in what might be termed the first of the marketing tools – industrial marketing research – that the major opportunities lie for setting the conditions of market leadership in an undifferentiated product situation.

Different Markets and Differentiated Marketing

The process of developing competitive 'plusses' must begin with a study of the basic purchasing propositions which, with non-differentiated products, will be largely the same. However, the first approach to establishing a difference is to examine whether the purchasing proposition can be subjected to what may be a unique, creative interpretation of that proposition. It is a basic rule of all marketing that the marketer should identify his 'plusses' and the part of his market to which those 'plusses' are most meaningful. While all products of a particular genre may exhibit the same characteristics the emphasis on the existence of any one or any grouping of them to one target segment of the market can readily create an association in the mind of the purchaser between product and supplier in a way which distinguish them from all other suppliers.

A firm of removers and packers specialising in works of art and antiques successfully marketed its services to manufacturers of sensitive instruments and fragile equipment. The heavy downside risk in all these product groups and the need for special equipment has a similarity, if only perceptual, of requirements and thus presented the opportunity to transfer the 'plus' from one market segment to another. If the product or its non-product factors have varying appeals to each segment of the market, it follows that the way of presenting these appeals will differ if only because the exposure, buying methods and needs of the segments also differ. A product which may be most economically sold through builders merchants to builders could well require direct selling to engineering concerns. Similarly, offices buying lithograph machines may respond to diversionary pricing tactics; a printing company is highly unlikely to do so.

The role of marketing is to see the purchasing appeal(s) of a product not from a product-orientated viewpoint but from that of the would-be purchasers, and to interpret them in terms of benefits to the purchaser. Differences between essentially similar products sharing the same basic purchasing proposition can be achieved by the re-interpretation of the proposition. In essence this is a matter of thinking creatively about the product and its use and meaning to the purchaser. The process of market segmentation by market or product preferences or perceptual characteristics is well-known but the concommitant of differentiated marketing tools to promote differentiated advantages is not widely practised.

Development of a Cluster of Non-product Advantages

It is now almost a decade since Theodore Levitt propounded the view that in highly competitive situations the process of getting and keeping customers requires that the generic product must be augmented in order to sell well,[6] that is, the product must be defined broadly in terms of the whole cluster of satellite attributes which produce distinct customer satisfactions. To do this an effort must be made to find out what the customer wants and values and, equally as important, to identify satisfactions which he may not as yet be able to express.

Non-product advantages which can be built into a non-differentiated product are numerous but they will rarely stem from sheer inspiration. The source of ideas for non-product features must come from the market and thus information on users' attitudes and needs, both total and limited, must be probed. For example:

● can the method of delivery be made compatible with the customers – handling facilities (or lack of them) or commercial needs perhaps by the supply or loan of handling equipment?

● will a self-imposed penalty clause for unreliable delivery move purchasers from present suppliers?

● would the provision of management aids improve the customer's operation? There is a well-documented precedent for this. International Mineral and Chemicals Corporation offered their customers who were manufacturers of fertilisers help in selling their fertilisers

● can end-user knowledge be improved to encourage sales of the intermediate producer? A Dutch glass fibre manufacturer developed an educational campaign among architects, builders and contractors to extend the use and knowledge of glass fibre

6 Theodore Levitt, *Innovation in Marketing*, Pan Books (London, 1968).

building products as an aid to their fabricator and moulder customers.

The list of possible non-product advantages is a lengthy one and can be developed both by a study of the buyers and by internal examination of a company's own strengths, so that they can be exploited fully in the market place.

Some of the non-product factors which can be applied to form a whole cluster of attributes and which are now considered are:

● guarantee improvement

● capture of a major distribution channel

● high quality selling

● image development and prestige spin-off

Guarantee improvement

With industrial products guarantees and warranties are not usually a feature of the sales approach. There is an in-built and usually quite erroneous view that the buyer is at least as knowledgeable as the seller, and can therefore make his own judgments without any need for guarantees and, in any case, the latter has a reserve defence under the Sale of Goods Acts and the Trade Descriptions Act 1968. When guarantees do exist they tend to be historical, based on the original assessment of safe product life or performance.

In both cases a realistic appraisal of the product and even a slight insight into buyer motivations indicates that guarantees can be used as a potent method of differentiating products. Security, notably job security, as has been shown in many studies, is a fundamental desire of everyone, buyers no less than sellers, and anything which enhances security commands attention and support. Guarantees offer additional security to the purchaser, provided they are presented in the correct way. A guarantee which is as long and as unequivocal as possible is a public affirmation of faith in the product by the supplier and, for the quality product, manoeuvres any competitive battle on a terrain where it can be fought to best advantage of the supplying company.

However, guarantees alone are of little use. Witness the cynicism of the average motorist towards the guarantees of the motor industry compared with the wide support and approval Marks & Spencer obtain by their policy of changing products virtually without question and without any formal guarantee. For most manufacturers of non-differentiated products these are the extremes. A guarantee as a competitive weapon must be seen to exist, have no 'small print' and be honoured in its implementation.

A cursory examination of most guarantees and analysis of guarantee claims will show that they can be safely extended for considerably longer periods and many of the restraints can be removed. Price wars are destructive, guarantee wars are creative since they encourage product and backing service improvement and the user is the final beneficiary.

Capture of a major distributive channel

In many markets the distributor may represent the difference between success and failure, e.g.: building materials, motor accessories, engineers' consumables, office equipment and supplies, electrical fittings, many timber products and photographic goods. The capture of a major distributive channel not only ensures outlets for the suppliers' products but can also block competition or restrain it. The National Coal Board's widespread network of builders merchants ensures outlets for their building products such as bricks.

'Capture' however does not necessarily imply acquisition although this is the most obvious route. Other methods of distribution channel control exist. Solus trading, as practised in the oil industry whereby special discounts are given in return for stocking only the product of the supplier makes it uneconomic to trade with competitors of the main supplier.

Franchise systems are another technique which can lead to the domination of the distribution channels. These contractual arrangements between supplier and outlet ensure that the franchisor's goods are stocked, merchandised, or serviced in strict accordance with the manufacturer's requirements. The most obvious and perhaps public example of this is operated by J. Lyons. The Wimpy franchise pre-empts the largest proportion of raw material purchases by the outlets and removes them from competitive attack. Although the outlets in this case are retail units the buying situation as between the Wimpy Bar operators and J. Lyons is an industrial one.

It can of course be argued that for many firms the acquisition or tying in of a distributive network to absorb a product is somewhat akin to having a suit made specially to match a button which has been found. While this might be valid where a wide range of products, all commanding different distribution systems or direct sales, is concerned, it is certainly not so for a large number of companies whose major output goes through homogeneous distributors.

In terms of non-differentiated products, the availability of the product through a particular distributor or distributive chain may be the factor which distinguishes it from its competitors and indeed in some cases the reputation and image of the distributor will 'rub off' onto the product, giving it what might be termed a 'patina' which cannot be copied by other similar products.

High quality selling

If it is difficult sometimes to differentiate products, it is not difficult to differentiate salesmen. Despite the tendency to demote selling in importance, it remains the spearhead of the industrial marketing effort. Outstanding salesmen can represent the difference between success and failure in non-differentiated products.

Paradoxically, manufacturers often reduce the quality of the sales force in markets where products are similar, largely because prices tend to move toward cost and the salesman is seen as an order taker whose job is to arrive at the buyer's office when an order is about to be placed. It is argued that because there is no difference between products, the buyer purchases at the most convenient moment, which might happen to be when the salesman calls. This view of the market and buying process is as primitive as it is incorrect. Non-differentiated products require high quality selling and indeed often executive selling. The conditions for making a sale are the same for all products:

- a need exists and the product is the correct one to meet this need;
- the company is capable of providing the product;
- price is acceptable;
- delivery time is satisfactory.

Within these parameters there might appear to be little room for the salesman to influence the course of the sale. It is precisely for this reason there is a need for salesmen endowed to an above average extent with those elusive qualities of empathy and ego drive. When all other things are equal, as indeed they tend to be in non-differentiated product markets, the buyer purchases from the salesman he prefers – and that after all is what personal selling is largely about. The salesman he prefers, apart from any personal charisma, will be the one who offers the greatest security, is enthusiastic and business-like, and on whom he knows he can rely for support. Conveying this quality is the major sales task and not one to be left to order takers, unsure or reluctant salesmen.

Thus with non-differentiated products the supplying company will always do well to consider how it can up-grade its sales force beyond that of its competitors rather than reduce sales costs by employing less than the best salesmen.

Image Development and Prestige Spin-off

Image factors are extremely important in non-differentiated product markets. Buyers' perceptions of products and suppliers are major influencing factors in many buying decisions. Tied in with a know-ledge of buying practices and attitudes, the most meaningful image development can be undertaken. Moreover, a strong positive image identification strengthens the 'instant recall' or association factor whereby a company thinking of a product associates it with a par-ticular firm. There is little doubt that to most buyers there is an immediate association between Lansing Bagnall and forklift trucks, Letraset and 'instant lettering', JCB and excavators, Accles & Pollock and tubes. Other makes may be bought but the firm first recalled clearly has major advantages.

Because perceptions play such an important role in differentiating products, there is considerable advantage to be gained from a linking with a well-known differentiated product or a prestigous customer.

Although lithography machines can be differentiated by the technically experienced, to the uninformed users they are largely similar. Gestetners contracted to supply the Vatican and the private audience granted by the Pope to members of their organisation certainly lifted them above the common run of printing equipment suppliers. The product may be non-differentiated but the customer is and thus the item is not one of a group of largely similar products but one which was supplied to the Vatican.

The image and 'spin-off' aspects of non-differentiated products form what has been called the 'fifth utility' (the other four are: *time*, *place*, *form* and *possession* utilities). This is the *image* utility – the ability of a product to provide satisfactions resulting from the user's perception of the social and personal meaning of the product in consumer terms and the commercial and corporate meanings in business terms. Once again, while products may be similar, images are not. The differences can be exploited.

Conclusion

By definition, the problem of the non-differentiated product is to distinguish it from all others of the same class or genre.

What this chapter has sought to point out is that if the product cannot be distinguished, it is possible to distinguish other factors which will influence its sale. The examples of ways of doing this are not complete but will take neither ingenuity nor inspiration to augment. A knowledge of one's own product and markets will rapidly reveal what non-product aspects can be promoted and offered as a real 'plus' to the buyer. Knowledge of the buying process and buyers, application engineering, non-product advantages such as guarantees, distribution channel control, high quality selling, and image factors represent but a small number of avenues for investigation. The firm manufacturing non-differentiated products need not adopt price cutting as the only expedient, nor need it be at the mercy of the market.

Indeed, as one marketing man has written: 'The firm that is at the mercy of its customers deserves sympathy and nothing else'. If products are not differentiated, suppliers and customers are, and it is not difficult to exploit existing strengths and avoid weaknesses.

Underlying all that has been said is the constant and insistent need for detailed and recent knowledge of the market, the customers, the products, the competition and the environment. Traditional acceptance of the state of non-differentiation tends to lull firms into either a false sense of security since all is thought to be known and nothing changes, or (an equally dangerous state of apathy) all is presumed to be immutable and nothing can be changed. Neither attitude is conducive to the creation of corporate policies which can bring about alteration in market dispositions or ensure survival of the company. Information used creatively is the one certain way of achieving leadership in a non-differentiated product group.

The check-list which follows is designed to generate the kind of information that can help a company develop significant competitive advantages in the market-place.

CHECK-LIST FOR NON-DIFFERENTIATED PRODUCTS

A. *The Product*

1. Is our product truly non-differentiated?

    (a) physical characteristics
    (b) performance characteristics
    (c) commercial characteristics

2. If not, do the aspects in which it differs from competitors' products represent a 'plus' to users?

3. Have we or can we exploit this 'plus'?

4. Are users aware of the 'plus'?

5. If not what steps can we take to draw users' attentions to the 'plus' and to demonstrate advantages to them?

6. If the product parameters are controlled by standards, is there any valid reason why we should not exceed the standards?

7. Is the users' attitude to price that of purchasing officers or of other members of the decision making unit?

8. Under what circumstances will price become of secondary or minor importance?

B. *Uniqueness*

1. Have we considered how we can introduce some aspect of uniqueness into the product, into the commercial conditions of supply or into our marketing?

2. Do we have detailed and recent knowledge of user attitudes, practices and unfulfilled requirements?

3. On what is this knowledge based, e.g.: salesmen's reports, formal marketing research, trade associations, and information, press, etc.?

4. Do we know what price premium users would pay for the introduction of features they regard as desirable? Can we ascertain this?

5. Would the introduction of such features lead to downward pressure of price on existing products? How do we know?

6. What features in existing products could be removed and still satisfy user requirements, e.g.: over-design features.

7. Are we capable of interpreting benefits of the product and commercial conditions as seen by the user and can we explain these to the users through our various marketing tools?

C. *Non-product Features*

1. What non-product factors can we develop to give our product a marketing 'plus'?

2. What is the relative value of these non-product advantages to customers of different types?

3. What member of the decision-making unit will understand these advantages?

4. Is it possible to develop optional non-product advantages so that customers may choose between various packages?

D. *Guarantees*

1. Do we offer any guarantees or warranties? If not, why not?

2. Are such guarantees and warranties – whether implicit or explicit – obvious to users?

3. What is our history of claims against guarantee or warranty?

4. What would be the cost to the company of extending guarantee periods?

5. What would the cost to the company be of widening guarantees?

6. What would the cost to the company be of more liberal interpretations of guarantee claims?

7. How can we exploit an improved guarantee position?

8. Ideally what sort of guarantees would users like?

E. *Distribution*

1. Is there any distributive channel the control of which would enhance our sales situation?

2. What percentage of sales could be expected through a controlled distributor channel?

3. Would obtaining control of the distributive channel antagonise existing customers?

4. Will competitive manufacturers supply any distributor which we control?

F. *Sales Force*

1. With whom in the buying companies do our salesmen have personal contact?

2. Is the quality of our sales force compatible with the level of authority and experience of those with whom they are in contact?

3. What steps are necessary to upgrade our sales force? (e.g.: training, replacement, short or call cycles, etc.)

4. Is the method of motivation and reward for our salesmen compatible with the qualitative and quantitative targets they are expected to achieve?

G. *Purchasing*

1. How is the decision-making unit of typical customers comprised?

2. Do we have knowledge and an understanding of the buying processes? How do we use this knowledge?

3. Do we know which factors in the product, in the commercial conditions and in marketing have particular appeal to the different members of the decision-making unit?

4. Should our marketing to different members of the decision-making unit be varied? If so in what way?

5. Can we convert a repeat purchase into a new purchase by introducing some innovative aspects in our offer?

H. *Application*

1. Do we know alternative uses for our product or uses which could be adopted if the product were modified in some way?

2. Do we have any formal application engineering activities?

3. Is there a second or secondary use for our product?

4. What additional market segments would be opened up by product modifications or by developing or exploiting second use?

I. *Image*

1. What is the 'ideal' supplier and product profile for the industries we supply? On what is this knowledge based (e.g.: formal research, salesmen's reports, trade comments, etc.)?

2. What is the image profile of our company and our products? On what is our knowledge based (e.g.: formal research, salesmen's reports, press comments, etc.)?

3. How far does our image fall short of or exceed the industry image reference?

4. How do images vary between different classifications of customers, e.g.: regular, sporadic, single transaction, discontinued customers, failed quotations, no contact?

5. How far are the images uncovered based on direct experience, knowledge by repute, heard of by name?

6. Is there any image variation among the decision-making units?

7. What factors influence image perception?

8. What method must we adopt to change our image?

CHAPTER 7

Marketing Purpose Made Capital Goods

The Contractual Consequences of Systems Selling, Large Projects and High Technology

By David Rowe

Introduction

Purpose made capital goods' selling is on the borderline between the selling of a service and the selling of a product. The seller is selling a *capability* to design, manufacture or construct something which does not yet exist. It may be an electronic control system or a chemical process plant, a factory, an aeroplane, all or part of a power station or a civil engineering project.

The purchaser has not merely to decide what he wants in terms of the end product. He has to satisfy himself of the competence and reliability of the seller to carry through the project to a successful conclusion and having done so he then has to place reliance on the seller to fulfil his promises as to the quality and performance of the ultimate product and the period within which it will be supplied. Purpose made capital goods are par excellence products where the purchaser is interested in security.

A distinguishing feature of the purpose made capital goods market is the risk created for the seller by the actual contract of sale. This is the risk which the seller has to assume in undertaking to provide the buyer with the security which is so important to him.

In the typical market situation risk is not something which is associated with the point of sale. The decision to invest in a new factory or to launch a new product involves risks, but not the actual selling of the product. Here we are faced with research into the market, the impact of the customer's needs on the design of the product, estimates of the numbers of units which can be sold, and finally the commitment of resources. These resources are put at greater or lesser risk according to the uncertainty of the market and the extent of the research the seller has carried out in order to reduce this uncertainty. But at least in these situations the company knows what its maximum risk is. It is the loss of the capital which has been irrevocably committed to the particular project.

The actual sale of the product itself of course involves the risk of bad debts, liability for injury caused through malfunctioning and claims under the manufacturer's guarantee. But, for the mass-produced product sold to big markets, losses in any of these risk areas can be monitored and controlled. Even if the steering wheel of a car comes off because of negligence in manufacture and as a direct consequence a tremendous multiple crash occurs on a motor-way, the resultant claims are unlikely seriously to dent the profits of the original manufacturer even if he does not have product liability insurance. The risks are capable of statistical treatment.

With purpose-made capital goods, however, the risk created by the actual sale is of a completely different order. There is no simple yard-stick to help determine the maximum loss the company can suffer. This is the risk which flows from the contract of sale itself, particularly when the sale is of an integrated system with under-takings as to its overall performance. In these cases it is not unusual for a company to wish afterwards that it had never made the sale in the first place.

A recent broker's circular[1] makes the following extremely relevant comment: 'It always amazes us how a single construction company is prepared to take on the £50 million risk (like the Hammersmith White City Scheme) when, if a £50 million issue was being raised in the City the risk would be split amongst a large number of houses.'

There is an increasing need for marketing theory to help firms in the capital goods business to develop a methodology for assessing and controlling contract of sale risk. Such a methodology might be called Contract Risk Analysis.

There are a number of factors which individually or collectively increase contract of sale risk. Some of the more important are:

Uncertainty. Obviously if one has undertaken a set of specific obligations any element of uncertainty about the environment in which they are to be carried out involves risk. Thus whenever the sale is of something which has yet to be designed or manu-factured or constructed, risk is very substantially increased

---

[1] *Investment in Construction 1972*, Green & Co.

because the uncertainty of the future is introduced. The longer the period of design, manufacture, or construction and the longer the period over which the price is fixed, the greater the risk. Two other aspects of uncertainty are the extent of knowledge of local conditions at the place where the equipment or system is to be put in use, and the degree of newness and sophistication of the technology involved.

Size of contract in relation to total turnover. The greater the size of the contract the less is it possible to rely on 'swings and roundabouts'.

The performance promises. The more the salesmen have had to promise to get the job the greater the risk that the promises will not be achieved in terms of the performance of the equipment and the period required to bring it into use.

The use to which the equipment is to be put. By definition capital goods are used in the production processes of the purchasing company. Thus any failure to deliver on time and any failure in performance involves the purchasing company in a loss of anticipated product and therefore profits and contribution to overheads. In the absence of protective language this loss may be recoverable from the supplier and is likely to be of a different order of magnitude from the value of the original contract. A failure of a newly originated pollution control system which was being relied on by the designers of a process plant might, with our growing awareness of pollution problems, make it necessary to halt all production for several months.

Degree of concentration of responsibility. When design is handled by one organisation, perhaps a consulting engineer, and the project execution by one or perhaps several other organisations, responsibility is divided and thereby diluted. The tendency to offer a 'package deal' as a means of product differentiation concentrates and increases responsibility and therefore risk.

Contracting

Of the factors which increase risk the most inevitable and intractable one is that which involves the uncertainty of the future, i.e. where the seller undertakes to supply something which has yet to be made, and perhaps designed, to a closely defined specification and within a certain time and at an agreed price. This, of course, is the essence of what we call 'contracting'. Strictly, of course, everyone who enters into a contract is a contractor. However, as a matter of language, we have long recognised that for some sellers who undertake future responsibilities the contract itself is so important that we call them contractors.

Inevitably we think of the building and civil engineering industry e.g. Laing, Wimpey, Taylor Woodrow, Costain and MacAlpine. And how often in this industry do losses on one particular contract destroy a pattern of steady growth?

The chief problems in building and civil engineering arise out of (a) product definition (i.e. what precisely did the contractor undertake to build?) and (b) price adjustment (i.e. have circumstances taken place which entitle the contractor to have the price adjusted?) Because this is an old and well-established industry it has built up norms against which to work particularly in the form of the model conditions of contract of the Royal Institute of British Architects and of the Institution of Civil Engineers. These conditions attempt to lay down acceptable solutions to the allocation of risk and responsibility. However it continues to remain a business in which much money can be lost as well as made.

Usually, however, the building and civil engineering contractor is working to someone else's design – the architect's or consultant engineer's – and he is working in an area which is well understood and where standards of performance are relatively easy to meet. Also he will usually have a multiplicity of projects of a relatively small size over which to spread his risks.

What we have to realise is that the nature and demands of the market place are putting many companies into a *contractor role* in much more dangerous areas than building and civil engineering.

We recognise this when we talk of defence contractors, aerospace contractors and process plants contractors, all of which are inevitably high risk businesses. Curiously we don't appear to realise that shipbuilding and heavy electrical plant have just the same problems.

For example, when Rolls-Royce undertook to supply the RB 211, it was contracting to supply something not yet designed or built, to a highly exacting performance specification at a price agreed. It involved extremely high technology and it represented a large proportion of the company's total turnover. But it had to take all

L

these risks in some form and some degree in order to survive. The market forced the situation.

In many fields over the next decade we shall face these agonising decisions. Manufacturing itself will become commonplace. We will sell our products by pursuing product differentiation – by doing something more than just supplying a product.[2] This is Levitt's 'cluster of consumer satisfactions'. Differentiation will come from designing and supplying systems, co-ordinating sub-contractors and guaranteeing the performance of the whole. The product that you started off trying to sell will be buried inside a system.

Furthermore, the projects in which we shall be involved are becoming larger, not merely in cash terms but in real terms. Growth has rightly or wrongly become so explosive that a single new project may easily double a company's productive capacity. One new power station may represent a five to ten per cent increase in the generating capacity of a medium sized country like the UK. During 1970 the book value of Rio Tinto Zinc's fixed assets went up by 50 per cent to £464 million, and the bulk of this increase was referable to expenditure during the year on only two immense projects.

Large projects usually involve taking technology to its limits because of the pursuit of economies of scale. It is less often recognised that they take our management and marketing techniques to the limits also. The job of controlling the network of relationships between designers, suppliers, constructors, carriers and bankers on a £100 million project is different in kind from that involved in a £10 million job. And the more a company pushes out in the attempt to satisfy its potential customers by assuming more and more roles and by designing the environment into which its equipment fits – the essence of systems marketing – the more the marketeer exposes his business to risk. And it is no good saying he should not – he has to. It happens in electronics, electrical equipment, in defence contracting, in computers, aerospace, process plants, steelworks, shipyards. In fact the more help you offer your client, i.e. the bigger the marketing package, the more risk you incur.

Negotiating

In order to keep risks under control, it is imperative that the seller

[2] For a fuller discussion of possible sources of differentiation in respect of industrial products and services, see Chapter 6 *The Marketing of a Non-Differentiated Industrial Product*, p. 138.

or contractor should put a great deal of effort into ensuring that he has a satisfactory contract with the purchaser. This is not a field where any longer can the contractor safely accept the purchasers' 'small print'. He must analyse and evaluate his risks and his contingency allowances, and where risks cannot be effectively covered by such allowances he must require that the wording of the contract modifies or removes the risk. There are many situations in which it is better not to get the business than to get it on the wrong terms.

In other words capital goods' marketing is increasingly more than just having the right product and services at the right price and purchasers who want to buy. Major sales have to be made against a background of extremely plain speaking. The terms of the contract have to be negotiated and where necessary compromises arrived at. These negotiations may take months and will draw heavily on top management time.

It is curious that 'negotiation' is not a word which marketing men use although it is an essential part of the purchasing man's vocabulary. Yet it must increasingly be a marketing function to establish negotiating objectives and to determine the company's position with respect to each major risk area. It thus becomes a vital matter to train salesmen as negotiators. Somehow the negotiation has to be conducted with toughness but at the same time without losing the relationship which has caused the purchaser to favour the company.

A contract for a project has two essential functions: 1. it defines the work, the price to be paid for it and the circumstances in which the price may be adjusted; 2. it defines liabilities in the event of failures of performance, delay, accidents, etc.

On most of these points the interests of the purchaser and the contractor are in conflict. The resolution of this conflict almost inevitably leads to complex solutions, and to an elaborate and lengthy contract. The outcome of the contractual negotiations will depend very much on the ability of the contractor to differentiate his offering from that of his competitors by introducing unique advantages. These may take the form of more proven experience on similar projects, a unique patent or know-how position, or, for example, an original financing package. In the absence of some significant distinguishing characteristics the buyer will tend to choose the lowest bid from a qualified contractor.

Price

Consideration of the question of price raises the most fundamental contractual issue – is the price to be lump sum or reimbursable cost or a mixture of the two? Many people are unaware of the extent to which contractors work on a reimbursable cost basis. There is also an assumption that reimbursable cost contracts are not in the best interests of purchasers. This is by no means necessarily the case. What is clear is that a contractor must have a policy against which to establish his position in particular instances; and he must have the arguments in favour and against each form of contract carefully organised. In certain fields it may well be a tenable marketing policy always to bid on a reimbursable cost basis with a separate profit fee. One firm which has very successfully developed and sold this approach is Bovis Fee Construction Ltd. who do so much work for Marks & Spencer. Bovis *only* work on a reimbursable cost basis. It take guts to take a position like this but sometimes it is no bad thing to show the market that one has convictions.

The report prepared by the National Economic Development Office[3] working party on large industrial construction sites contains an admirably clear and impartial statement of the relative roles of lump sum and reimbursable cost contracts

> '*We define a lump sum contract as one where the price for the specified work is a stated sum which may or may not be subject to variation by a prior agreed formula, for changes in the rates of materials and/or labour. It is a straightforward approach and the contractor carries the risks. Competition is also demonstrated. Given reasonable competition and specialisation and a very precise definition of what is required and when, it will secure the keenest bids. Contractors also have an incentive to complete the works economically (though this need not be the same as briskly) to make their profit. . . .*'

> '*Against these benefits we consider that the price factor can be given excessive weight. Estimating is not an exact science and a tender can be optimistic. A client is not immune to the repercussions. He cannot isolate himself from the risks and losses of his contractors because they affect the progress of his work, and the degree*

[3] NEDO *Large Industrial Sites. Report of the working party on large industrial construction sites*, HMSO, 1970.

of client contractor co-operation. But a bigger objection is that the client must be able to specify his requirements with considerable precision. He must also reduce to the minimum subsequent variations. Unless these prerequisites are met the contractor will include large sums for the uncertainties in the situation, or put in a low bid and exploit the charges for various frustrations.'

Of reimbursable contracts they say:

'We use the phrase "reimbursable contract" to describe the arrangement where engineering, procurement, and management costs, which include overheads and profit, can be fixed or be a percentage of the material and labour costs and can also be the subject of competition, but where material, labour and constructional plant costs will be reimbursed to the contractor. Sometimes a target cost, time bonus and penalty clause are linked with such variable costs as an incentive to timely and economic competition.'

'Reimbursable contracts are cheaper to prepare than lump sum contracts and generally take less time. Moreover competitive forces are not abandoned. Tenders may still be judged on the quotations for management fees, including overheads, but unreasonably large sums for contingencies are avoided. The greater security of the contractor makes for an easier relationship with his client which is not spoiled by inflated claims for variations. Most important, the client does not have to specify exactly what he wants when he goes out to tender. The contractor has more time to plan and organise his work and his expertise becomes available while designs are being completed. Finally, under reimbursable arrangements it is easier to call on a contractor to make good arrears that he had no part in making.

'There are drawbacks, however. There is no built-in strong incentive to finish the job on schedule and to the lowest cost, as there is in lump sum contracts. The fixing of "target costs" requires fine judgement and it has been argued that if sufficient is known about the work to fix a target cost, then a lump sum tender should be invited. This form of contract also requires an unusual relationship between the client and the contractor. The risk is now with the client and in his own interest he must monitor and control costs and progress day by day to an extent which he need not do with a lump sum contract.'

The primary reason for using the reimbursable cost route is to save project time. 'Only if the work has been settled in all its critical details is it reasonable to expect a contractor to tender for a firm price and a fixed period'.[4] The activity of settling the details of the project may take the client many months and may even be beyond the scope of his own technical resources. The period for lump sum bidding has then to be added and this can be a further two to four months. By contrast, the job can be started immediately if it is on a reimbursable cost basis and the contractor himself can be used to carry out the work of definition. At a later stage, once definition is complete, it may be possible to change the contract to a lump sum basis.

There is a great deal of sophistication available in the design of reimbursable cost contracts, and in the design of contracts which are in fact mixtures of lump sum and reimbursable cost. All this sophistication may be required to develop a satisfactory contract risk pattern with a particular client.

Price Variation

As will readily be seen, the importance of a fully detailed definition of the work to be performed depends upon whether the project is to be lump sum or open cost. However, the adequacy or otherwise of the specification is a technical and not a marketing matter. The question of price variation on a lump sum job is very much a marketing issue. Here there is need for meticulous care and reasoned persistence in negotiation. There are some risks which cannot reasonably be dealt with by a contingency allowance or which alternatively it may be expedient to exclude in order that the price which is bid will look competitive. These kinds of contingencies need to be reflected in a price variation provision.

For instance, one would not normally know how to assess a contingency for changes in taxes and customs and excise duties or for fluctuations in exchange rates on a project of several years duration. Today people are much more careful and sensitive on both these issues and are less and less willing to trust to hunch and sympathy. When profits become harder to come by it is extraordinary how irrelevant sympathy becomes.

[4] Report on the Planning and Method of Contracts for Building and Civil Engineering Contracts by the Bramwell Committee, HMSO 1962.

There are numerous other subjects for price variation – specification changes, unforeseeable difficulties with foundations, changes in laws and statutory regulations and prolongation of the work through causes beyond the contractor's control. In addition, one may or may not have a clause providing for escalation in materials and labour using a formula based on published indices.

The profitability of a project can also markedly be affected by its cash flow. Therefore one would expect negotiation over the details of the terms of payment and the provision of progress payments. Undoubtedly terms of payment are one area where a concerted company policy can be most effective in saving capital employed. It is also an area where clients are very prepared to be cooperative because they feel that a company which is careful in controlling its cash flow is likely to do a good job for them. It points to efficiency. Similarly one may have a policy to offer bank guarantees in place of retention monies during the defects liability period. For a first class company the cost of such a guarantee will always be substantially less than the cost of borrowing the equivalent sum of money.

Liabilities

The second essential function of a contract is to define and limit liabilities in the event of failures of performance, delays in the project, accidents, patents infringements, etc.

It cannot be stressed too much that irrespective of whether a project is lump sum or reimbursable cost these liabilities can attain enormous proportions. A failure to carry out one's contractual promises is a breach of contract and in assessing the damages payable for such a breach there is taken into account all the loss which could reasonably have been foreseen as a consequence of that breach, which of course includes the purchaser's own loss of profits. Many leading companies in the capital goods field, and perhaps particularly those of us origin, make it a matter of corporate policy that every sales contract must contain a clause excluding liability for consequential loss. Such an exclusion clause is becoming increasingly common in the United Kingdom and in fact a clause of this type is now included in the latest set of Conditions (the B3 Conditions) of the Institutions of Electrical and Mechnical Engineers, and also in the Model Conditions of the Institution of Chemical Engineers.

No exclusion clause can be completely effective because it can never do more than limit liability to the other contracting party. Thus, if any third party has a claim against a contractor, that third party's claim is unaffected. One consequence of this is that so far as liability for negligence is concerned, sub-contractors often are in a position of a greater risk *vis-à-vis* the ultimate client than is the main contractor. For example the manufacturers of instrumentation equipment for use in airliners are increasingly conscious of this liability, particularly when the size of a disaster which can be directly attributable to a failure in their instrumentation may be well beyond the limits of any insurance cover they could get on the market.

Clauses excluding liability will not be effective in protecting a contractor when he is in fundamental breach of his contract. The same position is arrived at in many other legal systems through the application of the rule that a person cannot exclude liability for his gross negligence or *faute lourde*.

With respect to plant or systems performance and completion time, the first line of the contractor's protection is that which identifies and clarifies the actual contractual obligations.

If a contractor is working on a design which is in any way developmental, he must find some way of recording this fact in the contract. It must be made obvious that the client is aware of the untried nature of the design so that it can be clearly seen that the client has accepted this risk and has not entered into this contract in ignorance. It is also important that the precise performance characteristics which are being guaranteed are laid down and that there is no room for argument as to how they are to be tested. Disputes can easily arise about the conduct of test runs, and margins of testing error.

It is usual to provide that deficiencies in performance up to a certain percentage may be discharged by the contractor paying liquidated damages. These are agreed sums of money to be paid on a scale proportional to the degree of deficiency. Wherever a contractor undertakes to achieve a particular standard of performance it is vital that he should agree a structure of liquidated damages because otherwise he may find that it is impossible to correct a slight deficiency or alternatively that the cost of such correction is totally disproportionate to the improvement.

In effect the use of a structure of liquidated damages buys the contractor a margin of error. If the plant or system yields a performance which is grossly inadequate and way outside tolerance limits envisaged in the guarantee, the extent of his liability will then depend upon the effectiveness of the exclusion clauses and upon the extent to which the contractor is able to show that the project was of a developmental nature and known to be such by the client.

Similar problems arise with respect to undertakings as to time of completion for a project. Here, however, it is essential to include clauses providing for extensions of time in the event of delays arising from causes outside the contractor's control. Many people are not aware that in the absence of such a clause the client is entitled to sue on the promised completion date regardless of the reasons for the delay.

If the contractor has to agree a specific date for completion then it is also strongly advisable that he should insist on a structure of liquidated damages which in effect entitle him to buy extra time for completion when the causes of delay result from his own fault.

The third major risk area is that of accidents, and here usually the critical risk is that which arises once the plant, or system, is operating. In all cases it is essential to define the precise extent of the contractor's liabilities and to match these against the programme of insurance The most difficult problem which a contractor faces is created by the fact that it is not possible to take out insurance against third party claims, sometimes known as public liability, beyond a specific financial limit. In other words a contractor's third party policy will always have a pecuniary limit of liability, whether it is £2 million, £5 million or £10 million with respect to any one accident. This limit of liability may well be inadequate in quite a number of circumstances. One just mentioned is the case of an airliner crash. Another could be an explosion of a plant in the middle of an operating oil refininery or power station. Usually, in these circumstances, it is possible to agree with a client that the contractor will only have a limited liability for damage to the client's existing installation. However, it is obviously important to negotiate this concession.

Consortia and Sub-contracts

In addition to the need to negotiate an adequate contract with the client, other sorts of negotiations are also necessary. On a major project it is increasingly common to form teams of sub-contractors and suppliers in order to qualify to bid. Such teams will usually be multi-national and quite often it will also be necessary to negotiate financing arrangements.

There always arises the problem of how the project risk is to be spread between the members of the team. Is one member prepared to assume the main contractor position with the others as sub-contractors, or will there be a consortium with risk and profit sharing? In the latter case, if there is a joint and several liability to the client on the part of the members of the consortium, how is each member going to limit his liability *vis-à-vis* the others?

*   *   *

Throughout all negotiations concerning capital probjects, it is essential that a contractor, in whatever business he may be, should be aware of his risk but at the same time flexible and innovative in his approach. In most companies in the capital projects and capital goods field, much work needs to be done by lawyers, financial men, insurance experts, salesmen and other marketers in analysing and quantifying the risks in their respective areas, with an awareness of how these risks interact so that those who price and bid may do so with the minimum of uncertainty as to the risks involved.

CHAPTER 8

A Systematic Approach to Effective Pricing

By André Gabor and C. W. J. Granger

Introduction

Price is only one of the many elements in the marketing mix which determine the extent of the success or failure of a product[1], and since in any actual marketing situation price exerts its influence in combination with all the other factors, it would seem justified to ask whether it is at all reasonable to lift price out of the complex and discuss it by itself.

There is a twofold answer to this question. First of all, the essence of any promising approach to a complex problem must consist in the effective separation and individual investigation of all the important determinants before proceeding to the study of their interactions. It is therefore clear that it is desirable to consider price by itself, though not so much in isolation from the other factors as rather by keeping them as constant as possible. This is perfectly feasible, but just because it can be done, it does not follow that it should also be attempted. The justification for undertaking this analysis lies in the unquestionable importance of price, and in the recognition that in the present economic situation even the prices of established products must be looked upon as variables rather than as constants.

It has recently been pointed out by a well known American business consultant that 'price is the *only* variable in the marketing strategy mix that generates income, all the others – product development, packaging, advertising and sales promotion, etc. – generate

[1] 'I once made a list,' says Garrit Lydekker of the Thompson company, 'of all the factors that can influence sales. I had forty-five of them written down before I got bored with it, I'm sure there are more.' Martin Mayer, *Madison Avenue USA*, Penguin Books, Harmondsworth, Middlesex, 1958, p. 57.

costs.'[2] While this is undoubtedly true, we would prefer to paraphrase it and say instead that the purpose of all the other elements in the marketing mix is to make the product sell in appropriate quantity at the desired price, and add that all the merchandising effort may be wasted if the price is not right. Furthermore, since in this competitive world profit margins tend to be slender, slight differences in price can greatly affect profitability.

There was a time in the not too distant past when the price of a product somehow arrived at was then taken as given, largely because of the widespread conviction (founded on belief rather than proper evidence) that while an increase in price would heavily reduce the demand, a reduction in price would not materially increase sales. The almost complete elimination of retail price maintenance in Britain (engendered by the introduction of American-styled marketing methods and subsequently reinforced by legislation) coupled with the general inflationary tendency has drastically changed this situation. In most fields, price revision has become a more or less continuous process, and more and more businessmen realise that fluctuations in the market shares of their products can to a large extent be ascribed to changes in relative prices.

Pricing principles and practices

A systematic approach to the problem of price determination must proceed by stages. We shall start with the fundamental aspects, taking the basic purposes of pricing first.

Pricing objectives

It is a self-evident and yet very often neglected principle that the ideal price is one which is optimal from the point of view of the company as a whole, and since this is frequently different from that of the salesman or even the product manager, it is the task of top management to clarify the objectives and to issue directives in a form which the lower echelons can both understand and effectively carry out.

The first part of the task is to clarify the objectives and to see that they are not inconsistent. For example, it may not be possible to achieve maximum profitability and maximum market share at the

[2] Daniel Nimer, 'Does your pricing pay?', *Marketing*, April 1970, p. 24.

same time, though the latter may be a legitimate short-term aim, which will duly serve the purposes of the former in the long run.

Let us take the most fundamental objective first. It is generally agreed that within the framework of the law and accepted conventions, the purpose of a business enterprise is to make profit for its owners and all other things being equal, a larger profit will always be preferable to a smaller one. This is what we mean by profit maximisation. It follows that it is not the same thing as striving for excessive profits at the expense of all other considerations.

However, profit maximisation can be interpreted in at least three different ways. It may refer to (a) the rate of return on turnover, (b) the rate of return on capital or (c) the amount of profit per year (or other time period). It is easy to see that even a highly increased rate of return (or mark-up rate) on a reduced turnover may well reduce both the rate of return on capital and the total amount of profit per year, and the reason why (b) and (c) generally call for different measures is that the effective capital of a firm is not a fixed quantity but one which can be varied almost any time.

With the exception of certain co-operative enterprises, the profit of which is shared by its members according to some principle other than the amount of capital contributed by them, maximisation of the rate of return on capital must be the proper aim of a business. What still remains to be clarified is the meaning of capital in this context: should it be interpreted as the value of the total assets of the firm, or merely as its net worth, i.e.: the capital of its owners?

It is sometimes argued that only the capital of the owners needs to be considered, since any loan capital which earns even a modicum of profit in excess of the interest payable on it, will contribute to the wealth of the owners, whether the net return is handed out in the form of dividends or retained in the firm. While this is not untrue, it is, unfortunately, often misinterpreted, to the detriment of profitability. *Capital should always be directed to its best available use, whether this appears within the firm or outside it: it is a mistake to allocate funds according to the interest charge on them, and allow 'cheap' monies to be put to a less profitable purpose if there are better opportunities in sight.*

Price can play a decisive role in investment decisions, but this is an aspect which we shall not pursue further in this chapter.[3] It must

---

[3] The interested reader is referred to André Gabor, 'Marketing's Role in Investment Decisions', *Marketing*, September 1970, pp. 44–7.

be pointed out, though, that the fullest extent of pricing discretion occurs when a manufacturing company takes up a new product, and this is generally coupled with an investment decision.

Larger companies, which consciously plan ahead, mostly set themselves a profit target in the form of a certain rate of return on capital.[4] Setting an apparently modest target rate is often interpreted as a deliberate departure from the maximisation principle, whereas this would be the case only if the Board of the company should consider it just as reprehensible to exceed the target as failing to attain it. In actual fact, there can be little doubt that the target is merely an indication of the minimum which should qualify as a satisfactory performance in the year concerned, and it is not therefore at variance with profit maximisation as we have defined it above.

It has, however, been argued that the executives of a company look upon growth of sales and market share as their primary objectives, with the target rate merely as a constraint on the means whereby growth is to be achieved. The answer to this is simply that growth for its own sake is not in the long run a desirable aim: growth is laudable only as a promise of higher profitability, and if this promise is never redeemed, the reputation of the firm and its executives is bound to suffer.

This is not meant as a denial of the fact that 'the modern firm is not a monolithic entity and that its objectives are necessarily compounded out of the divergent views of a variety of individuals and groups within the firm'.[5] What we do suggest is that rational business policy demands the proper ordering of all objectives, otherwise the very existence of the firm may be in jeopardy. Growth, price stabilisation, adequate utilisation of capacity and even a quiet life are all legitimate objectives, as is the maintenance of the good name of the company, but if any of these should demand a sacrifice of profits, the cost so interpreted must not be disregarded in any executive action, least of all in pricing decisions.

[4] Cf. Robert F. Lanzilotti, 'Pricing Objectives in Large Companies,' *American Economic Review*, December 1958, pp. 921–40. Reprinted in *Price Policies and Practices* (D. F. Mulvihill and S. Paranka, eds.), John Wiley and Sons, New York, N.Y. 1967. – For a comprehensive bibliography of related studies cf. Aubrey Silberston, 'Price Behaviour of Firms', *Economic Journal*, September 1970, pp. 511–82.
[5] William J. Baumol, 'Company Goals, Growth and the Multiproduct Firm' in *Theory of Marketing* (R. Cox *et al.*, eds.), Richard Irwin, Homewood, Ill., 1964, p. 330.

Pricing policies

There is no generally accepted nomenclature of pricing activities. Some authors consider the whole complex as one of policy or strategy or even as procedure, and this has led to some confusion. Here we shall endeavour to give precise meaning to each of the terms used, and we define pricing policy as being concerned with the desired image of the company. Broadly speaking, there is a choice between various ranges according to whether the price should imply top quality, good value for money or that the firm's products are the cheapest in the field.

This is sometimes described as an aspect of market segmentation, which is certainly not incorrect. It is seldom if ever possible for a firm to cater simultaneously for the luxury trade, the well-to-do middle class and the masses, but an appropriate product line policy can go a long way towards securing a foothold in at least two adjacent segments, by using different brand names and separate marketing organisations.

It follows from our definition of pricing policy that the crucial decisions are those taken when the introduction of new products is considered, also that it is desirable that the pricing decision, in broad terms at least, should precede product development, and that the latter should purposefully be directed towards the selected price range. This is sometimes described as *backward cost pricing* and will further be discussed in the next section.

While the elimination of resale price maintenance necessarily means that the manufacturer has little, if any, direct control over the actual price charged by the retail distributors of consumer goods to the final purchasers (and frequently no precise knowledge of the prices charged either), the price variations which are possible for the retailers can extend over a relatively narrow range only and will not permit the distributors effectively to cross the segment boundaries.

However, the image of a brand, and even that of a company, can seriously be affected if there is no proper control over marketing policy. Those distributors who cater for the masses buy in bulk and insist on appropriately low wholesale prices, and if these enable them to undercut the quality trade, the latter are apt to retaliate by refusing to stock the product concerned. There are well known instances of manufacturers having suffered severe losses by allowing this to happen, even though it could have been avoided if they had thought of the consequences in time, and had developed separate lines for each of the markets. We will return to this issue again in the section on pricing strategies and tactics.

Pricing procedures

Objectives and policy should determine the method by which actual prices are arrived at, and it is a difficult but highly important task of top management to delegate price determination to the lower echelons with instructions which ensure that the central aims of the company will be duly served by each decision.

In small companies, these decisions will generally be taken by top management itself, but even in the largest companies, pricing decisions should generally be submitted to high executive levels or even to the Board, since a price which promises to ensure success to one division, might fulfil this promise at the expense of overall profitability by adversely affecting the returns of another division. This does not mean that competition between different brands of the same firm is necessarily undesirable, but it should not be engendered in ignorance of the likely consequences.

It has been related that when the Vice-President of the soap division of a large American firm found his sales dwindling because of the successful incursion of the detergent division into his market, he petitioned for permission to meet the internal competition by introducing detergents himself. On his first attempt he was told that his business was to make and sell soap, but when he kept insisting that this was wrong, his proper business being to produce profits, the permission was eventually granted. The result of the ensuing fight was that the company greatly increased both its share of the soap and detergent market and the profitability of the two divisions taken together.

The outcome of internal competition is not invariably so happy, and it is generally better to harmonize the activities of the different divisions instead of pitting them against one another.

The actual pricing procedure can be cost-based, competition oriented or customer oriented. These different approaches are important enough to deserve detailed examination.

The simplest form of cost-based pricing is known as the rigid cost-plus procedure. As implied by its name, it consists in adding a predetermined percentage to the estimated unit cost of the product, generally combined with the application of some more or less systematical quantity rebate schedule. It has two variants, one of which is based on direct cost only and the other on the full absorption cost, as estimated by the cost accountant of the company.

Direct cost is a relatively unambiguous concept, provided it is meant to include only items which can be allocated from time sheets and material vouchers. All the other cost constituents plus the profit margin are then to be covered by the mark-up, which must therefore be based on some estimate of capacity utilization in the period concerned.

The full absorption cost procedure differs from the above only insofar as each of the elements of supplementary and overhead costs is individually allocated to the different products, or even to each separate order. The mark-up has to account then for the profit only, though not infrequently it is calculated so that it should also cover the estimated marketing costs.[6]

It is, of course, of vital interest to the firm to have some idea of the cost of its different products, but this does not mean that a rigid mark-up system should be looked upon as a sound pricing procedure. It has often been claimed that it represents the proper approach to the pricing of industrial products, on the grounds that the industrial buyer is an expert who will not tolerate more than a modest conventional profit margin on each of his orders. However, the expertise of the buyer seldom extends beyond the knowledge of the prices charged by different manufacturers of similar products, and it has been found that even in firms the executives of which claim full adherence to the rigid cost-plus system, actual pricing is competition-oriented and that their mark-up varies heavily from one quotation to another.[7]

Absorption costing may, on occasion, be very useful in gauging the price of a competitor, and standard costing within a given industry is sometimes advocated on the grounds that it will facilitate effective competition.

The danger of undue preoccupation with costs is that it tends to

---

[6] For a detailed critical exposition of cost-based pricing methods cf. Spencer A. Tucker, *Pricing for Higher Profit – Criteria, Methods*, McGraw-Hill Book Company, New York, N.Y., 1966.

[7] For two exceptionally revealing demonstrations of this point cf. I. F. Pearce, 'A Study in Price Policy', *Economica*, May 1956, pp. 114–27, and I. F. Pearce and Lloyd R. Amey, 'Price Policy with a Branded Product', *Review of Economic Studies*, XXIV.1, 1956/57, pp. 49–60.

M

disregard the fact that cost is not so much a justification for the price charged as rather for accepting or refusing the price tolerated by the market. And while competition-oriented pricing is certainly more realistic, it can be detrimental if driven too far, not only because it can develop into cut-throat competition, but also because it may lead to the neglect of the customers' true requirements. It is generally more profitable to develop the latent demand in the market than to fight over the already heavily exploited portion.

This is where backward cost pricing comes into its own, and whether openly acknowledged or not, it plays an important role in the field of many manufactures. Its essence is that instead of costing a product to find a price for it after it has been developed, the price is selected first, and the product shaped so that it should meet with the requirements of those customers to whom the price in question is attractive. In the past, the price points for new products had to be selected more or less by instinct; now there are research methods available which can be of considerable help in dealing with this problem. More will be said about this later, in connection with the psychology of pricing.

Finally, a word about the practice known as marginal pricing, but more properly designated as incremental costing. A manufacturer who has empty capacity may find it advantageous to accept an order at a relatively low price, well below the full absorption cost of the product, as long as it will cover the additional cost thereby incurred. However, it is also essential that by accepting such an order he should not spoil his regular market. If this condition is satisfied, it may be desirable to accept an order even somewhat below the direct cost if thereby labour which would otherwise have to be dismissed can be retained on the payroll because, quite apart from humanitarian considerations, this may be more advantageous and less costly than re-recruitment at a later date.[8]

Pricing strategies and tactics

What we mean by a pricing strategy is the purposeful application of the selected principles to specific products and markets over a certain

[8] For a sound appraisal of cost-based pricing cf. John Sizer, 'The Accountant's Contribution to the Pricing Decision', *Journal of Management Studies*, May 1966, pp. 129–49. Reprinted in *Pricing Strategy* (B. Taylor & G. Wills, eds.), Staples Press 1969, pp. 381–400.

period of time. Ideally, a complete strategy should include instructions for tactical moves to meet all certain and probable future situations, such as seasonal changes in consumer demand, temporary or permanent price cutting by competitors and even the emergence of new rival products. While it is hardly practicable to develop such an all-embracing strategy in advance, it is not only possible but highly desirable to estimate the likely life cycle of each product, to decide whether appropriate effort should be made to maintain its price at the original level throughout, or start with a low output at a high price and then gradually reduce it as increasing output lowers unit cost. Needless to say, strategies should be under constant review all the time.

Seasonal changes can be met in different ways. Where seasonality is very marked, it is often found best to withdraw the product from the market during the slack periods; where the variations in demand are less severe, the choice is between two alternatives: leave the price unchanged and accept the reduced off-season turnover, or lower the price when demand slackens and endeavour to smooth out fluctuations in sales in this way. It depends very much on the product and the nature of its market which of these strategies hold out the best promise.

The strategy may also include instructions for temporary price promotions and for appropriate moves to counter such action if initiated by a competitor. It is interesting to note that at the retail level the practice of withdrawing the brand from the shelves while a nearby competitor sells it at a cut price appears to be spreading. Clearly, this cannot be made a general rule of behaviour, and the real choice is between ignoring the action of the competition, matching the price cut or countering it by some other method of promotion.

Price changes of competitors which promise to be permanent should not find the marketing division unprepared either. The good old principle of not crossing our bridges before we come to them may have served us well in the past; nowadays it can be dangerous to leave the decision until the emergency has occurred.

Some typical pricing situations

Pricing situations can be classified in many different ways, a few of which will be discussed here.

In the first instance, there is the dichotomy which distinguishes between negotiated and declared prices. The difference is, however, more apparent than real, since even firms which issue price lists complete with quantity rebates, generally find that actual orders are the result of negotiations, and the listed prices serve merely as the maxima they hope to achieve. Exceptions are strong monopolies and, at least to some extent, those product fields where resale price maintenance is still legal.

Jobbing firms, such as contractors, etc., have to tender separately for each order, and since pricing is a daily task for them, it is particularly important that any delegation of pricing decisions should be accompanied by clear and comprehensive instructions designed to ensure conformity with the basic objectives and selected policy of the firm.

Product Analysis Pricing, or PAP for short, is a pricing system which claims to comply with these requirements and may therefore deserve brief mention. Its originators suggest that pricing should not be based on cost but on the value placed by the buyer on four essential characteristics of the product, which are materials, bought components, product properties and special features, each of which is measurable in one way or another. While PAP is based on the laudable principle of market orientation, it has not spread beyond the company where it was originally developed, because it suffers from a fundamental weakness: it offers no other way for determining the rules by which the value of each of the characteristics should be assessed except the evidence of past sales as evaluated by the chief pricing executive.[9]

While it is true that negotiated prices are largely dominant in the industrial market, they are not entirely absent from the consumer market either. Builders, decorators and other tradesmen generally have to quote separately for each job, and there can be little doubt that their pricing is aimed at the level which the market will bear, with some regard to their reputation in the long run. Like all small firms, they could not possibly afford either a sophisticated pricing system or market research.

Another instance of negotiated prices is the market for consumer durables. Since the abolition of resale price maintenance, the buyers

[9] Readers who desire further information about PAP should consult Leon Simcns, 'Product Analysis Pricing' in *Pricing Strategy* (B. Taylor and G. Wills, eds.), Staples Press, 1969, pp. 334–45. The book written by the originators, Wilfred Brown and Elliott Jaques, which bears the same title (Heinemann 1964) makes more difficult reading.

of consumer durables often start shopping around for the cheapest price after they have decided on the item of their choice, especially if they are prepared to pay cash. Here a good reputation for reliability and efficient after-sale service can help to counter the price cutters.

In the field of repeat purchase consumer goods the emergence of the modern supermarket has materially changed the situation in the course of the last 15 years or so. While prices may be said to be declared at any given moment of time, they are not fixed from one day to another, and the practice of having always a few items on special offer while the prices of the other products are more or less systematically fluctuated around a predetermined level has become widespread. The real or apparent 'loss leaders' have the purpose of enticing the customer, while the fluctuating price level aims at the prevention of selective shopping.

The soundness of this practice is very much in doubt. On the one hand, it has been found that whereas formerly most housewives regularly patronised one grocer, now they customarily visit two or three, and many of them systematically hunt round for bargains. It is also known that those chain stores which deliberately eschew fluctuating prices and are careful to offer genuine bargains only, have gained a reputation for fair trading which is paying them handsome dividends.

Recommended prices, which are still allowed under the law, have fallen very much into disrepute since the spread of the 'so much below the manufacturer's recommended price' gimmick. They do not even serve any longer as secure upper limits to the retail prices since the public have tacitly accepted the inflationary situation and do not complain if they find that the label with the price which they paid was placed so as to cover up an original lower price.

We will not discuss here price formation in commodity markets and the stock exchange, since where such markets exist, price determination cannot be influenced by the deliberate action of any single firm or individual, and rings, corners, take over bids and such like fall outside the scope of this chapter.

The psychology of pricing

So far we have only hinted at the principle that if pricing is to be fully effective, it must be customer oriented.

The question is, how is this to be achieved. In the past, many a large fortune has been made by businessmen who could identify with their customers, adapt to their point of view and develop their products and prices accordingly. Those who are blessed with such empathy need no help with this side of their business, but the gift is rare and it is therefore of considerable importance that modern research methods, capable of replacing a great deal of intuition, are now available. We shall briefly outline these methods and their utilization in pricing decisions. Though they are largely concerned with the attitude of consumers, the findings are not without relevance to industrial buyers either, who are, after all, human beings even while they act in their official capacity. Furthermore, it is the final user who counts most, and it often pays to look beyond the industrial buyer, since he cannot afford to be indifferent to any proposition which promises to have a favourable influence on the sale of the products of his firm.

Price awareness

The extent to which price can be used as an effective marketing tool must necessarily depend on the price consciousness of the prospective customers, and price recall can be used to measure its extent.

In the case of repeat purchase goods, this can be tested at two levels: on leaving the shop immediately after the purchase, and in the home. Not unexpectedly, it has been found to vary somewhat with the socio-economic group of the subjects, but very much higher variability of price recall has been found between different products.

The extent to which customers can correctly remember the prices paid for their recent purchases is not independent from the frequency of purchase or from the relative importance of the products concerned in their budget, but cannot directly be inferred from them. Research is needed to ascertain it, and especially in the case of highly competitive markets and variable prices, the shopfront method is more appropriate.[10]

The relevance of price awareness to marketing decisions should be obvious, since the higher is this awareness, the more likely is price to be an effective element in the marketing mix, and *vice versa*.

[10] Techniques and findings are described in André Gabor and C. W. J. Granger, 'On the Price Consciousness of Consumers', *Applied Statistics*, 1961, pp. 170–88, also in 'How Much Do Customers Know About Retail Prices?', *Progressive Grocer* (USA), February 1964, pp. c. 104–6.

Price as a quality indicator

For the prospective customer the information content of the price has two aspects, since it tells him both about the cost of acquisition and about the implied quality of the item. It has been suggested that this second connotation of price is simply a reflection of the ignorance of the consumer, but this is not entirely correct, insofar as the price paid remains an important attribute of the article also after the purchase, just as much as the brand name, the packaging and the composition and quantity of the product.

This means that a price higher than those of some of the competitive brands is not necessarily a deterrent to the customer, and that the reason why this is so is only exceptionally self-deception. In most highly developed countries price differences are on the whole reasonably reliable indicators of quality differences: experience has taught the public to accept this as the general rule. While manufacturers could not be said to be unaware of this relationship, its systematic utilization in pricing decisions is of relatively recent origin.

Some small-scale experiments were carried out in the United States, but the main advances owe their origin to the work of French researchers.[11]

The principal tool of research is the buy-response curve, the theory and practical application of which was developed in Britain. Both are described in detail in the references;[12] here we shall restrict ourselves to a simple outline of the technique.

An appropriately selected representative sample of consumers has to be interviewed and each subject asked if he would buy the product named (or a given brand, according to the purpose of the enquiry) at certain selected prices. The proportions of those who answered in the affirmative is then plotted against the price, and connecting the points so obtained yields the buy-response curve.

[11] Cf. H. J. Leavitt, 'A Note on Some Experimental Findings About the Meaning of Price', *Journal of Business*, July 1964, pp. 205 ff., E. A. Pessemier, *Experimental Methods of Analyzing Demand for Branded Consumer Goods*, Washington State University Press, 1963, esp. Chapter 6, pp. 74–125, D. S. Tull *et al.*, 'A Note on the Relationship of Price and Imputed Quality', *Journal of Business*, April 1964, pp. 186–91, Jean Stoetzel, 'Le prix comme limite', in *La psychologie économique*, P. L. Reynaud, ed.), Marcel Rivière et Cie, Paris 1954, pp. 184–8, Daniel Adam, *Le comportement du consommateur devant le prix*, SEDES, Paris, 1958.

[12] André Gabor and C. W. J. Granger, 'Price as an Indicator of Quality', *Economica*, February 1966, pp. 43–70, and, by the same authors, 'The Attitude of the Consumer to Price', in *Pricing Strategy* (B. Taylor and G. Wills, eds.), Staples Press, London, 1969, pp. 132–51.

(Those who respond with 'no', may be asked if the price was too high for them or so low that they would not trust the quality, but the resulting limit distributions are of more relevance to the theory of consumer psychology than to practical pricing decisions.)

If the range of prices was appropriately selected, a bell-shaped curve will emerge[13], the shape of which will be in general conformity with the relevant theory of consumer behaviour. However, any deviations from the generic shape deserve special attention since they reflect the peculiarities of the market, especially with respect to the sensitivity to price changes.

Each of the subjects is also asked about the price paid for the last purchase of the product (or brand) concerned. In this way, a measure of price consciousness is obtained, but the main use of the price recall data is that if plotted on the same diagram as the buy-response curve, the relationship of the two will reveal whether the public are on the whole satisfied with the price-quality combinations available or consider the product overpriced.

Properly obtained and interpreted, the buy-response curve can be a powerful aid to any price revision, and has in fact found widespread use by manufacturers and market research organisations in a number of countries.

An illustration is provided below, in the section on New Product Pricing.

Price sensitivity

Reference has been made above to the different regions of price sensitivity revealed by a buy-response curve. Generally, there will be three distinct price ranges: a central range embracing the price which is of interest to the highest proportion of consumers, a range to the left of it, where, as we move away from the centre, we find increasing proportions of customers who consider the price too low, and a range to the right, where higher prices deter more and more of the potential customers.

In the case of some products, the central range displays a more or less sharp peak, and is thus relatively narrow; in the case of others, we find a plateau instead of a peak, indicating low price sensitivity of the market over the range concerned. This does not necessarily mean

[13] In spite of the broad similarity, it will not be a Gaussian curve, but its central portion will approximate the shape of a log-normal distribution.

that the same customers are prepared to purchase at any price within the range, but merely that the proportion of interested subjects remains fairly constant.

The slopes of the two outside ranges may be gentle or steep, as the case may be. It is not possible to generalize these findings since the specific characteristics of the market must be ascertained separately in each instance.

Apart from revealing these broad ranges of sensitivity, the actual shape of the buy-response curve also reveals the attitude of the consumers to the so-called 'psychological prices', which are generally a fraction below the next round figure.

The practice of this type of pricing is even more widespread in the United States than in Britain, but its efficacy has never yet been conclusively assessed. The results of our own enquiries strongly imply that the consumers' attitude to these 'charm prices' is more a reflection of the traditional conventions of the price-makers than of their own subjective price scale. It seems also that it is the retailers rather than the manufacturers who cling to the traditional pricing points of the trade, presumably because strict adherence to them is tantamount to the elimination of fine pricing as a tool of marketing.[14]

New product pricing

Broadly speaking, new products can be classified into two separate categories: true novelties which, according to a well-known authority on managerial economics, 'have a protected distinctiveness which is doomed to progressive degeneration from competitive inroads,'[15] and those which are new to their manufacturer but, being functionally similar to existing products (or even functionally identical with them), are in fact merely new brands which have to find their place in established markets. Novelty is, however, a matter of degree, and

[14] This issue is further discussed in André Gabor and C. W. J. Granger, 'Price Sensitivity of the Consumer', *Journal of Advertising Research*, December 1964, pp. 40–44. (Reprinted in *Readings in Market Research* (K. K. Cox, ed.), Appleton-Century-Crofts, New York, N.Y. 1967; *Readings in Marketing* (C. J. Dirksen *et al.*, eds.), Revised Edition, Richard D. Irwin, Homewood, Ill., 1968; *The Environment of Marketing Behavior*, R. J. Holloway and R. S. Hancock, eds.), John Wiley & Sons, New York, N.Y., 1969. – Cf. also, by the same authors, 'Price as an Indicator of Quality', *Economica*, February 1966, pp. 43–70 (reprinted in *Pricing Strategy* (B. Taylor and G. Wills, eds.), Staples Press, London, 1969), especially Figure 12(a) and the discussion appended to it.
[15] Joel Dean, 'Pricing Pioneering Products', *Journal of Industrial Economics*, July 1969, p. 65.

hence it is possible for a new product to be on the borderline between the above two categories – which is another way of saying that the protective distinctiveness is not invariably a strong one.

It might seem that it is the true novelty which presents the more difficult pricing problem, but this is not in fact the case, since it is almost invariably possible to launch it at a price which is a heavy multiple of current production cost, and then gradually reduce the price as the increasing acceptance of the product makes mass manufacturing possible, which will also help to make the market less attractive to potential competitors. This might look as an encouragement to exploit the temporary monopoly situation, whereas all it means is that, in the case of a true novelty which is favourably received by the market, returns should make appropriate early contribution to accumulated development expenses and marketing cost, both of which are likely to be relatively heavy at this stage.

In the case of a new industrial product the search for the proper price generally involves the estimation of the cost saving or extra revenue which may accrue to the user. If the product is a capital good, such as a new machine, and the advantages which it offers are really unique, the most effective method is to hire it out and to charge according to the extent to which it is used, instead of selling it outright. If it is a component which enhances the value of the product in which it will be embodied, it can be of great help to find out by market research the price difference final users would be prepared to pay for its advantages, and negotiate on this basis. Where a new component will also find a sale as a spare part or replacement, the manufacturer is faced with two separate markets. It is not unusual to let the original component go at cost or even below it, and to charge a profitable price to the spare part trade.

If an industrial product is not much more than a new brand which does not confer any special benefits on the user, the price will have to adapt itself to the prices of those products for which it is offered as a substitute. This does not necessarily mean that the competition should invariably be undercut, since a low price implies low quality also to industrial buyers.

The proper pricing of a new brand for the consumer market is an intricate problem. It does not readily yield itself to the skimming price policy which is appropriate for the true novelty only, though it may on occasion be applicable provided the new brand is appropriate for starting its life in the luxury class. For a new brand not so blessed, it is essential to find the right price at the outset, that is to say, the strategy adopted must be that of the penetration price.[16]

Whereas a genuine novelty will generally arise as a result of an invention, as the fruit of research which, even if purposefully conducted, cannot in advance aim at a definite price or unit cost of production, the development of a new brand can do just that. Brief reference to such backward-cost-pricing was made above, in the sections on pricing policies and procedures, now we will show how the buy-response curve can help to locate the most promising price.

The broad approach starts with a survey in which an appropriately selected sample of the actual users of the existing brands should be interviewed. For the sake of example, let us assume that the product in question is shoe polish. The first question to be asked should then be: '*Do you buy shoe polish?*' and the interview will be continued only if the answer is in the affirmative. Next, the subject is asked '*If you went out to buy a tin of shoe polish of the normal size* (a sample tin without the brand name may be shown) *and found one which looked acceptable to you, would you buy it if the price were X pence.*' After recording the answer as 'yes' or 'no', the interviewer will say: '*I will now name a few more prices, please answer to each "yes, buy" or "no".*'

Experience indicates that up to eight prices can safely be put to each subject, and if this should be insufficient to cover adequately the actual price range of the market, the sample will have to be subdivided. In each case the first price named should be from the middle range, the others in randomized order.

Then the subject is asked for the price of his last purchase and the brand bought; also, if desired, the name of the retail outlet where it was obtained, but it will generally be sufficient to record merely the category of the establishment, e.g. 'Chain Store', 'Chemist', 'Department Store', 'Grocer (independent or symbol)', 'Shoe Shop', 'Supermarket' and 'Other'. The interview is concluded with the usual classification questions.

The buy-response and price-last-paid curves can now be plotted. The former will indicate the percentage of potential customers at each price, and the latter will reveal if there happens to be a gap in the price structure into which the new brand could effectively step. The

16 The terms skimming and penetration price policies are due to Joel Dean (in whose vocabulary strategy is included in policy). Cf. his *Managerial Economics*, Prentice-Hall, Englewood Cliffs, N.J., 1951, especially Chapter 7, pp. 397–467.

shapes and relative position of the two curves will also indicate whether it would be advantageous to introduce the new brand at the most popular price or below or above it.

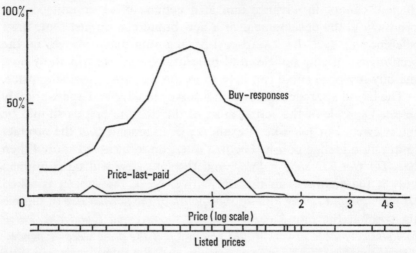

Figure 1 Household Cleaning Product *A*. Positive responses of 1,971 subjects.

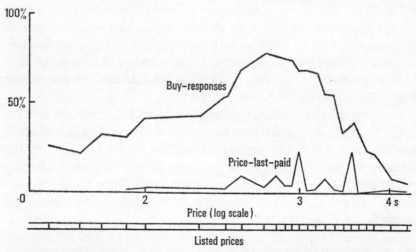

Figure 2 Household Cleaning Product *B*. Positive responses of 1,100 subjects.

Figures 1 and 2 show buy-response and price-last-paid curves obtained by questioning in their homes two different but comparable samples of housewives. Each of the original lists contained about 2,000 addresses, selected by a clustered quasi-random method, but information was taken only from those subjects who declared themselves actual purchasers of the household cleaning product concerned.

In the diagrams the percentages of positive responses are measured on the vertical axis, and the horizontal axis shows the prices on a logarithmic or ratio scale. Below each diagram the 24 prices used in the questioning are indicated by the vertical divisions.

Product A has been on the market for a long time. It has a very high penetration and its buy-response curve conforms well to the basic theoretical shape. It is roughly symmetrical and its peak coincides with the most popular price. The inference is that the purchasers are generally satisfied with the price structure, i.e.: that they consider the pricing equitable.

Not so in the case of Product *B*, which was of relatively recent origin at the time of the survey and had a very much lower penetration. Here the rough conformity with the generic shape and symmetry are still discernible in the buy-response curve but its peak and bulk are both well to the left of the range of the most popular prices. What this shows is that high proportions of the purchasers considered the product overpriced. The reason why the high priced brands were still the market leaders was that at the time the cheaper brands were markedly inferior in quality, also they were available only in a small proportion of the retail outlets.

A manufacturer thinking of developing a new brand for the market of Product *A* would have been well advised to select a price point somewhat above 9d., which was at the time the most popular price. He would then have encountered a proportion of potential purchasers as large as he could have expected by going below the peak by a similar price difference, while the higher price held a better chance of good profitability. Having chosen his price, he was able to identify the competition and thereby ascertain what quality (in the widest possible sense) purchasers would expect from the new brand.

The potentialities of the market for Product *B* were markedly different: here a price below 2s. was indicated, and if one of the leading national brands had stepped down with its price, it might have swept the market. (What actually happened was that several cheaper brands, largely own label, appeared all over the place and substantially reduced the market shares of the leading brands.)

The method here outlined and illustrated is capable of many modifications and can be adapted to a great variety of situations. The procedure itself is straightforward, but it should be noted that both the design of the enquiry and the interpretation of the results require expert knowledge.

From any selected retail price appropriate deduction will be made for distributors' margins, marketing expenses and profits, and the task is then to determine whether the remainder is sufficient to cover the manufacturing cost and overheads of a product which consumers are likely to judge as acceptable at the target price. Once a small quantity has been produced, a consumer panel, selected from the appropriate segment of the consumers, can be consulted to find out how the new brand compares with what the market expects at that price.

The panel may also be asked if they would be prepared regularly to purchase the new product, but the answers should be treated with great caution. It is advisable to follow up with test-marketing and to pay special attention to the repeat purchase rate.

The procedure here outlined is certainly not costless but, if properly conducted, may prove much more conducive to success than the present general practice; it being an established fact that only a small proportion of the hundreds of new products launched each year proves to be profitable in the long run. The great majority fail and result in losses instead of profits.[17]

Product line pricing

The term product line may refer to a collection of items very different from one another but connected by their use, such as, e.g.: motor car accessories. While such a line may contain more than one item for each purpose, differing in quality and price, the whole line should preferably be governed by the same pricing policy: economy, good value for money or luxury. It would be difficult to pursue this particular topic further without explicit reference to the specific market concerned; thus, for example, comparable items will be priced

---

[17] Cf. *New Products in the Grocery Trade*, Kraushar Andrews and Eassie Limited, London, 1971, p. 5, where it is shown that out of a total of 1,492 new food products introduced in 1959–66, only 464 (37 per cent) could qualify as successes by 1970.

The method outlined in this section and also an alternative are described in André Gabor and C. W. J. Granger, 'The Pricing of New Products', *Scientific Business*, August 1965, pp. 3–12. Reprinted in *European Marketing Research Review* (ESOMAR), 1966; *Price Policies and Practices* (D. S. Mulvihill and S. Paranka, eds.), Wiley & Sons, New York, N.Y., 1967; *Pricing Strategy* (B. Taylor and G. Wills, eds.), Staples Press, London, 1969. – For a critical discussion of the relevant ideas of Alfred R. Oxenfeldt and Joel Dean, cf. André Gabor, 'New Product Pricing', *Marketing*, February 1971.

differently if they are for the use of cyclists, motorists or aircraft operators.

Another kind of product line contains only items of much greater similarity, such as, for example, motor cars, washing powders or overcoats. Here it is well possible to cater for the needs of different strata of users, at least between certain limits, and the main question which arises is what gaps should exist between the prices of the various qualities.

The traditional principle appears to be to space the prices sufficiently apart, so that each user stratum should be catered for by a distinct grade. Until a few years ago, this had been the practice of American automobile manufacturers, presumably with the idea that such an important status symbol as the automobile should clearly indicate the socio-economic group of the owner. More recently, automobile manufacturers adopted a different policy, and have made the price ranges of their brands overlap, so that, for example, the cheapest Oldsmobile costs less than the de luxe Buick. Whether this form of internal competition is beneficial to the company or not (both Oldsmobile and Buick are brands of General Motors), could not be decided in general.

A third form of product line exists if the same brand is available in different sizes, which is the case with large numbers of repeat purchase household goods. Here there is a clear-cut principle to be advocated, which has recently been tested in an experiment.[18] It is simply that since it is more advantageous both to the manufacturer and to the retailer to sell larger packs, the prices of the packs of different weight should be so set that the purchaser should obtain better value each time he switches to a larger size, meaning that the price per unit weight should decline as the size of the pack goes up.

Actual practice seems to neglect this principle, and the tendency appears to be to set the sizes so that they should represent odd units of weight (or cubic capacity), presumably to prevent the potential purchaser from making precise value comparisons between competitive brands. What is less comprehensible is the fact that neither the prices charged by the retailers nor the price lists of the manufacturers display systematic structures, thus the so-called large economy size is often found to be more expensive per unit weight than the smaller packs.

[18] Cf. C. W. J. Granger and A. Billson, 'Consumers' Attitude to Package Size and Price: An Experiment', *Journal of Marketing Research*, 1972.

Observation and experimental results indicate that purchasers do in fact tend to be confused by these practices, and also that if pricing is consistent with the principle that the larger the pack, the better the bargain, and appropriate information about the price and size relationship is provided, purchasers will react rationally.

The example below illustrates the principle of purchaser's advantage consistently increasing with size. The additional pound becomes *progressively* cheaper at each step.

Size lbs.	Price £ p.	Price per lb. p.	Price of additional lb. p.	Difference p.
1	0·50	50	50	
2	0·96	48	46	4
3	1·36	$45\frac{1}{3}$	40	6
4	1·68	42	32	8
5	1·90	38	22	10

Price as a weapon of competition

As mentioned in the introduction of this chapter, the importance of price in the marketing mix has increased in recent years. Whereas formerly product differentiation appeared to be the main guiding principle, the striving for being distinctly different has given way to an effort to be similar but preferably superior, at least in a number of product fields. The purchasing public recognise the similarity and have limits to what they are prepared to pay for the real or alleged superiority, and if they fail to perceive a qualitative difference, price will become the major influence on market shares. This is what marketing men mean when they say that a brand market has deteriorated into a commodity market.

Such phenomena are not in any way contrary to the role of price as an indicator of quality. The salient point is that there are limits to the effect of any factor in the marketing mix, and what matters is not so much the mere existence of a relationship, but its nature and magnitude. The latest research methods have made it possible to determine the former and to measure the latter.

The first point to consider is the identification of competition. It would be rash to assume that it is invariably the product which is most similar in its physical characteristics to one's own will also be its closest competitor. For example, it is known that canteens of cutlery bought as wedding presents have to compete with plate silver, cut glass and such like, and an investigation into the multi-brand market for a household cleaning product has revealed that the housewife's order of preferences is mostly different from that of the expert. Market research can obtain the relevant information, but the methods must be appropriately selected and expertly adapted to the peculiarities of the market to furnish reliable data.

Once the competition is identified, a controlled price variation experiment can be applied to establish the price/market-share relationship between the brand concerned and its main competitor. The fact that there is now a tested theory of such relationships is of great help here and makes it possible to separate brand preference from brand loyalty. A measure of the former is the price difference needed to make the market shares equal (or, alternatively, the difference in market shares when the prices are identical), and brand loyalty can quantitatively be assessed by the effect of successive price differences on market shares.

If certain basic conditions are satisfied, it may be safe to eschew the actual pricing experiments in retail outlets and use hypothetical shop situations instead.

The methods and conditions of applicability are described in the references.[19]

Decimalisation and the consumer

The decimalisation of the British currency provided a rare occasion to observe and investigate how the public react to a full-scale social experiment. Since, however, the most important effects will fully develop only when, with metrication completed, commercial arithmetic has become as simple and straightforward in Britain as it is in most other industrialised countries, the immediate consequences are of temporary significance only.

From the marketing point of view, it is unfortunate that the pound was selected for the base because, until inflation has substantially eroded its value, the relative magnitude of the smallest unit will render fine price adjustments of cheaper items well-nigh impossible, and is

[19] A. P. Sowter, A. Gabor and C. W. J. Granger, 'The Influence of Price Differences on Brand Shares and Switching', *British Journal of Marketing*, Winter 1969, pp. 223–30; 'Real and Hypothetical Shop Situations in Market Research', *Journal of Marketing Research*, August 1970, pp. 355–59; 'The Effect of Price on Choice: A Theoretical and Empirical Investigation', *Applied Economics*, November 1971, pp. 167–81. Further references are listed at the end of each of these articles.

N

therefore bound to perpetuate the practice of varying the contents of the pack when costs change. This is inevitable with the so-called 'count lines' (small chocolate bars and packs of sweets largely bought by children or for them), but should not have been allowed to spread to other product fields. However, the present position is that only in the case of a few products, such as, e.g.: instant coffee, do legal regulations prescribe the size of the packs in which the product may be offered for sale.

Contrary to some early claims, decimalisation has not meant the end of the system of conventional price points and charm prices, but has certainly upset the traditional structure. For example, 2/6 and 3/9 were generally judged to be attractive prices, whereas their decimal equivalents (or near-equivalents) could hardly be called that.

It can be said that, on the whole, decimalisation was very quietly accepted. Price awareness was somewhat affected in the months immediately after Decimal Day (15th February, 1971), and it was also found that, with the exception of the simplest cases, people had difficulty in identifying the equivalent of a decimal price in the old units. In spite of all this, the attitude to prices and price differences as ascertained by buy-response curves and experimental techniques, showed quite remarkable degrees of constancy, as did also actual purchasing behaviour.

The investigation of attitudes also revealed that people heavily overestimate the current rate of inflation, which makes it all the more remarkable that there has not been any serious public outcry against it. About two-thirds of the housewives questioned were trying to counter inflation by looking round for cheaper prices, almost one-third said that they were cutting down on expenditure, and only a very small proportion asserted that they were doing extra work or asking for more housekeeping money.[20]

20 Cf. the summary of the Interim Report of the Nottingham University Consumer Study Group on Decimalisation and the Consumer in the *SSRC Newsletter*, November 1971. The project was sponsored by the Social Science Research Council and a full report will be published at a later date.

CHAPTER 9

Developments in Physical Distribution Management

By Digby Brindle-Wood-Williams

Introduction

The 1960's will be remembered as a decade in which British industry became particularly aware of the importance of effective physical distribution management. Rising costs, growing international competition and a revolution in transport techniques – especially the large-scale introduction of unit load and container services – combined to stimulate a new approach to an area which hitherto had been widely ignored.

Physical distribution has been defined[1] as 'the process of interpretation of an order to effect the movement of goods from the point of manufacture or storage to the customer in accordance with company policy'. It broadly covers all the events which occur between the end of a manufacturer's production line and the receipt of goods by his customer, and includes: warehousing and handling, documentation, packaging and transport.

These activities add nothing to the inherent value of a product. It was, however, the fundamental realisation by management that they can add greatly to its cost and that badly planned distribution methods can adversely affect both the production and marketing processes, and thus overall company profits, that has contributed so much to discussion about and research into physical distribution techniques over the last few years.

A major problem to most companies was, and still is, the isolation of the distribution activity and its costs from those of production and marketing. In many organisations, for example, warehousing has

---

[1] *The Marketing of Industrial Products*, Hutchinson, 1965, edited by A. Wilson, pp. 134 *et seq.*

historically been the responsibility of the production manager, and packaging and forwarding that of the sales or marketing function. The identification of what is and what is not distribution is important.

All parts of the distribution system are interrelated and affect one another from cost and efficiency points of view. Methods of packing, and therefore packing costs, are determined by the transport method; this in turn is partly determined by the company's policy with regard to field warehouses and overseas distribution systems. The choice of handling equipment may depend on transport methods, too, and on the number and size of warehouses.

The distribution activity, as a whole, affects other parts of an organisation, and its isolation is only important for examination and effective management purposes; it cannot in fact be treated as something outside the total company context. Warehouses, for example, not ideally placed in a perfect distribution chain and therefore adding unnecessarily to direct distribution costs, might in the final analysis be of greater value from an overall company benefit point of view in that they allow longer and more economic production runs of a particular article.

The management technique which became known, in the 1960s, as 'the total cost approach to distribution', falls therefore into two parts. It is the treatment of physical distribution as one identifiable company activity, the interrelated divisions of which must be managed as a whole in order to attain the most efficient and most economic distribution system; and it is the method of relating the effects of alternative systems, or indeed individual parts of the distribution chain, to other company activities so that the optimum overall benefit to that company is achieved.

The 'total approach' technique has special relevance to marketing. Distribution costs naturally affect the final selling price of an article, and this may be a crucial factor particularly when selling overseas in competition with local producers. Of equal importance, an efficient distribution system will ensure that the right, properly documented goods are delivered to the right customer at the right time, in the right place, in the right quantity and in the right condition. Good distribution can thus be regarded as a marketing tool and can be used as a means of sales promotion by offering a high level of customer service.

The achievement of a high level of customer service depends, however, on what the individual customer requires; and it is the task of the marketing manager to ensure that the distribution system meets these requirements before he can use it for marketing purposes. In some circumstances, the customer's needs may involve an increase in direct distribution costs. To meet delivery dates, for exmaple, consignments might have to be shipped by air; or to eliminate the risks of damage in transit or deterioration in storage, the use of sophisticated packaging materials and methods might be necessary. Applying the total approach concept, customer satisfaction and the possibility of increased sales must be measured in terms of overall company benefits against higher distribution costs.

Such measurements are not always easy. The marketing manager's perfect distribution system may not be that of the production manager, and this may in turn differ from that of the company accountant. All may have excellent reasons for their preferences, and each may show apparently parallel benefits. An important role of physical distribution management is to act as a kind of referee between conflicting company interests by evaluating what has become known as the 'trade-offs' of opposing distribution methods. This may involve the use of operations research techniques or computers to quantify the side effects of alternative systems, and finally to arrive at an optimum overall solution – even by proposing an entirely new method. The marketing manager therefore does not necessarily get exactly what he wants; but with manufacturing industry becoming more and more customer orientated, his needs are usually of prime consideration.

Theory Into Practice

Although physical distribution management theory was thoroughly debated during the 1960s, and the 'total approach' concept and all it implies widely accepted by British industry, the conversion of theory into practice from a management structure point of view has been comparatively slow. Part-implementation of the theory, without structural changes, has certainly taken place on a larger scale, but even so only about half a dozen British companies are believed currently to be practising physical distribution management in its purest form.

One reason for this slow progress is a fundamental misunderstanding – despite a multitude of seminars, books and articles on the subject – that physical distribution management is mainly concerned with cutting distribution costs; that is, the treatment of distribution as a separate company activity without properly relating it to the marketing and production sides of a business. It is only when distribution is regarded as a possible profit generating source, rather than merely as a cost, and when it is accepted that more expensive distribution methods might increase profits by increasing sales, that a company can be said to have grasped the real physical distribution principle.

Effective physical distribution clearly requires top management involvement, a Board director or senior executive who not only supervises all aspects of the distribution chain but who is also in a position to liaise with marketing, production and finance management at the highest levels. Here lies another reason for the slow implementation of the physical distribution concept. In most companies it involves a basic management reorganisation, a redistribution of responsibilities which many might applaud in theory but – as human animals jealously guarding hardly won territory – will resist in practice. The production manager sees the reallocation of warehouse and transport fleet control to another, and possibly new, executive as demotion for himself; the export sales manager fights to keep control of route selection; and so on. Resistance to change is not peculiarly British, but it is an undeniably common characteristic.

The 1970s should be a decade in which these problems are resolved and in which the theories of the 1960s are put into practice. Situations vary greatly between companies and methods of execution will also differ widely. In every case, success much depends on the personal calibre of the appointed distribution executive, on his ability – without creating internal political problems and thus further resistance to his aims – to ensure that he controls all he should and to keep the physical distribution function firmly within the total company context.

Aiding the trend towards implementation of the theory is the increasing use, in business as a whole, of data processing techniques which have the effect of cutting across traditional departmental responsibilities, lines of information and control. The computer, itself invaluable to the distribution executive with a mass of data to quantify, could be said to be paving the way for physical distribution practice in that change-resistant management is already having to adapt to new business methods.

Helping implementation, too, is every firm's growing concern with costs and profits – and effective physical distribution can offer both a reduction in the former and an increase in the latter. The customer is becoming no less concerned with the same problems, and will be making ever greater demands on his supplier's distribution system in order to keep his own costs to a minimum. He may, for example, decide to reduce his stockholding investment and require instead smaller, more frequent and absolutely reliable deliveries. To maintain a high level of customer service, the manufacturer might have to change his whole distribution system and establish field warehouses where there were none before. Whatever the situation, expert management approach to these problems will become more and more imperative.

The 1970s are also seeing the wider application, by large international companies, of the 'business logistics' approach. Physical distribution management is concerned with the packaging, storage and movement of finished products and is thus sales orientated. Materials management, on the other hand, is purchasing orientated, and concerns the acquisition, movement and storage of raw materials before and sometimes during the manufacturing process. Business logistics embraces both, and is therefore a comprehensive management approach to a firm's total inwards and outwards materials and goods movement programme.

Such an approach is particularly advantageous to those organisations which manufacture parts of what is to become the final product in different countries (possibly near raw material sources), assemble these in one or more other countries (often market centres) and then export a proportion of the assembly runs throughout the world. The movement of raw materials and finished goods, the coordination of supply and demand, can be extremely complicated and requires not only a completely integrated distribution system but also the closest cooperation between all sides of the organisation concerned.

The vehicle manufacturing industry specifically illustrates the business logistics approach. Motor cars, or their parts, are increasingly being transported in knocked down form for assembly in overseas consumer centres – reducing distribution costs and at the same time the whole pattern of production, distribution and marketing. Final selling price apart, 'home' assembly implies from a marketing point of view a readier availability of the product and improved after-sales service; and also takes advantage of some consumers' inclination for home-produced goods.

The transportation of parts for final assembly is essentially regarded as an extension of the production line or of the production 'flow'. This, on the one hand, proves the need for a total company approach to the distribution question, and on the other, requires the physical existence of a distribution method to provide a complementary movement 'flow'; and the flow-line principle is exactly what modern transport techniques aim to emulate.

Intermodality and Through-transport

Since the mid-1960's Europe has been experiencing the greatest technical revolution in transport since the advent of steam. The key to change has been intermodality, the door-to-door movement of goods in uniform, easily identifiable units which may quickly be transferred from one mode of transport to another without intermediate handling of the contents.

The intermodal freight container, which was developed in the United States during the immediate post-war period, has been applied to most major trade routes of the world over the last six or seven years, the system's tremendous growth reflecting its inherent advantages. The principle of consolidating many small packages into a large standard unit and their carriage, as a unit, from point of origin to destination has several effects. From the operator's point of view, handling and labour requirements are considerably reduced, automated loading/unloading techniques take such little time that the total number of vessels or vehicles needed on a particular route can be decreased, and long-term cost savings (bearing in mind the heavy initial investment in facilities) can be achieved. The shipper or supplier benefits from faster transit times, less danger of damage to his goods, reduced packing requirements and protection against the freight rate increases to which labour-intensive methods are subject.

Part of the International Organisation for Standardisation's definition of a freight container is 'an article of transport equipment'. Containerisation is basically a transport method in itself (not a packing method as some mistakenly believed a few years ago) providing through-transit from origin to destination. That the container may travel by road, rail, sea or a combination of these should not be, operators believe, of prime interest to the user. Nor should he necessarily be concerned with the route the container takes. The user should rather concentrate on the speed, simplicity, costs, efficiency and reliability of alternative container services and the comparison of these with other transport methods; and indeed it does seem that traditional attitudes towards the physical presence of ships, ports, road vehicles and railway wagons are gradually changing.

Containerisation's *modus operandi* is helping this trend. The system has, first of all, engendered an entirely new kind of operator, who may take the responsibility for the goods throughout their total journey and who assumes all the roles previously held by road, rail, sea and sometimes air carriers. The container operator may own all the vessels and vehicles used to carry the unit, only some of them or, as in the case of some freight forwarders, none at all. However this may be, the operator can quote a through rate for a door-to-door transit, and the consignor no longer has to obtain quotations from a multitude of carriers.

Secondly, the speed of intercommunicating services and of container transfer between transport modes means that the most direct route may not necessarily be the right one for a particular consignment. Containers for the United States may be shipped via East, South or West Coast ports, or even via the Continent and, at the other side of the Atlantic, via Canadian ports and their complementary rail container links. So far as the manufacturer is concerned his factory or, in the case of part-load consignments, his nearest Inland Clearance Depot or Freightliner terminal, is the point of departure and his customer's premises the point of arrival. What occurs between these points is the operator's choice, reflected in the standard of his through-service.

Although, therefore, an operator/owner might be marketing a particular route because his vessels or vehicles are serving it, or an operator/forwarder various routes because of special arrangements with carriers and agents, the user's choice of container operator is becoming more and more determined by the levels of service provided and is only confined by his consignment's destination and the number of operators who offer a service to it. That his containerised goods might travel, say, to Japan by sea or principally overland via the Trans-Siberian railway is becoming of peripheral interest to the user, who is concerned more with the speed, economy and reliability offered by operators serving the destination in question.

Shippers or suppliers are, of course, intimately involved with the details of the container method, especially at points of origin and destination and where it requires a changeover from traditional handling and marketing techniques. Container services initially grew faster than many industrial companies' ability to cope with them, and there were, firstly, problems of physically being capable of receiving and loading containers at factories and warehouses – and similar restrictions at customers' premises. There was the difficulty of adapting packing methods for the new system, and of stowing goods safely in the container. There were new insurance and documentation problems to overcome. On the marketing side, there was delay in the attempt to sell by the container load to obtain the most benefit from the system and delay, too, in the exploitation of new markets which the speed of container methods and the adaptability of the unit itself (temperature controlled units, bulktainers) opened for some companies.

Teething troubles certainly remain; but technical developments in handling equipment, experience in the use of container methods and the still growing application of the system by the world's transport industry to more and more routes should see all these overcome within the next few years. The 1970s can be regarded as a decade of wide-scale adaption to intermodal containerisation, for adaption there must be. The future of general goods transport undoubtedly lies with intermodality or, in those cases where intermodal techniques cannot be applied, with other unit load methods. Industry's concern to hold down distribution costs and its need for a transport flow to complement production flow-line techniques imply the gradual phasing-out, if not entire elimination, of traditional fragmented break-bulk movements.

Statistics emphasise this trend. In 1965 the container system, apart from non-standard units operated by European railways, was confined to a few American transport companies. January 1972 saw the sailing of the containership *Kamakura Maru* from Tokyo to Hamburg, Rotterdam and Southampton, inaugurating a service on the world's last remaining major deep-sea trade route (between developed countries) to be containerised. In the space of seven years some 40 deep-sea container services have come into operation, with another ten planned. Specially-designed cellular containerships are carrying about 200,000 units on these routes, and the world's estimated container population of between three and four hundred thousand is expected to rise towards one million in a few years' time. By the end of the decade, at least 70 per cent of international general cargoes should be travelling on container systems.

Within the United Kingdom (and indeed within all geographically small countries), carriage of goods by freight container for home distribution accounts for only a small percentage of the total. Deliveries by ordinary road vehicle, which has enormous flexibility and the maximum element of control, remain the most popular method for manufactured goods – and will probably remain so.

Nevertheless, the development of Britain's Freightliner system, the envy of many foreign railway administrations, has shown that – over the longer distances at any rate – 'home' containerisation can pay dividends. Freightliners Limited currently operates 160 services on 67 routes, with scheduled nightly services between 21 centres of industry and population. Such services have the advantage over road haulage in that trains can travel at consistently high speeds and, where overnight services are concerned, a container may be delivered to a Freightliner terminal before 20.00 hours one evening and reach its final destination the next morning. The immediate transfer of containers between road and rail vehicles is effected at all Freightliner terminals by specially designed electric cranes.

The 1970 figures showed that Freightliners carried about $4\frac{1}{2}$ million tons of freight in that year, a tremendous achievement after less than five years of operation, yet still only 0·2 per cent of the inland freight total. By 1980 Freightliners' share is expected to grow by some ten or twelve times.

Growth of rail container traffic can also be anticipated in and between European countries, including Britain, especially in view of recent and forthcoming developments. Railway administrations have had to face two basic problems when attracting prospective users. Firstly, railways run on fixed lines and unless a consignor or his customer have their own sidings (which is unusual) goods have to be delivered to and collected from rail terminals by road; and since shippers have come to expect a door-to-door, 'flowline' service, this complication is often unacceptable. Many of the world's railways have therefore been investing in their own road transport fleets, so that a through-service can in fact be offered directly by them (bearing in mind that freight forwarders can always provide shippers with a door-to-door service by arranging all transport requirements).

Secondly, railways have for some years had a reputation for unreliability with regard to delivery times. The creation of regular, scheduled departures and arrivals of container trains has gone some way in overcoming this problem; and Intercontainer – the Basle-based organisation which represents 19 railway systems and handles nearly all intra-European rail container traffic – has been introducing scheduled block train services with guaranteed delivery times on certain international routes. When this network is complete, these routes are expected to carry 4 million containers a year – a substantial increase on the 1970 European total of under a quarter of a million.

The establishment of many reliable, high-frequency block train services, not only on the Continent but throughout the world, should have a significant effect on the transport mode and route decisions taken by container operators. Trains can travel in a straight line, but ships must follow coastal configurations. To take a simple example, sending a container from Hamburg to Barcelona is much quicker by rail (or road) than all round the Iberian Peninsular by sea. The same 'landbridge' principle applies to traditional sea routes: a new railway system planned between Singapore and Istanbul will cut out the long sea journey to Europe round the Cape; developments on the Trans-Siberian Railway should soon cut transit time from London to Yokohama (Japan) by at least a week over the sea route.

LASH

Another example of the logical use of natural resources (land and water) is the LASH or Lighter Aboard Ship vessel which, simply, is a mother ship for a number of 'float-on float-off' barges. Operated in a similar way to the container system, each barge is a vast unit load – some can hold more than 400 tons – which can carry a variety of bulk and general cargoes. Scheduled LASH services have already been successfully established between the Continent, UK (Sheerness) and the US Gulf. Designed to take the fullest advantage of inland water-ways and rivers, barge loads may travel, for instance, from a Rhine port in the middle of the German Federal Republic right through to St. Louis on the Mississippi without ever touching land.

Up till now the LASH system has mainly been of real interest to those shippers with bulk consignments and who – with their custo-mers – have waterside premises in locations accessible to LASH barges. However, it seems likely that the system, where it operates, will become of increasing interest to shippers of general cargo and especially on those routes not served by satisfactory containership alternatives. One great advantage of the LASH system is that it is not dependent on sophisticated shore installations; tugs to push or tow its barges are all that are required. Therefore routes to those under-developed countries whose return traffic is principally unfit for containerisation and who have neither the means nor sufficient commercial and labour reasons to invest in expensive container ports, will be particularly suitable for LASH operation. As for the door-to-door needs of modern shippers, LASH operators are already catering for these: the Holland America Line/Hapag Lloyd 'Combi-Lash' service which started in March 1972 offers collection and delivery facilities anywhere in the UK, Continent and United States.

TIR

As has been mentioned above, road transport is the most popular and most widely used method for the distribution of goods to home markets. The introduction, in the 1950s, of roll-on roll-off ferries and the TIR (Transport International Routier) carnet enabled road vehicles to be used for door-to-door deliveries to places as widely spaced as Oslo, Lisbon, Naples and Teheran.

The TIR carnet is a Customs facility which allows a road vehicle or freight container (provided that the latter travels at least part of its journey by road) to cross international frontiers without Customs inspection or payment of duties – save at those frontiers of countries of departure and destination, or at Customs approved inland depots within them. By eliminating physical Customs examination of goods at intermediate frontiers, the TIR system has considerably speeded up European road transport and, by so doing, has cut down its costs.

TIR service operators provide a variety of trailer, box van and container types, including those for specialised traffics – refrigerated units for perishables, tank trailers and containers for bulk liquids and powders, knock-out rear-axle low-loaders and step-frame trailers for large items of machinery. Indeed, the only loads that cannot travel under TIR carnet are those so large that they exceed the width of the trailer (8 ft.) and thus cannot be covered and Customs sealed.

Full-load door-to-door TIR transport is particularly advantageous. Goods undergo no intermediate handling, are less liable to be damaged and require 'home' rather than the more expensive export packs. Driver-accompanied vehicles, especially, offer tremendous flexibility and speed; journey time between Britain and Italy, for example, is only two days. The statistics show that TIR transport is becoming increasingly popular with British physical distribution and marketing management. Carnets are controlled by the International Road Transport Union on behalf of member states, and in the United Kingdom are issued to professional hauliers by the Road Haulage Association and to own account operators by the Freight Transport Association. In 1969 the RHA issued 17,000 carnets as compared to 23,500 in 1970 and 33,800 in 1971. A similar growth percentage is expected over the next few years, always providing that certain quota arrangements between Britain and some European countries allow it. Plans announced in June 1972 allow for the phasing-out of the TIR carnet between member countries of the EEC, and by the end of 1974 new customs procedures should be in operation.

TIR operators, incidentally, by no means have to stick to the road. Various Continental railway systems run 'piggyback' trains for road trailers and vehicles, and those operators using freight containers can also make the best use of road/rail combinations on any particular route. The shipper should not really concern himself with the methods chosen by his operator/agent, so long as he receives the level of service he expects.

Groupage Traffic

Shippers of manufactured goods often do not have enough traffic to fill a large unit load like a freight container or TIR trailer. Most operators, therefore, offer groupage or consolidation services. These basically involve the grouping or collection, at one central point, of many small consignments from different shippers but all bound for the same general destination; and then forwarding them as one unit load and under one consignment note to a central point in the foreign country concerned for onward distribution.

With groupage, many of the advantages of door-to-door travel are lost: tougher packaging is, for example, necessary as goods must be transported to and from groupage depots and might be stowed with or under other goods incompatible in weight and shape. Nevertheless, groupage services can show great cost savings, and the recent and continuing establishment of regular, scheduled departures offers the shipper increasing delivery reliability. Groupage service operators have been particularly concerned, too, to create excellent overseas storage and distribution facilities with their agents or partners.

'Smalls' traffic travelling on unit load systems will undoubtedly grow further – as indeed it must if the majority of general cargo is to be carried in this way.

Air Freight

The consolidation of small consignments into larger units is crucial to the air freight industry, and will play a prominent part in its development over the next decade.

Depending on the airline, between 50 and 80 per cent of freight is currently carried in the bellyholds of passenger aircraft. Planes may touch down at an airport for less than an hour, and it is during this time that they have to be loaded. Air freight primarily consists of low volume, low weight packages and, to achieve the necessary speed of ground handling, it has become clear that these must be consolidated into larger unit loads which can be taken out to the aircraft as soon as it arrives.

To meet these needs, at any rate in part, many airlines have already built modern cargo terminal facilities incorporating the most sophisticated mechanical handling and sorting machinery. The new BOAC and BEA terminals at London Airport (Heathrow) are cases in point. Such facilities can, however, only physically handle a certain amount of traffic and an additional solution to the problem has been the encouragement of shippers and air freight forwarders to present cargoes to the airlines already made up into unit loads.

Such 'encouragement' consists of rating incentives, a handling rebate and a tare weight allowance, i.e. an allowance on the weight of the container, if shippers or forwarders use a unit load device (ULD) registered with IATA – the International Air Transport Association – and conforming to one of IATA's dimensional standards. IATA is the world organisation of the scheduled airlines, and its major purpose is to ensure that all airline traffic anywhere moves with the greatest possible speed, convenience and economy. During the early 1960's IATA first introduced a container programme, a 'Register of Containers and Pallets', which has since been revised and the aim of which is to simplify inter-airline handling, reduce ground handling costs and to achieve optimum aircraft loading densities.

With effect from January 1973 the IATA container programme was reduced from 22 to eleven standard sizes. Those ULD's which have been retained are all modular to the standard aircraft pallet sizes of 88″ × 108″ and 88″ × 125″, and the largest six are contoured to fit aircraft furselage profiles. It is anticipated that in the not too distant future the number of IATA standard sizes for these non-aircraft ULD's (i.e. shipper or agent owned containers) will be reduced to five.

The container programme has not been a success with shippers. The cost of buying an IATA registered ULD is often greater than the rebate received for using it, and the tare weight allowance which is of most significance when air cargo rates are high has not generally been of sufficient incentive to shippers to pack their goods in special containers. Advantageous use of the scheme has, however, been made by the larger air freight forwarders. Some ULD's can be used for as many as 50 trips, and the more re-use a forwarder can make of a container – by having a wide network of overseas branches or agents and thus return or onwards traffic – the less significant does its initial cost become.

Handling a number of consignments from different shippers but all for the same destination allows the air freight forwarder to make up unit loads of a size eligible for the best rebates and allowances, and gives him the opportunity to exceed the minimum chargeable weight ('pivot weight') for any one consignment and take advantage of the lower freight rates thereafter. It thus becomes cheaper for the shipper of a small consignment to send his goods via a forwarder's consolidation service than to deal with an airline direct and pay the minimum rate.

Size is indeed becoming crucial to the air freight forwarding industry: the larger the agent, the more traffic he is able to handle; the more traffic he has, the greater the possibility of profitable unit loads and the more frequent his services to a wider variety of foreign destinations; the more widespread his international network, the more efficient becomes the door-to-door or through service he can offer to shippers and the more opportunity he has to re-consolidate consignments at intermediate airports (a forwarder may, for example, send goods bound for Johannesburg on a consolidation to Frankfurt, where they can be re-consolidated for their ultimate destination).

Also favouring larger-sized agents has been the arrival of wide-bodied Jumbo aircraft and the increasing use by airlines of all-cargo flights. Both Jumbo and freighter aircraft have their own 'suites' of airline-owned containers and other ULD's, of which there are ten international standard sizes. Some of these units, which are a part of aircraft equipment, are of such delicate construction and so awkwardly shaped that most airlines are reluctant to let them off the airport concerned. It is, therefore, primarily those agents with airport premises and who have enough traffic to fill such containers that benefit from the use of airline-owned ULD's; for buying aircraft space, as it were, wholesale, forwarders are offered large incentives.

Some air freight forwarders have already become or are becoming large by means of mergers and amalgamations, or by forming consortia; and this trend will undoubtedly continue. By 1980 there should be a small number of large agents serving UK industry, a reduction from some 300 to about twenty. These, a significant new force on the air freight scene, will be handling most of air cargo shipments on the ground, making up large unit loads at, probably, off-airport Customs approved depots and breaking down import containers for inland distribution.

Another development which could well be expected over the next few years is a simplification in scheduled airline rating structures. The current IATA-pegged rates, which are based on traditional passenger aircraft operation and its costs, are extremely complicated and do not compete favourably with those charter cargo carriers who are not members of IATA. It could be said that the inconsistent and rigid IATA structure must change if too much lucrative high volume traffic is not to be lost to non-IATA members.

Air Freight Marketing

In 1970 IATA forecast that international air cargo traffic would grow 20 per cent per annum to 1980, reaching in this year a total of 66,000,000,000 tonnes-kilometre. This represents an increase from a current 2 per cent share of international general goods traffic to between 10 and 15 per cent by the end of the decade. Some optimists in the industry hope for as much as a 20 per cent share. 1971 was, however, a particularly bad year on some routes and IATA's overall forecast was certainly not achieved in this period.

Air freight faces serious competition from the new surface methods, which offer simple, door-to-door movements to the shipper whilst air cargo – with the multiplicity of forwarders, airlines, air brokers and charterers selling air space, the numerous and often difficult-to-handle ULD's and with puzzling alternative rates and incentives –

o

might appear to present complications other methods do not have. Nevertheless, the rationalisation or 'shaking down' of the industry which is currently in progress should go some way in solving these problems. The trend is very much for the air freight forwarder to offer shippers a door-to-door service, and the fewer and larger forwarders become the simpler it will be for shippers to grasp the real advantages of air cargo distribution.

Air freight still primarily consists of urgent, high value consignments, since the direct costs of air transport are so high compared with other methods. When the 'total cost approach to distribution' concept is, however, applied, it is sometimes found that the use of air freight in fact contributes to improved overall company profitability. Naturally enough, the air freight industry has done its best to initiate and encourage 'total cost' attitudes in the minds of shippers and it is largely due to firms like Emery Air Freight Corporation and the larger world airlines that the management technique has become – in theory – so widely accepted; though as has been said, its widescale application in practice has yet to be achieved.

A few direct costs savings can be made by the use of air freight: packing materials and thus packing labour charges, insurance, documentation and loading/unloading costs. The indirect savings which arise from the speed of air transport are, however, by far the most important: capital investment in stocks and in goods in transit is considerably reduced, accounts are paid quicker by the customer since delivery is earlier and, from the marketing point of view, customer service can be immensely improved by faster, more frequent deliveries. Perhaps the most tangible advantage, especially in view of growing interest rates, is that of reduced capital investment.

	Surface $		Air $
Warehouse	2,000	.. ..	460
Obsolescence	1,000	.. ..	Nil
Capital investment..	6,088	.. ..	1,264
Insurance	750	.. ..	300
Packing	1,000	.. ..	240
Shipping	2,500	Air cargo	9,200
Total	$12,804	.. ..	$11,464

This study by the Harvard Graduate School of Business

Administration[2] comparing the costs of one delivery by surface and air methods shows that from production line to consumer the surface route took 91 days and air freight only 21.

This example shows a total cost saving from the use of air freight of $1,340; and to this must be added the fact that the customer received his goods 70 days earlier.

Time and speed, the essence of air freight marketing, become more significant the further away an export market is situated. The short-haul routes, like those between Britain and Europe, arc however quite a different matter and face strong competition from TIR and freight container methods. A shipper must study very carefully whether the extra 24 or 48 hours saved by air freight will warrant the higher transport costs.

As for the long-haul routes, there are various reasons why the advantages of air freight have not yet been seized upon with greater enthusiasm by many shippers, despite the educational and promotional efforts of the air freight industry.

The change from surface methods to air cargo distribution involves or should involve a basic reorganisation of thinking and indeed of physical operation throughout a company. The marketing and financial sides of a business are clearly affected, warehousing and other distribution requirements change substantially and, less obviously, production has to be reoriented towards smaller, more frequent runs to gain most benefit from distribution by air. Production can be matched with demand, and expensive stockholding considerably reduced if not eliminated altogether.

Such changes require the ultimate in physical distribution management, and it is only when PDM theory is really put into practice that British industry will seriously consider air freight as a viable alternative to surface methods for goods other than the most urgent or the most valuable. This situation is gradually coming about, and new management attitudes must contribute greatly to the anticipated growth of air freight.

Conclusion

Besides discussing, in general terms, the progress of physical distribution management, this chapter reviews developments in modern

[2] *The Role of Air Freight in Physical Distribution*, 1956, co-sponsored by Emery Air Freight Corporation.

transport techniques. Although transportation is only one part of a company's total distribution activity – materials handling, documentation, packing and packaging, warehousing and warehouse location are others – it is on the transport method that the other parts depend. The choice, therefore, of a transport method becomes the most important one and sometimes the selection of an operator offering the transport service is of equal significance.

Modern transport techniques aim to give the manufacturer or shipper a door-to-door through service, a flowline extension to his production line. Many operators, whether they offer surface or air services or a combination of these, can also undertake the necessary documentation, storage and packing activities – and by so doing may provide a complete distribution service. Subcontracting, as it were, the whole distribution chain allows a firm's total resources (capital, space and staff) to be concentrated on production and marketing; at the same time the isolation of total distribution costs and the pricing of finished products becomes much easier.

There is certainly a trend towards giving professional transport operators a whole distribution 'package', and this in no way detracts from the responsibilities of physical distribution management who must constantly be assessing and re-assessing the alternative methods and means of distribution and their effect on the total company business.

A similar trend, in that it conserves capital for investment elsewhere, is that towards the leasing of equipment – mechanical handling, storage and transport. Again, the pros and cons of hire or purchase must be carefully weighed up by the distribution manager, in close consultation with the company accountant.

Physical distribution techniques are constantly developing, particularly in this the aftermath of the unit load 'revolution'. The management of goods distribution is a continuous process and one which affects the whole of a company's production, marketing and financial policies; it requires executives of the highest calibre and with a clear understanding of the implications of the distribution activity. To be effective, the physical distribution manager needs the cooperation and understanding, too, of all other company executives. This fundamental reappraisal of an area which for so long has been considered of little importance will undoubtedly assume new dimensions over the next decade and British industry, spurred on by financial and competitive pressures, should be converting the much applauded management theory into practice.

CHECKLIST

1. How far has your own organisation gone in establishing an identifiable physical distribution management function?

2. Are you sure that you and your colleagues really understand and apply the total cost concept?

3. How many customers are satisfied/dissatisfied with your company's distribution system?

4. How often do you ask your customers whether they are happy with the distribution system, and how often do you discuss with them ways of improving it?

5. How often do you consult with your own physical distribution management and state the marketing case?

6. How far have you assessed the marketing impact of the following alternative transport methods:

   (a) Containerisation?
   (b) TIR?
   (c) Air freight?
   (d) Groupage or consolidation services?

7. How often and in what way do you bring yourself up-to-date on developments in distribution methods?

8. How often do you weigh up the marketing advantages – in cost, speed and delivery reliability – of such developments if they were applied to your own customers?

9. How often do you explore the possibilities of new markets by making use of modern and developing distribution techniques, e.g. temperature-controlled and other specialised containers, charter flights, new air and surface routes?

CHAPTER 10

Social Marketing

BY NORMAN MARCUS

Introduction

Over the past few decades business methods have proved effective in solving the problems set before it. In recent years 'business' has evolved new approaches to confront the increasingly complex factors it faced. Business had to come to terms with the interrelatedness of all factors in any given situation. Perhaps at one time it was good enough to launch a product and hope for the best.

The gathering of information now becomes very important. Additionally, the large-scale introduction of computers into the business world has facilitated the classification and systematisation of information flowing in from many different sources. Paralleling developments in science a new approach was formulated – known as a 'systems' approach. Systems theory holds that all elements in a given structure or 'environment' are interrelated, to act on one will affect all the others. Thus the creation of a new product changes the nature of the market, and factors such as 'feedback' become intimately linked with effective strategy. The co-ordinating concepts of marketing can be seen as an offshoot of the systems approach.

Marketing in Business

Marketing is the effective co-ordination, within an organisation, of all those separate functional activities that contribute to overall effectiveness of the company in satisfying consumer needs. The degree of effectiveness must be capable of being measured and controlled. The word 'marketing' refers to activity *in toto*; the co-ordination of different, but related specialist functions. Marketing is involved, in any business activity, from the conception of a new product until either its eventual demise or supersession by a newer product. The feedback mechanism, i.e. measuring the effectiveness of any marketing plan which includes problems particular to the product, ensures a continual evolution both in the development of products and in marketing plans related to those products.

A meeting of management within a business organisation to discuss the deployment of the sales force in connection with a new product is *not* a marketing planning meeting. But it could be a marketing planning meeting if there was discussion on *all* aspects of bringing a new product to the market of which the deployment of the sales force would be one element. An essential of effective marketing planning is the preparation of a marketing plan involving a clear statement of background and objectives, the functional plans to be undertaken to achieve these objectives, and the methods to be utilised in order to measure and control the plan. The employment and deployment of salesmen, the selection of different advertising media such as newspapers, magazines, commercial radio, or television however expertly undertaken, is unlikely to be effective in business unless it is part of the total plan.

Business Advertising as Part of Marketing

Advertising in business can truly play an important role. But its use is a matter of tactical decisions as are decisions concerning selling techniques and the other separate specialist functions. When coordinated these functions are referred to as being part of a 'marketing mix'. It is not difficult, especially in certain industrial markets, to consider cases where advertising would not be utilised as part of a marketing strategy. Although it may not be used to contribute to the plan to market an individual product or group of products, it may be used instead to promulgate the name of the manufacturing company and to develop a healthy corporate image. In utilising advertising in this manner, there is still the consideration of the requirement to 'communicate'. Advertising is not being used in this instance as part of the product marketing mix. It is nevertheless part of an overall plan. However, not all marketing communication is undertaken by advertising. There could be instances when the strategy decided would be to make greater use of press or public relations techniques. The communication in the case of the press relations techniques would be through editorial comment, features, articles, or programmes in the press or on television. In the case of public relations, there could be other activity to communicate as directly as possible with prospects who might be interested in the product or service as well as with shareholders, employees, etc. The word 'advertising' usually refers to paid advertising appearing in newspapers, magazines or hoardings, radio or television, or in the cinema. This media listing, sometimes with the addition of direct mail is frequently referred to as 'above-the-line' promotion. But the marketing manager may equally decide to use 'below the line' promotional strategies. More frequently known as sales promotions, these include sales demonstrations, gift offers, trading stamps, and coupons etc.

Information is one very important element in advertising. It states that such and such a product is available. But advertising is interested in more than just relaying information. Advertising is used primarily to persuade the potential customer that not only will product X satisfy his needs but product X will satisfy his needs best. Thus for our purposes communication can be defined as: (a) relaying of information, (b) persuasion. It wishes to motivate action to achieve the goals set by the marketing plan. But advertising is only one, albeit an important one, among many different methods of achieving the marketing goal. The marketer strives to co-ordinate advertising with the other means of communication, so that they reinforce each other. All the different possibilities for communicating – including the salesman or shop assistant, packaging, corporate symbols and logos on road vehicles and factory frontages – make a communicating contribution of varying importance. The above-the-line advertising that is seen daily in newspapers or on television is, then, but one specialist part of this communication activity.

Business has explored in depth the various problems of communication; but outside industry and business there has been little effort to understand, much less utilise effectively, communication processes to solve pressing social ills. We find the advertising that is used tends to be isolated from the remainder of the activity, and is not considered as one specialist function in a total plan. For instance, public service advertising for road safety campaigns, for health service benefits, against smoking, or to promote charities are frequently completely isolated from other campaign activities. Where they are truly co-ordinated the term social advertising may be validly used. Social advertising must be part of social marketing. The techniques of advertising must be considered in relation to a total social programme with all functional tasks co-ordinated as they are in business. Functional elements being co-ordinated include deployment of and instruction to field workers, distribution of literature, inducement to participate in or to sample a particular proposition.

Distinction between Public and Social Advertising

Let us examine the three existing forms of 'public' advertising and see how far they conform to our definition of social advertising.

Public service advertising refers to advertising by a social agency (e.g. welfare board, local council or national government). It can advertise family planning aids, benefits that can be claimed by welfare recipients, road safety etc. But as we have mentioned (and we shall examine more fully) their advertisements tend to be created in a vacuum without supporting programmes to reinforce their effectiveness. Thus each year we see the toll on roads mounting, increase in incidence of VD, etc. Obviously, something is going wrong; the advertisements are not effective. Questions must be asked why and what can be done to change that situation.

Public interest advertising is undertaken by a business organisation utilising regularly purchased advertising space to make known the contribution that they as a company are making to some problem in society; perhaps a problem that society has recently become aware of, and where pressure group activity is strident. In the case of public interest advertising the approach would be in some problem area connected with the company's activities. The techniques used in the advertising copy might be to suggest that the company's products or services were fighting against social malaise. Such advertising might declare that the company had taken some positive action, that it was aware of the problems that perhaps its own operations had caused, and action that the company had taken meant that it no longer contributed to the problem, for example, to the pollution of the atmosphere. However, although not unimportant, public interest advertising is not social advertising, and should not to be considered as part of social marketing.

Public issue advertising is undertaken by a company donating space to social causes, using its own donated funds and employees' skills (and possibly also those of its advertising agency). Public issue advertising directs its attentions to social programmes or social causes (usually the sponsor's name appears in a discreet form). But public issue advertising is not social advertising, and once again, is not part of social marketing.

Public interest and public issue advertising may draw attention to situations requiring social communication. But the reasons for their appearance are seldom that the company has an altruistic motive. Their advertisements remain part of a larger marketing mix and in the end, business is concerned with profits and growth (the targets it sets for itself).

However, there can be so many public interest and public issue advertisements directed at the public at any one time, that the audience becomes confused and unable to make a decision as to which proposition is of more importance to them than the next. Thus any possible useful effect of such activity is negated. The decision as to which social matter is to be the subject of a campaign is a boardroom decision. The area selected for attention is likely to be the one that is less controversial, or at least one that will not harm the image of the company when they are known to be associated with the particular advertising appeal. Even the system that applies in the United States, where most of such activity is co-ordinated through the Advertising Council, appears to suffer from similar faults.

Marketing in a Social Context

The concept of social marketing comes close to marketing as practised in commerce and industry. It involves strategies used in business marketing translated for use in a social context and, if advertising is used, it will be social advertising directed towards a social cause, problem or programme *without commercial consideration*. Companies that utilise strategies such as sponsored publications in the interest of a social cause are not engaged in social marketing. True social marketing cannot be undertaken by a commercially profit-motivated organisation.

It has been suggested that any segment of the marketing mix in isolation, may not be effective; also that there are difficulties in assessing the contribution, of say advertising, to a marketing activity when other influences exist. However, a statement that all public service, public interest and public issue advertising make little or no contribution to society's problems or social programmes can be just as strongly faulted. It would be as erroneous to dismiss all the advertising undertaken by the Central Office of Information in England and the Advertising Council in America as it would be to dismiss the effectiveness of any advertising campaign undertaken in business without assessing its contribution which is of course difficult, if not impossible, to do.

By re-emphasising that marketing is a co-ordinated activity and that its segments are unlikely to be effective in isolation, and by defining a concept of social marketing which excludes public service, public interest or public issue advertising, we can see that marketing should no longer be viewed as being concerned exclusively with the functional tasks in business directed towards products and services. Professor Philip Kotler[1] has recently written 'the similarities between the marketing of commercial products and the marketing of other things – organisation, persons, places and ideas – are too striking to be ignored'. Kotler explains that the fact that marketing means markets, markets mean transactions, and transactions mean money-flow is overruled by allusions to marketing that are constantly appearing. He cites American examples where 'driver education programmes' are marketed, 'political candidates' are marketed, 'the police department' is marketed. Churches must modernise their 'product', and the 'Post Office' must improve its image.

Opportunities for Social Marketing

Criticism in society of commercial marketing is likely to be mounting substantially in the years ahead. The environmentalists will see to that. Indeed, some campaign bodies would have us completely abandon technological progress and return the environment to its pre-industrial purity. We should retreat to a world without drab cities, without the litter and waste of modern industry, without the slag heaps, without the poisoned air and water, without polluted beaches and congested roads. Others agree with the mayor of a town in the north of England whose council recently gave permission for the extension of an existing plant: 'If we want the town to grow and prosper, it's got to stink a bit too!'

The social marketing concept as outlined can improve the quality of life by addressing itself beyond commerce and industry, and by being aware of both sides of competing arguments. Its decisions and

[1] Philip Kotler, *Market Management: Analysis Planning and Control.* (2nd Edition). Prentice Hall, Princeton, 1972.

plans must be 'socially profitable' and 'socially accountable'. There is ample evidence of a greater appreciation of society's unwillingness to further countenance any action that is harmful to the environment. Marketing can no longer afford to ignore society as a whole, but given true perspective this is its most exciting challenge to date. Business men like scientists must change their directions! It has been suggested that business men might have the opportunity of directing their expertise at local or national level to the most worthwhile product that they or any other marketing men have ever marketed, a better quality of life for every citizen.

Can one in fact market a better quality of life? Marketing activity has developed in commerce and industry nourished by technological advance. New products satisfy new 'needs'; the ability to produce goods in quantity to satisfy more people at prices that more people can afford – this in itself has made life easier for many. Even those that are critical of 'material possession' would hardly wish to return to the life of a past where women toiled endlessly to prepare food; where the housewife satisfied her family's demands without the aid of hygienic cleaning agents and cooking stoves that merely require a touch of a switch. The use of marketing in its normal and legitimate business role satisfies human needs, co-ordinates and brings together production and consumption, and thus contributes to much that is improvement in the quality of life.

But social marketing, concerned directly with safety and health, the encouragement of fraternity and the abolition of selfish behaviour and prejudice, goes further than the provision of goods and services by profit or even non-profit organisations. Instead of marketing 'needs', social marketing markets propositions which concern living and new attitudes to life by utilising tried and proven marketing techniques. The programmes usually already exist. The problems are already appreciated. What is not thus far accepted is the contribution that marketing could make, if used in accordance with the practices and principles that have now been developed.

Marketing organisation in local and central government, or in Parliament, could be directed towards problems that are frequently considered as an inevitable but unsatisfactory by-product of the technological age and of democratic government. Frequently voiced discontent with 'bureaucracy' and 'red tape' can be the result of unsatisfactory team work possibly due to inadequate definition of a common goal. The principles of marketing, and the incorporation in its use of quantitative measuring techniques, provides barriers and controls where human action is likely to be selfishly motivated. In a commercial organisation a marketing plan should be available for all to see – the chairman, the chief accountant, the new recruit to the marketing department, and even those whose responsibilities might at first sight appear to be less relevant to the plan – works managers, union officials, research and development technicians. All of these have a degree of joint responsibility for the success of a programme, and in fact are in direct communication and have complete information, along with others who have major or even minor involvement. Much that is criticised as wasteful administrative detail can be eliminated – lack of communication, and thus lack of trust, is the harbinger of administrative over-documentation. Marketing calls for communication and co-ordination. There is little doubt that institutional organisations with local, national or international responsibilities are often lacking in effective internal as well as external communication.

A need exists to persuade those not directly concerned with, or those violently against, the conduct of commerce and industry to consider the validity of marketing principles for social causes and social problems. Education on what marketing means and what it does is necessary. Once such activity exists and a case has been established, the benefits to all could be realised. The results could be dramatic. Even the most vociferous critics might soften their views. Society is now concerned about people in a way that has never previously occurred. And marketing *is* 'about people'!

There are many who have suggested that the motivating techniques associated with marketing can have possible deleterious effects such as brainwashing. There are some who would confine all advertisements and marketing activity to an informational function and restrict or otherwise prevent any action which was designed to motivate. Such a view demonstrates a total misunderstanding of human motivation. The transfer of information is, of itself, a motivating factor.

Marketing as used in business by those who fully understand its potential and methods, aims at achieving more than the task of merely imparting information about a product or service. It is being used to implant a proposition or sequence of propositions that ultimately will lead to action – usually to make a purchase.

This is seen by some as having dangers. Nicholas Kaldor suggested that advertising as we knew it was wasteful, and that the information could be presented in a catalogued form without encouraging the consumer to give consideration to one product rather than that of a competitor, which is the essence of marketing strategy. Information alone will not achieve the effect. The prospective target audience for a marketing programme has to be motivated towards decision making by sophisticated appeals to reason and to the emotions. It has to be informed, but it also has to be carried beyond information – to action. It is the argument against the motivating force of advertising that leads people to suggest that the use of techniques of marketing to bring about social change is dangerous. In the context of such arguments the suggestion that well established marketing tools should be used to enrol students at colleges, presenting the competing opportunities from different educational establishments other than in the most factual terminology, would receive adverse criticism.

Is it not true that young people are in any case requesting more guidance? That they want the guidance in a form which is authoritative but which, at the same time, leaves the choice to them as adult individuals? Informative guidance – providing a true and honest situation but incorporating persuasive elements leading towards decision and action *is* marketing. The strategy will be rejected if it lacks credibility! And as there will be competing announcements from other educational establishments, or prospective employers of youth, which may appeal more to some individuals within a target group than to others at whom the marketing effort is directed, true choice exists.

Parental and even schoolteacher advice is no longer considered sufficiently compatible with the attitudes of youth in a confused world. Target group identification is mandatory in commerce and industry where proper marketing plans are formulated. In the instance quoted, the opportunity would exist to alter the approach to satisfy different attitudes – attitudes that differ because of different hereditary or environmental backgrounds. The appeals to young people would differ where interests are more likely to be directed towards arts or sciences career futures, and to those who wish or require to start work at an earlier age. Marketing can cater for different segments of society. The motivations behind marketing campaigns for further education would be based upon stated objectives, which would then take into consideration the different attitudes, lifestyle, expectations and other considerations of growing generations. This is *not* what happens at present. Educationalists

appear to scorn the use of anything approaching marketing techniques
– although at some colleges where this very attitude prevails, marketing is taught as a subject!

All marketing activity requires the use of research techniques.
Market research has developed from social research and the poverty
surveys of the turn of the century. Although today's social researchers
are critical of some of the methods used for research, for instance in
consumer marketing fields, social researchers are making greater use
of the data produced by commerce. Market research does not
necessarily involve field work; much can be used from published
sources, including international and government papers, and from
data within an organisation which has been prepared for some other
purpose, possibly for accounting purposes. The same would apply
in social marketing, including behavioural research.

Behavioural research goes further than finding out who and what.
It is concerned with finding out why! It frequently uses the techniques
of clinical psychology and group analysis in order to understand
people's attitudes to and habits in a given situation. It can be used
in order to plan a marketing campaign, as well as to measure the
effectiveness of such a campaign by discovering whether in fact any
changes in attitude have taken place. Behavioural research could
make a valid contribution to the effectiveness of social marketing.
A greater understanding of the purpose of such research has to be
engendered, because the public's concept of behavioural research is
that its methods and techniques threaten to interfere with human
freedom and liberty. In fact, in depth interviewing techniques would
enormously aid in the development of social marketing plans concerned with better quality of life. However, this is not an easy
proposition to present in society with a deep-grained distrust of the use
of psychological research methods other than for clinical purposes.

It would be useful at this point to examine marketing's lack of
credibility when it comes to social questions. We have already
noted that a profit-making concern cannot involve itself in social
marketing, for obvious reasons. However, what are some of the
other factors indicating the use of marketing expertise in the
attempt to solve social problems? The lack of ethical and moral
concern in business provides a barrier to a greater interest in the
concept of social marketing and in the potential application of
established marketing methods to the solution of social problems.
Attacks on certain business practices and the tardiness of business in

responding constructively have helped to develop a favourable climate for consumerism. Corporate marketing strategies need to be re-examined in the light of the changing social environment to reflect a greater awareness and sensitivity to society's evolving ethical values and non-materialistic aspirations.

The tendency of business to disengage itself from discussion about the philosophy and the fundamental nature of marketing has been an inhibiting factor in the development of social marketing. Business reluctance to enter into the debate, and answer charges of exploitation of consumers and excessive and anti-social profiteering, has prevented any serious consideration being given, other than by a few academics, to the opportunities which exist to widen marketing's area of activity beyond the strictly commercial level. Extravagant and unsupportable claims in advertising copy, 'party selling', 'pyramid selling' and other direct selling techniques in which the sales force is encouraged to use aggressive methods which many consider to be anti-social are given extensive publicity. These and other sales strategies are and will become increasingly subject to regulatory action. But it should be action by those who appreciate that the consumer has and does practise his right to say 'No', that the marketing of unsatisfactory products by firms who understand and use the full panoply of marketing techniques is self-defeating in the end. The encouragement of efficient and socially responsible marketing is a powerful restraint on the unscrupulous. But there is still, especially as far as advertising is concerned, much to be done.

Codes of conduct can now be shown as being capable of working effectively in practice. They often work more effectively, and certainly are able to 'stamp on' malpractices more quickly than legislation. Notable examples of codes of conduct are the British Code of Advertising Practice and the code of practice of the British Market Research Society. Attempts are being made to introduce similar codes of conduct elsewhere and in other segments of marketing. Sometimes laws and statutes are needed as safeguards; but codes devised and conducted on a voluntary basis by responsive, responsible, and socially aware business groups do have advantages.

The Role of Advertising

Although it has been emphasised that public service, public interest and public issue advertising are not social advertising or a part of social marketing, the need for an advertising segment in any valid social marketing campaign cannot be ignored. Advertising is a major element of marketing communication; it has developed as a flexible, persuasive, and powerful tool. Advertising effectiveness demands direct approach to the audience to whom some proposition is being addressed. Language and visual communication readily comprehensible to the target group must contain acceptable and believable messages.

Criticism of consumer goods advertising can be seen as arising from a lack of understanding of the techniques. It is said that 'advertising talks down to people' or 'advertising concentrates on the mundane or on trivia'. But viable and effective advertising is not possible unless it is directed to those for whom the message would have some meaning. It should not contain complex or over-literal language where this would inhibit effective communication. Effective advertising as part of marketing communication may contain colour and other aesthetic attention-getting symbols and signals. Frequently there is a combination of drawn or photographed illustrations together with crisp slogans or concise sentences. The message is written within the constraints set down in a statement of communication objectives (or copy platform) aimed at a particular target audience within a defined market. This creative activity is intended to contribute towards action, perhaps including changes of habit and attitude. The techniques outlined are far from new. Ancient scholars laboriously produced illuminated manuscripts aimed at their own limited target groups to proselytise and to promulgate religious beliefs.

Throughout the world, there is a wide and growing use of posters, newspapers and magazine advertisements, and radio and television spot announcements to communicate messages, and to endeavour to motivate some desired action or change of attitude. But as already stated this is done almost exclusively on behalf of commercial interests.

Let us turn back now to the problem of social advertising. It seems obvious that the major agency in the development of social advertising will be existing public service advertising. Public service advertising is undertaken by governments, social welfare and charitable organisations. Public interest and public issue campaigns are sometimes undertaken by industry. The public service campaigns include recruitment advertising for the armed forces, the police,

P

schoolteachers, nurses, etc. Public service campaigns also communicate the social harm that is done by cigarette smoking and driving under the influence of alcohol. Attempts are made to direct advertising announcements in the media towards more emotive and controversial areas such as race relations and industrial relations.

Advertising, as part of a total commercial activity, is concerned with the transfer of attitudes of prospective purchasers through the stages of unawareness, awareness, comprehension, conviction and finally motivating them to action. The marketing director knows that the advertising plan has to be part of the total marketing mix. Advertising as one element in the marketing mix is unable to work effectively in isolation. But acknowledgement of this is by no means as widespread as it ought to be among those concerned with public service advertising.

A well-designed poster, embodying acceptable or even outstanding creative standards together with cleverly contrived wording, is accepted too readily as being all that is necessary to motivate people to action. The question 'What is its real contribution?' is not asked. Let us visualise a committee meeting of an organisation concerned with a particular social problem. All aspects of their future plans are being discussed. It is decided that as part of their programme it will be necessary to use advertising. The discussion then continues with a discourse as to how much finance is, or is not, available to meet 'advertising expenses'. A figure will be arrived at by methods which would be anathema to a marketing director of any efficient commercial organisation. Whenever advertising is to be used effectively, the advertising budget must take into account what has to be achieved in order to successfully accomplish marketing communication objectives within the total planned marketing strategy. An amount has to be appropriated to cover the cost of accomplishing each stated marketing communication objective, or at least those aspects of the marketing communication job which are to be undertaken by advertising.

Public service advertising in the United States is mainly coordinated through the intermediary of the Advertising Council. In the United Kingdom, public service advertising is handled on behalf of government departments by the Central Office of Information. In both the United States and the United Kingdom, advertising agencies are concerned with these campaigns. Advertising councils and comparable bodies have been formed in other countries, while systems similar to that which operate in Britain exist in other parts of the world. However, the fact remains that there is little evidence that public service advertising is being operated, except by a few progressive social agencies, as an integral part of a total marketing strategy.

We have attempted to constructively criticise public service, public interest and public issue advertising. As advertising tends to be viewed as the visible manifestation of marketing and business, it is understandable that many academics, politicians, consumer protection groups and others direct their criticism of the marketing function at advertising. A greater understanding of the role of advertising and marketing among a wider section of the public, including opinion leaders, is essential. To take but one example, which we have already briefly mentioned, the problem of a greater awareness of the purpose of target group identification. We need to explain why some people become involuntary audiences of marketing communication propositions which, in all probability, will never be of interest to them. Advertising media and production costs are such that today's advertiser must do everything possible to ensure that his messages reach as many of the prospects who in the end are likely (and sometimes more immediately) to be interested in the product or service that is being offered. Media owners publish copious demographic data regarding their audiences and readership composition. Scientific methods, aided by the computer, are directed towards the task of media selection, media planning, and media buying.

There will always be an element of wastage because some people will, for various reasons, have no interest in the produce or service that is being marketed, or at least will not regard themselves as potential purchasers. But an increasing ability to segment markets into groups, classes, or other defined social collectives and to tailor one's messages to specific audiences will lead to greater efficiency in communication in terms of reaching the right people with the right messages in the most economical medium. Perhaps some will always complain of over-simplicity; others express disagreement with the lack of restraint shown in newspaper advertisements, posters, television spots and the like which to them over-project certain connotations, e.g. sex, self-indulgence, snob-appeal. The accusation is frequently voiced that advertising over-concentrates on sexuality to promote products. But effective advertising must talk in the idiom of the day. If censorship in cinema, theatre, or the novel becomes more tolerant why expect advertising to communicate in a manner which to present generations will be considered stilted, dated and inhibited and lacking honesty and sincerity? There is no logic in expecting advertising addressed to adult audiences to restrain its approach to the extent of blunting the very powers of communication and motivation that are its strengths.

Marketing managers of business concerns are aware that the identification of different markets and the identification of potential consumers are crucial to every aspect of a total marketing plan. To plan marketing strategies in fast-moving consumer product markets requires knowledge of the segments of markets to which different campaigns will be addressed. In consumer markets pricing strategy, packaging decisions, choice of distribution outlets, and merchandising strategies are dependent on the knowledge of habits, attitudes, sex, age and lifestyles (and even idiosyncrasies) of the consumers. Plans evolved will be measured, evaluated and adjusted – or sometimes totally withdrawn – and remodelled as a result of changing circumstances in the company, in the market, in society or even internationally. The marketing manager's awareness of differences is not confined to knowledge of differences in people. The nature of his product, the image, standards of conduct and philosophy of his company, and a great many external factors over which he has no control, are relevant to the skilful practice of his profession.

Conclusion

Social marketing and social advertising would utilize tried principles and be practised in such a way that they may help to stay and reduce the growing antagonism towards business activity generally and certain marketing methods in particular. The requirements of social marketing, as of commercial marketing, must be to define needs, to determine goals, to consider total plans, to be aware of social needs, and to look for new needs.

It is indeed curious that whereas marketing has tended to be deemed inapplicable or neglected outside business and commerce the same has not necessarily been true of other business practices. Cost accounting and value analysis have certainly found a place within non-profit organisations. Distrust of selling, and the still widely held view that marketing is only another name for salesmanship, has probably been largely instrumental in creating the attitudes which have inhibited the use or even consideration of marketing techniques and strategies outside commerce and industry.

In predicting a greater appreciation and use of marketing techniques to social causes and programmes, it is suggested that there will also be further activity on the part of companies to increase their interest in producing products and services which reflect a much greater degree of social awareness or social concern. Despite the apparent decline in Britain of religious affiliations, Christmas has not declined as a period when well-meant greetings are exchanged among family and friends. Charity Christmas card marketing has become a sizeable industry, where the strategies used by commercial greeting card producers are exercised in the interests of charities. Here sophisiticated marketing, including retail or direct mail distribution and merchandising techniques are ably demonstrated. We have also only to think of the campaigns directed in Britain by such charitable organisations as Oxfam, Christian Aid, Shelter and the Salvation Army.

Every marketing plan must take into account changing attitudes and environments within society as a whole and within individual segments of the market. Consumerism is no passing fad! The question can rightly be asked as to whether the strength of public feeling would be as great on many issues, e.g. car safety, had it not been for the strenuous efforts of a few very articulate campaigners. Many of the campaigners have been successful because they have utilised marketing principles. Ralph Nader has demonstrated how to use modern marketing communications media that would do credit to some of the more advanced marketing orientated companies.

There is no doubt that telecommunication developments will be important to social marketing. One has only to look to the potential growth of commercial radio, the further expansion of commercial television, the development of cable television with commercial as well as non-commercial channels, to see new possibilities for the greater use of social marketing. The same is true of visual facilities connected to household and business telephones and systems. Some futurists suggest that every home telephone will incorporate a computer bureau terminal and document producing facilities for facsimile news-sheet production 'on site'.

For those who understand that marketing can go beyond its current limitations the possibilities of serving the interests of society are truly exciting. The advance of social marketing will enable us to devise social marketing plans which will have as their objectives improvement of the quality of life for all our citizens. In the opening years of this decade many business men, marketing men among them, have become increasingly aware of the disparity between the way we plan and organise our resources to develop and market technical innovations and the way we plan and organise our resources to develop and market social innovation. A potentially powerful body of expertise exists, trained and practised in the marketing discipline, and is anxious to enter the field of social marketing. Many of the best practitioners would be only too ready to put their creative ideas and talents to work in the public interest on many of the problems which beset society – community planning, law enforcement, the drug question, vocational and educational guidance, traffic reorganisation, welfare service planning, racial harmony and integration, industrial relations, protection of the environment and so on.

If only the opportunities could be recognised and seized and the jobs created, what advances in social engineering, social planning and social innovation might we be capable of achieving by the end of this century?

Author Biographies

Chapter 1

Leslie W. Rodger, the editor of this work and also the author of the opening chapter, is General Manager of the Central Marketing Services Division of Mullard Limited, manufacturers of electronic components for a wide range of consumer, industrial and professional applications. Prior to this he was a marketing management consultant, and also held market research and marketing appointments with the British subsidiaries of two leading American advertising agencies. He was Marketing Director and Member of the Board of McCann-Erickson Advertising from 1960 to 1965. Earlier experience was gained with the Economist Intelligence Unit and in the Export Division of Tube Investments Limited.

He is the author of *Marketing In A Competitive Economy* published by Associated Business Programmes (new revised edition, London, 1971), a member of the Institute of Marketing and former Chairman (1971–72) of The Marketing Society. He is an honours graduate in economics of University College, London.

Chapter 2

Ronald Hurst is author of *Industrial Management Methods*, Hutchinson (London, 1969). He is known for his contributions to leading management journals. He writes with the authority gained from fifteen years of practical work in the engineering industry before he became a journalist in 1962.

Having edited a variety of major technical publications he is now an established commentator in the field of industrial reportage; a specialisation which has involved him in innumerable visits to factories and plant throughout the UK and Europe, and in intensive discussions with the managements concerned. This background has given him a remarkably detailed knowledge of the industrial scene, and in particular, of the marketing problems which continue to challenge every producer.

Chapter 3

Harry Sasson joined Hambros Bank in 1972 as Head of UK Financial Services. He was previously a senior consultant in the Strategy Division of the P-E Consulting Group, specialising in business appraisals, corporate strategy and organisation studies, and has worked in these fields for a wide range of organisations in the UK, the USA, Australia and elsewhere. Before joining P-E in 1966 he was for six years a director of a high-technology company in the industrial and process heating equipment field, and previously to that spent another six years in economic resource appraisal in the petroleum and mineral resources industries as a consultant and a manager in the UK, in Europe and in the Far East. He is a frequent lecturer and has written numerous articles for the business press.

Chapter 4

Aubrey Wilson is Managing Director of Industrial Market Research Limited. He is the author of six books on marketing and one on industrial archaeology, and is a well-known lecturer in the UK and overseas. The early part of his career was spent in the textile industry and towards the end of the 1950's he became a director of a firm of international marketing consultants. In 1960 he formed Industrial Market Research Limited, which is now the largest company of its kind in Europe. Mr. Wilson is also a founder director of Associated Business Programmes, which is recognised as a leading private company organising business seminars in Britain.

Chapter 5

Philippe Bieler is Managing Director of European Operations in the International Division of Milton Bradley Company, a leading American-based educational and play toys and games manufacturer with subsidiaries in Holland, West Germany and France. Prior to to this he was an Executive Director of New Court & Partners, the venture capital subsidiary of N. M. Rothschild & Sons Limited, following positions with the Singer Company as Planning Manager and subsequently Director with its Canadian subsidiary, and as Director of Planning and Development for Europe. Earlier, he had sales experience with Alcan Aluminium in Canada and was also a security analyst with Merrill, Lynch, Pierce, Fenner & Smith in New York. He holds an M.B.A. in International Business from Centre d'Etudes Industrielles in Geneva, as well as a degree in Mechanical Engineering from McGill University, Montreal.

Chapter 6

Jeremy Fowler is a graduate in Civil and Municipal Engineering from University College, London, and a Masters graduate in Industrial Engineering and Management from the University of Technology, Loughborough. On leaving university, he obtained marketing and sales experience with a United States producer of industrial gases and chemicals. At present, Jeremy Fowler is Head of the Research for Planning Group at Industrial Market Research Limited, a unit established to provide a unique and comprehensive research service to executives concerned with strategic planning.

Jeremy Fowler is a contributor to the leading management journals on strategic planning and marketing topics and lectures to public and private institutions, such as the Institute of Marketing and the Administrative Staff College, Henley. He has travelled widely in Europe and North America and supervised projects for many large organisations at home and overseas.

Chapter 7

André Gabor is Senior Lecturer in Economics in the University of Essex and Director of Pricing Research Limited, London. He and Professor C. W. J. Granger are founder-members of the Nottingham University Consumer Study Group, the work of which has received international recognition. André Gabor is a graduate of London and Berlin. He held posts in industry and in the Agricultural Economics Service of the Ministry of Agriculture before he returned to the academic fold. He is the author of a number of papers on economic problems, of which those on various aspects of pricing are best known.

Clive Granger holds the Chair of Applied Statistics and Econometrics in the Mathematics Department at the University of Nottingham. He graduated with First Class Honours in the same department in 1955 and was awarded his Ph.D. in Statistics in 1959. He has spent his whole career at Nottingham, apart from periods as visiting lecturer at Princeton University, Stanford University, University of California at San Diego and the Institute for Advanced Studies in

Q

Vienna, being promoted to Reader in 1964 and to Professor in 1965.

His main research interests are in the fields of time series analysis, forecasting, stock and commodity markets, consumer pricing and analysis of spatial data. The result of this research has appeared in three books and over forty research papers.

Chapter 8

David Rowe is the Legal Adviser of Kellogg International Corporation, one of the world's leading oil refinery and chemical plants contractors. He has an M.A. from Oxford where he read law, and is a barrister. He started his business career in the legal department of The Distillers Co. Ltd. working chiefly on problems which concerned their chemicals and plastics interests. Whilst working for Distillers he transferred to the Plastics Group and spent several years marketing plastics' raw materials. He was for three years Legal Adviser of the British Electrical & Allied Manufacturers Association where he specialised on engineering contracts and represented the industry on the various bodies who devise model forms of contract. Mr. Rowe is co-author with Ivan Alexander of *Selling Industrial Products* Hutchinson (London, 1968). He also contributed the chapter on Industrial Selling in Aubrey Wilson's *The Marketing of Industrial Products,* Pan Books (London, 1972). He is a member of the Contracts Committee of the Institution of Chemical Engineers.

Chapter 9

Digby Brindle-Wood-Williams took an M.A. at Oxford in 1962 and spent the following six years marketing the distribution services of a large international transport group, the Proprietors of Hay's Wharf Limited. This also involved studying in depth the effect of distribution methods on marketing itself. A freelance journalist for the last four years, he has written widely on distribution matters for a number of technical freight journals and national newspapers, and is co-author with D. John Aylott of *Physical Distribution in Industrial and Consumer Marketing* (Hutchinson, 1970). He has also acted as a consultant to various freight forwarding and shipping companies, is a member of the Institute of Public Relations and of the British Association of Industrial Editors.

Chapter 10

Norman Marcus, with some twenty years industrial marketing experience behind him, culminating in a Directorship with Gold Seal Office Furniture Ltd. with responsibility for marketing and diversification, took up a senior lectureship in Marketing and Management at the North Staffordshire Polytechnic in 1968. He is a campaigner and researcher on the possibilities of utilising marketing and advertising techniques in connection with social problems and social programmes, a subject about which he has written and lectured in the USA and Canada as well as the UK. He is a member of the Institute of Marketing, National Marketing Teachers Committee, and is also a member of The Marketing Society, the British Institute of Management and of the International Advertising Association (UK chapter).

The views expressed by the various authors are entirely their own and do not necessarily represent those of their firms.

Bibliography

Readers may wish to pursue in greater depth some of the important subjects and issues raised in this book. The following selected bibliography and references are recommended by the author of each of the chapters.

The Coming Age of Marketing Maturity

M. L. Bell and C. W. Emory: 'The Faltering Marketing Concept', *Journal of Marketing*, Vol. 35. American Marketing Association (Chicago, October 1971).

P. Kotler: *Marketing Management: Analysis Planning and Control.* Prentice-Hall (Englewood Cliffs, New Jersey, 1972).

T. Levitt: *Innovation in Marketing.* Pan Books (London, 1968); *The Marketing Mode*, McGraw-Hill (New York, 1969).

L. Rodger: *Marketing In A Competitive Economy.* Associated Business Programmes (London, 1971).

R. Willsmer: *Directing The Marketing Effort.* Staples Press (London, 1971).

A. Wilson: *The Art and Practice of Marketing.* Hutchinson (London, 1971); *The Marketing of Professional Services.* McGraw-Hill (London, 1972).

Marketing Strategy for Technology-Based Enterprises

B. Achilladelis, P. Jervis and A. Robertson: *Project Sappho – a study of success and failure in innovation.* Science Policy Research Unit, University of Sussex. Science Research Council, 1971.

F. J. Aguilar: *Scanning the Business Environment.* Collier Macmillan (1967).

H. I. Ansoff and J. M. Stewart: 'Strategies for a Technology-based Business', *Harvard Business Review* (Boston, November/December 1967).

W. E. Duckworth: 'Determination of Total Research Effort', *Operational Research Quarterly*, Vol. 18. Pergamon Press 1967.

C. Freeman: 'Research and Development: a comparison between British and American industry', *Economic Review*, No. 20. National Institute of Economic and Social Research, 1962.

A. Hart and S. A. Gregory: 'Productivity in Research', Symposium. London Institution of Chemical Engineers, 1963.

National Economic Development Office: *A Handbook for Marketing Machinery*, NEDO/Machine Tools EDC. HMSO, 1970.

Central Advisory Council for Science and Technology: *Technological Innovation in Britain*. HMSO, July, 1968.

Planning A Diversification Strategy

H. I. Ansoff: *Corporate Strategy*. McGraw-Hill (New York, 1965).

G. A. Steiner: *Managerial Long-range Planning*. McGraw-Hill (New York, 1965).

T. A. Andersen, H. I. Ansoff, F. E. Norton and J. F. Weston: 'Planning for Diversification Through Merger', *California Management Review*, Vol. 1. Summer 1959.

J. Fowler: 'The Necessities of Strategic Corporate Planning', *Engineering* (January 1972).

P. Hilton: *Planning Corporate Growth and Diversification*. McGraw-Hill (New York, 1970).

Patterns and Developments in Multi-National Enterprise

C. Tugendhat: *The Multinationals*. Eyre & Spottiswoode (London, 1971).

C. Levinson: *Capital, Inflation and the Multinational*, Allen & Unwin (London, 1971).

Marketing a Non-Differentiated Industrial Product

There is no bibliography as such on the marketing of non-differentiated industrial products, but readers may find Theodore Levitt's *Innovation in Marketing* and Leslie Rodger's *Marketing in a Competitive Economy* of value as background to the issues raised in this chapter. Although both of the above-mentioned books concentrate on differentiation of consumer products they nevertheless provide some insights into the problems facing manufacturers of industrial products.

Marketing Purpose Made Capital Goods

K. F. A. Johnston: *Electrical and Mechanical Engineering Contracts*. Gower Press (1971).

P. D. V. Marshall: *Contracting for Engineering and Construction Projects*. Gower Press (1970).

I. N. Duncan Wallace: *Hudson's Building and Engineering Contracts*, 10th Edition. Sweet & Maxwell (1970).

National Economic Development Office: *Large Industrial Sites*. Report of the NEDO Working Party on Large Industrial Construction Sites. HMSO (1970).

A Systematic Approach to Effective Pricing

Over thirty books and articles are quoted in the references of the chapter and are particularly recommended for further reading. In addition, three American textbooks might be found instructive:

D. V. Harper: *Price Policy and Procedure.* Harcourt, Brace & World (New York, 1966).

R. A. Lynn: *Price Policies and Marketing Management.* Richard D. Irwin (Homewood, Illinois, 1967).

A. R. Oxenfeldt: *Pricing for Marketing Executives.* Wadsworth (Belmont, California, 1966).

Developments in Physical Distribution Management

D. J. Aylott and D. Brindle-Wood-Williams: *Physical Distribution in Industrial and Consumer Marketing.* Hutchinson (London, 1970).

P. Jackson and W. Brackenridge: *Air Cargo Distribution.* Gower Press (London, 1971).

Social Marketing

O. A. Brewer: 'Is Business the Source of New Social Values?' *Harvard Business Review* (Boston, November/December, 1971).

S. A. Greyser: 'The Social Impact of Advertising'; *The Advertising Quarterly*, No. 3. Advertising Association (London, Spring 1972).

P. Kotler: 'What Consumerism Means for Marketers'. *Harvard Business Review* (Boston, May/June 1972).

P. Kotler and S. J. Levy: 'Broadening the Concept of Marketing', *Journal of Marketing*, Vol. 33. American Marketing Association (Chicago, January 1969).

P. Kotler and G. Zaltman: 'Social Marketing: An Approach to Planned Social Change'. *Journal of Marketing*, Vol. 35. American Marketing Association (Chicago, July 1971).

F. Luthans and R. M. Hodgetts: *Social Issues in Business.* Collier Macmillan (London, 1972).

J. R. Wish and S. H. Gamble (Eds.): *Marketing and Social Issues.* John Wiley & Sons (New York, 1971).

Index

Page references in italics indicate a diagram